THE GUARDIAN BOOK OF THE SPANISH CIVIL WAR

The Guardian Book
of the
Spanish Civil War

Edited by

R. H. Haigh
D. S. Morris
A. R. Peters

WILDWOOD HOUSE

First published in Great Britain in 1987
by Wildwood House Ltd
Gower House, Croft Road,
Aldershot, Hants GU11 3HR,
England

ISBN 0 7045 3080 5

Typeset in Great Britain by
Guildford Graphics Limited, Petworth, West Sussex
Printed by Billing & Sons Limited, Worcester

Contents

List of Maps   vi

Acknowledgements   vii

Editors' Introduction to the series   ix

Editors' Introduction   xi

Chronology of the Spanish Civil War   xvii

Selected Guardian reports of Spanish Civil War   1
   January 17 1936 to March 30 1939

Appendix 1: Spanish political parties   327

Appendix 2: Major political figures in the Spanish Civil
   War   330

List of Maps

1   Battle of the Sierras – July 1936   4
2   Seville to Toledo – August–September 1936   26
3   Advance on Madrid – October–November 1936   42
4   Attack on Madrid – November 1936   54
5   Corunna Road and Jarama Battles – December 1936–
    January 1937; February 1937   65
6   Màlaga Campaign – January–February 1937   73
7   Battle of Guadalajara – March 1937   86
8   Capture of Bilbao – March–June 1937   96
9   Brunete – July 1937   136
10 Santander and Asturias campaigns – August–
    October 1937   154
11 Aragón – August–October 1937   155
12 Teruel offensive – December 1937–February 1938   185
13 Ebro offensive – July–November 1938   228
14 Catalonian campaign – December 1938–February
    1939   277

Acknowledgements

A number of people have made our task in producing this book a great deal easier than would have otherwise been the case. Michael Harkin, Social Sciences Librarian at the Central Library in Manchester, responded most readily to our request for microfilmed copies of the *Manchester Guardian* and, by so doing, greatly reduced the time and effort expended on producing the manuscript. Roger Hines, Margot Madin, Ray Thompson and Laura Tolley of the Eric Mensforth Library, Sheffield City Polytechnic, all gave willingly of their time and never failed to meet the many arduous demands we made of them.

Joanne and Ann Gould cheefully undertook the mammoth typing effort entailed in preparing the manuscript for publication and did so with a speed and accuracy which exceeded our most optimistic expectations.

Finally our thanks are owed, as on many previous occasions, to our families. Without their tolerance and support, our task would have been that much more difficult. To them we dedicate this book.

R. H. Haigh
D. S. Morris
A. R. Peters
Sheffield, 1986

Editors' Introduction to the Series

The historian is blessed with many advantages. He can assemble all of the available facts relevant to any particular past event, analyse each in turn, assemble his accumulated knowledge into a comprehensive and logically sequential pattern, and present a rationally sound appraisal of all of the elements which have contributed both directly and indirectly to a social phenomenon considered by him or by others to be worthy of special attention.

In marked contrast to the historian stands the journalist. Not for him the luxury of wide-ranging and detailed information; instead he is confronted by a complex blend of fact, rumour and innuendo which falls far short of being comprehensive in character or cohesive in format. Working from partial information he can at best offer his reader a rational assessment of what he has gleaned from a multiplicity of sources, with but little hope or opportunity of being able to verify and validate every element of his story by reference to other knowledgeable or accepted authorities and accounts.

Yet despite the advantages enjoyed by the historian and despite the disadvantages which beset the journalist, there is an immediacy about journalistic accounts which the historian can only try to capture in his own scholarly labours. Social events rarely happen in a causal sequence, decisions are invariably taken on the basis of limited knowledge, and the complexity of societal phenomena makes total comprehension and a fully rational response an impossibility. Perhaps, therefore, the historian may be not unreasonably accused of enforcing a rationality and order on to events which is largely his own, and of attributing motives which accord with his perceptions rather than being the motives which underlay human actions at the time of his chosen event.

In short, the journalist offers a 'snap shot' of the world as he perceives it in the present, an assessment which has an immediacy even though it affords an interpretation which may well lack comprehensiveness. The historian, working from accumulated past knowledge and enjoying the benefit of hindsight is able to offer a fuller account of past events but one which will almost inevitably fall short of conveying the immediacy which is a feature of the journalistic report.

Let it not be forgotten that the work of a journalist can, of itself, be a factor which influences the actions of others. Journalistic accounts are themselves elements which are capable of influencing the perceptions and behaviours of social actors and can, therefore, be an integral part of significant events in man's social activities. The historian may point to past 'errors' and may influence current and future events by so doing, but it is most unlikely that his work will ever, by its very nature, be as significant a determinant of current events as that of the journalist.

This is not to deny or denigrate the art of the historian. It is simply to state that in order to gain an understanding of a past event and to acquire an appreciation of it that was available to the majority of those living at the time it was unfolding, it may well be more fruitful to give consideration to journalistic accounts of the day rather than simply being restricted to the more academically oriented accounts of historians. Journalists offer living history, historians offer considered history. Neither is, of itself, better than the other, nor are the two mutually exclusive. We have chosen to utilise the former to provide an insight into the origins and causes of the Spanish Civil War and, by so doing, have consciously sought to offer a counterbalance to the many voluminous and more profoundly academic accounts which have been produced over the years.

Whether we have succeeded, indeed whether we should have even attempted such an exercise, must be left to the judgement of the reader.

R. H. Haigh
D. S. Morris
A. R. Peters
Sheffield, September 1986

Editors' Introduction

The fourth decade of the twentieth century will be remembered as a period which left an indelible scar on the Spanish people and shocked and horrified the world. The outbreak of the Civil War in Spain in July 1936, unleashed a whirlwind of destruction, persecution and terror which over the course of three years claimed half a million lives and tore the heart out of the Spanish nation. Yet although the opening of hostilities took much of the international community by surprise the tensions that erupted in 1936 had bubbled barely beneath the surface of Spanish society for over a century. Behind the facade of a modern liberal democracy, Spain was in reality a nation deeply divided by cross-cutting religious, class and regional differences with political power still effectively concentrated in the hands of the rural aristocracy and the professional classes that dominated the highly centralised state apparatus. Despite radical rhetoric and an outward commitment to reform, it was evident that the sympathies of successive governments lay more firmly with the twin bastions of Spanish conservatism, the Roman Catholic Church and the army, than with the growing groundswell for radical change.

The demands for modernisation, however, could not be indefinitely suppressed. The rising industrial and commercial wealth of Catalonia and the Basque regions represented deeply entrenched pockets of resistance to the traditional ascendancy of Castille. In addition, the emergence of a growing industrial workforce in the northern provinces and the major cities of Spain reinforced the pressure being exerted by the rural peasantry for a more equitable redistribution of land and wealth.

With the conclusion of the First World War, the forces of conservatism appeared to be in retreat as the working classes responded to the economic recession with a campaign of strike action, assassination and bombings in an attempt to follow the revolutionary pattern set by the Bolsheviks in 1917. In response the government turned initially to police repression but ultimately to the power of the army. The imposition of an effective military dictatorship, led by General Primo de Rivera, in 1923 has been seen by some observers as the last desperate attempt to stem the tide of change. Despite a range of impressive reforms Primo de Rivera was no more successful than his predecessors in regenerating the ailing Spanish economy.

Furthermore, the prestige and morale of the army had been severely impaired by the loss of Spain's empire in the Americas and a series of defeats inflicted by Rif tribesmen in Spanish Morocco. It was, therefore, amid growing economic and financial problems and increasing self-doubt within the officer corps that Rivera tendered his resignation in January 1930 to be followed within sixteen months by the abdication of the monarch, Alfonso XIII. These dramatic events suggested that Spain had at last shed itself of the feudal alliance which had held the nation in a vice-like grip for almost three centuries.

The promise of modernisation and progress was provided by the establishment of the Second Republic in 1931 founded upon a broad coalition of moderate liberal and socialist political factions. From the outset, with a series of reforms designed to reduce the size and influence of the officer corps and to limit the formal privileges accorded to the Church, the Republic displayed a refreshing willingness to strike against the alliance of the crucifix and the sword which, for many, symbolised the perpetration of inequality and injustice in Spanish society. Furthermore, with the recognition of trade union rights and the initiation of land reform, the government strove to accommodate the grievances of the urban and rural working classes and to undermine the power of the aristocracy and the industrialists who had treated the workforce with contempt and brutality within the confines of a semi-feudal society. Such an upheaval, however, was unlikely to pass unopposed but with the crushing of a military revolt led by General Sanjurjo in August 1932, and with the granting of autonomy to Catalonia in the same year, the Republic showed a marked determination to sweep aside the last vestiges of the old order and to propel the Spanish nation into the twentieth century.

Yet, while well-intentioned and progressive, the Republic was unwittingly releasing forces within society which had been simmering under the yoke of Castillian authoritarianism for centuries. Within a year of the granting of trade union rights, membership of socialist (UGT) and anarchist (CNT) trade unions had spiralled dramatically. Within their ranks the reforms initiated by the Republic were interpreted as simply the first steps in the complete reshaping of Spanish society. Their demands for equality were shared by the rural working class. Traditionally, seen as little more than the chattels of the landed aristocracy, the peasantry now looked to the Republic to satisfy their hunger for land and independence.

In the face of such a challenge, the forces of Spanish conservatism rapidly began to marshal their defences. The formation of the CEDA, a broad right political alliance under the leadership of Gil Robles, was indicative of the revulsion and fear generated in many sectors of Spanish society by attacks on Church property and the attempts to neutralise the political influence of the army. In addition, the industrial and rural reforms initiated by the Republic were interpreted as the first moves in the surrender of Spain to the godless barbarity of the communist and anarchist creeds.

In reality, such radical goals were beyond both the intentions and capabilities of what was still primarily a government composed of moderate liberal politicians. Caught between the pull for revolutionary change and the forces of conservatism the Republic followed a path of moderate reform and compromise which won few friends and led to electoral defeat in November 1933. In the following two years, under the guidance of the Radical Republican Party and CEDA, Spain swung once again to the right of the political continuum. The advances made by the rural and urban working classes were brutally and ruthlessly suppressed while Catalonian autonomy, which had symbolised the breakdown of Castillian authority, was rescinded. Yet the expectations generated by the establishment of the Second Republic were difficult to eradicate and, although often bitterly divided on political goals and means, in the face of adversity the various communist, anarchist and socialist factions were united in their hatred of Gil Robles and the CEDA which symbolised the attempt to re-establish the corruption and élitism of the old regime.

It was, therefore, the accession of three CEDA ministers to the government in October 1934 which provoked uprisings in Barcelona and the northern province of Asturias. While the rising in Barcelona was quickly suppressed, the Asturian miners conducted a bitter military campaign against the government forces for several weeks. The rebellion was only extinguished following the introduction of native troops and the Spanish Foreign Legion. In the course of a brutal campaign, in which atrocities were committed by both sides, up to 4,000 casualties were incurred and tens of thousands were imprisoned on suspicion of being left-wing political sympathisers. Although the uprising resulted in a defeat for the Asturian miners it had shown quite clearly that the Left was capable of mounting a serious threat to the government if the various communist, anarchist and socialist factions were prepared to pool their resources.

The decision to form a broad coalition of the political parties of the Left to contest the general election of February 1936 suggested that the lessons of the Asturian uprising had been fully absorbed. Under the banner of the Popular Front the parties of the Left scored a resounding electoral victory over the CEDA yet, beneath the semblance of unity, it was evident that the divisions within the Front were deep and probably insoluble. The support of the anarchist movement (FAI) was only bought at the price of a pledge to release political prisoners and it was clear that the FAI would not participate formally within a coalition government. More seriously the major party of the Left, the Socialist Party (PSCE), was divided between the moderates led by Indalecio Prieto and a group which supported Largo Caballero in demanding that the party adopt a more extreme and revolutionary stance. The burden of government, therefore, fell upon the minority Republican Left Party led by Manuel Azana which was dependent upon the support in the Cortes of the PSOE and the Communist Party (PCE).

Through the restoration of Catalan autonomy, the widening of agrarian reform and measures to limit the control of the Church over education, Azana sought to restore Spain to the path of moderate reform associated with the Second Republic. The decision, however, to extend the emergency measures contained in the 'Estado de Alarmo' and retain censorship of the press was indicative of his appreciation of the growing tensions in Spanish society.

The anarchist and socialist trade unions and elements of the PSOE and PCE clearly expected the government to accelerate the pace of reform and were prepared to use strike action and mass demonstrations to pressurise the authorities into action. At the other end of the political spectrum, the demands of the Left heightened the apprehensions and fears of those who saw the Popular Front as a menace to the traditional pillars of Spanish society. In the form of the Carlist movement and the Falange, led by Jose Antonio, it was apparent that elements of both established Spanish conservatism, upholding the authority of the Church and the monarchy, and the 'New Right', associated more closely with the Italian fascist movement, were mobilising to defend Spain against the spectre of communism and anarchy. Furthermore, following the electoral defeat of the CEDA, a new champion of the Spanish Right was emerging in the person of Calvo Sotelo. A former Finance Minister under Primo de Rivera, Sotelo hinted darkly that only the intervention of the army could cleanse Spain of Bolshevik influence.

In May 1936 Azana assumed the Presidency and was succeeded as Premier by Santiago Casares Quiroga. Measures had already been taken to forestall the army with the posting of senior officers of dubious loyalty to the Republic to relatively minor garrisons. Quiroga now sought to restore confidence in the government by confirming his determination to both pursue a programme of reform and also to suppress displays of intimidation and violence by factions from either end of the political spectrum. However, in a climate where the major political parties were assembling units of armed militia, and assassination of opponents was increasingly commonplace, support for a policy of moderation and compromise was being rapidly eroded. Such was the polarisation of opinion in Spanish society that it seemed probable that one small spark would be sufficient to unleash forces bubbling beneath the veneer of liberal democracy which would see no alternative but the settlement of their differences through violence and confrontation.

The reports in this book, all from the pages of the *Manchester Guardian*, were selected by three independent historians who also wrote the annotations, introduction and appendices.

Chronology of the Spanish Civil War

	Spain	Europe
1936		
February	Popular front wins General Election. Manuel Azana Prime Minister. Amnesty for political prisoners.	
March	Violence between left and right-wing factions. Falange banned and José Antonio imprisoned.	Germany seizes the Rhineland. Britain and France reject military response.
May	Azana assumes Presidency with Casares as Premier.	
July	Assassinations of Castillo and Sotelo followed by army rebellion in Morocco. Uprising on the mainland coordinated by General Mola seizes Seville, Cordoba and areas of northern Spain. Army of Africa airlifted into southern Spain. Uprisings in Madrid and Barcelona suppressed by workers and units loyal to the Republic. Casares succeeded by José Giral.	Hitler and Mussolini promise aid to Nationalists. French Premier, Blum, declares that France will remain neutral.
August	Nationalists take Badajoz and massacre Republican garrison. First German aircraft arrive in Spain.	Britain and France announce embargo on arms sales to Spain. Italy, Germany and USSR accept non-intervention in principle.
September	Nationalists capture Irun, San Sebastian and Toledo. Largo Cobollero heads Republican Cabinet of socialists, communists and left-wing Republicans.	Non-Intervention Committee meets in London. Recruiting for International Brigade begins.
October	Franco appointed Head of State and Commander-in-Chief. Increasing internationalisation of the war as Italian forces occupy Ibiza and Soviet arms and advisers arrive to organise the Republican Popular Army. First Soviet tanks and aircraft arrive in Spain.	

	Spain	Europe
November	German Condor Legion joins Nationalist forces and first International Brigades arrive in Spain.	Germany and Italy recognise Franco's government.
	Nationalist attempt to capture Madrid causes Republican Government to move to Valencia as people of Madrid are mobilised to resist the Nationalist assault.	
December	Nationalist assault on Madrid contained. First Italian volunteers arrive in southern Spain.	
1937		
January		Anglo–Italian 'Gentleman's Agreement' signed.
February	Italian volunteers capture Malaga.	Britain and France implement measures to ban the flow of volunteers to Spain from their territory.
	Republican forces resist attempt by Nationalists to cross the Jarama river to the south of Madrid and cut the Madrid–Valencia road. Resulting Battle of Jarama ends in stalemate.	
March	Republican forces contain and ultimately rout Italian forces seeking to cut Madrid's communications with the north. Battle of Guadalajara a major setback for Italian morale.	
	Nationalist forces turn their attention to a campaign against the Basque provinces.	
April	Guernica bombed by the Condor Legion.	Non-Intervention Committee establishes patrols to supervise imports into Spain.
	Franco extends his control over factions in the Nationalist coalition.	
May	Rivalry between communist, anarchist and socialist factions leads to the suppression of an anarchist uprising in Barcelona and the replacement of Cabollero by a communist government headed by Juan Negrin.	Neville Chamberlain succeeds Baldwin as Prime Minister. Germany and Italy leave naval patrol scheme after alleged attacks on the 'Deutschland' and the 'Leipzig'.
	German warships bombard Almeria after alleged attack on the 'Deutschland'.	
June	General Mola killed in aircrash. Nationalists capture Bilbao. Trotskyist movement POUM banned by Republic and its leaders arrested.	

	Spain	Europe
July	Battle of Brunete. Massive Republican assault to the west of Madrid contained and eventually repulsed by Nationalists.	
August	Republican offensive in Aragon. Nationalists take Santander. Unidentified submarines attack merchant shipping in the Mediterranean supplying the Republic.	
September	Attacks on merchant shipping continue. Republican offensive in Aragon grinds to a halt after the capture of Belchite.	Nyon conference. Nine powers agree to instigate naval patrols to sink submarines attacking merchant shipping in the Mediterranean. Germany and Italy refuse to attend conference but Italy subsequently accepts a patrol zone.
October	Nationalists take remaining sections of northern Spain.	
November	Republican government moves to Barcelona.	
December	Republican offensive against Teruel.	

1938

	Spain	Europe
January	Republicans capture Teruel. German and Italian aircraft bomb Barcelona.	
February	Nationalists recapture Teruel.	Eden resigns from Chamberlain Cabinet.
March	Massive Nationalist offensive drives Republican forces out of Aragon. Bombing of Barcelona stepped up.	Germany occupies Austria. French reopen frontier with Spain.
April	Nationalists reach the Mediterranean at Vinaroz and cut the Republic in two.	
May	Franco only willing to accept unconditional surrender.	Blum replaced by Daladier and French frontier closed.
June	Nationalists take Castellon. Campaign to take Valencia successfully resisted by Republican army.	
July	Battle of the Ebro. Republican army recrosses the Ebro.	Non-Intervention Committee unveils plan for withdrawal of volunteers from Spain.

	Spain	Europe
August	Republican Ebro offensive contained by Nationalists. Basque and Catalan Ministers resign from Republican Cabinet.	
September	International Brigades withdrawn from active service under League of Nations agreement.	Munich Agreement kills hopes that Britain and France might intervene to 'save' the Republic.
November	Republican army pushed back across the Ebro. International Brigades leave Spain.	
December	Nationalists launch assault against Catalonia.	
1939		
January	Nationalists capture Barcelona.	
February	Catalonia falls to Nationalists. Azana leaves Spain for France along with a large number of Republican soldiers and refugees. Negrin attempts to negotiate peace.	Britain and France recognise Franco Government.
March	Colonel Casado leads coup against Negrin Government in Madrid and establishes National Defence Council. After fighting in Madrid communists defeated and Negrin leaves for France. Casado opens negotiations with Franco. Franco ends negotiations and Nationalists enter Madrid.	German troops disregard Munich Agreement and enter Prague.
April	Franco announces end of the war.	

SELECTED *GUARDIAN* REPORTS
OF THE SPANISH CIVIL WAR
JANUARY 17 1936 to
MARCH 30 1939

DISORDERS IN SPAIN
Astonishing Estimate

Madrid, June 16.

The Spanish Chambers (the Cortes) gave the Government a vote of confidence to-night after a bitter attack had been made on it by deputies of the Right, led by Senor Gil Robles and Senor Calvo Sotelo. The latter declared that recently 170 churches had been burnt and 251 persons had been burnt to death. In addition 269 persons had been killed and 1,267 injured in disorders arising out of 331 strikes. Ten newspaper offices had been burnt down and 200 political clubs attacked.

There were stormy scenes when allusions were made to a recent revolt in the army and to attacks on Civil Guards. The Premier, replying, declared that it was the deputies of the Right themselves who were responsible for disaffection in the army, and he would hold them to their responsibility. At present the army was loyal to the Government and ready to defend the Republic.–Exchange Telegram.

It is surprising that so significant a debate in the Cortes received so little coverage and that certain aspects of the report do not correspond with the record of the debate as printed in the 'Diario de Sesiones de las Cortes Espanolas'. Firstly, the speech attributed to Calvo Sotelo was made by Gil Robles. Secondly, there are minor discrepancies between the figures given in the report and those in the 'Diario'. The 'Diario' reports Robles as stating that, in the four months since the election, 160 churches had been burned, 269 mainly political murders committed, 1,287 assaults perpetrated, 69 political centres attacked, 113 general and 228 partial strikes undertaken, and 10 newspaper offices assailed. Robles concluded his speech by arguing that Spain could live under any form of political régime except anarchy and that anarchy was what existed in Spain. Calvo Sotelo, the monarchist leader, blamed the problem of Spain on the Constitution of 1931 which he saw as an inadequate base for a viable state, and declared himself to be an advocate of an integrated state even if that state might be labelled as fascist. He ended his speech with remarks which many took to be a hint that the army should save Spain from its government. The warnings, recriminations and subtle encouragement to the army to seize power that were voiced in this debate were noted by all political parties and factions throughout Spain and brought the advent of civil war that much nearer.

3

Battle of the Sierras – July 1936

1,000 FASCISTS ARRESTED
Spanish Plot Charges

Madrid, July 6.

Over a thousand Fascists were arrested throughout Spain to-day following the alleged discovery late last night of evidence of plans for a coup d'état in Madrid.

Information on the position is difficult to obtain, as official quarters are extremely reticent. It is understood, however, that large hauls of firearms and ammunition have been made in houses of Fascists and that documents have been discovered instructing Fascists up and down the country to foment strikes where possible and to do everything in their power to prevent the settling of strikes where these are in existence.

This drastic action by the authorities follows the 'massacre' of Socialists on Saturday, when seven Socialists were killed and twelve wounded by Fascists armed with sub-machine-guns, who poured a hail of bullets into them from passing cars as the Socialists were leaving a political meeting. On the same day two other Socialists were murdered in a working-class district, presumably by Fascists.

Another political murder mystery which is occupying the attention of the Madrid police to-day is the discovery of the body of an 18-year-old youth who has been missing from his home for four days. He was found lying dead in a ditch a few miles from Madrid, completely naked and bound hand and foot, with five revolver bullets in him. He was known to be of Fascist sympathies, and so the police theory is that he was kidnapped by gangsters of the extreme Left and murdered.

Reports received from the north say that many cars are being greeted on the main road with the Fascist salute. One case of this was unfortunate for the saluter, as the car contained the local chief of police. He jumped out, produced his certificate, and with the help of his bodyguard arrested the man.– Reuter.

These arrests were the culmination of several days of fighting between socialists and fascists throughout Spain, first reported in the 'Manchester Guardian' of 4.7.36, but which did not end the factional feuding.

BITTER FEUDS IN SPAIN
Fascist Murdered

ARREST OF POLICE OFFICERS
Revenge Theory

From a Correspondent

Madrid, July 13.

The mutilated body of Senor Calvo Sotelo, the leader of the small Monarchist party, was found in the River Manzanares at Madrid to-day. The murder is believed to be in revenge for the murder last night of Lieutenant Jose de Castillo, a chief of police with anti-Fascist tendencies.

That murder in turn was announced as a reprisal for earlier murders by the other side. One of the worst of the series was the murder of Socialists as they were leaving their headquarters by Fascists waiting in a motor-car.

Senor Sotelo was considered by the Right and the Left as the only possible serious future leader of the Fascist party in Spain. He was a strong and clever man, aged about 42, a lawyer, an economist, and a member of the Cortes, and was Minister of Finance in the Government of Primo de Rivera.

ARRESTED EARLIER IN THE DAY

In the Cortes he had been speaking strongly against political murders and against the leniency of the Government towards murders committed by the Left. He was arrested by the police this morning, and so his friends had considered him safe from assassination, for the son of Primo de Rivera, the titular leader of the Fascists, whose life had also been threatened, has been safe in prison for some time.

It is believed to-night that a general strike is imminent in support of the strikers in the building trades in Madrid, who have been ordered to return to work by the Government. The attitude of the army is not clear, but it is believed to be unfriendly to the strikers.

CABINET'S LONG MEETING

Madrid, July 13.

A captain, four lieutenants, and five men of the Shock Police have been arrested on suspicion of having murdered Senor Sotelo.

The Government crisis which it was feared might arise

to-day has not come about, but the situation in Spain is ugly. For the fourth time the 100,000 strikers in the building trade have defied the Minister of the Interior's order to return to work on terms approved by the Government. At the same time the murder of Senor Sotelo may cause an out-burst among Conservatives. The Cabinet met this morning to consider the position and sat most of the day.

Senor Sotelo's murder is probably the most remarkable outrage in the feud between Socialists and Fascists, which has led to the death of nearly a score of persons in the past week and is calculated to inflame party passions to fever-heat.– Reuter.

Lieutenant Jose Castillo of the Asaltos had played a prominent part in the suppression of violent rioting at the funeral of a member of the Civil Guard who had been shot in Madrid in April on the occasion of the fifth anniversary of the Republic. From that time on, he had been a target for Falange revenge. News of Castillo's death inflamed passions at the Asalto head-quarters at the Pontejos barracks in the Puerta del Sol. Captain Condes, a member not of the Asaltos but of the Civil Guard – a man noted for his left-wing tendencies and only recently reinstated by the Quiroga Government – together with members of the Asaltos and left-wing organisations, arrested Sotelo, drove him away from his home, shot him and deposited his body at Madrid's East Cemetery without disclosing Sotelo's identity. It is thought that Gil Robles was also an intended victim of Condes' hit squad but Robles was safe in Biarritz.

Wednesday July 15 1936   *p.14*

THE SPANISH MURDERS
Revenge the Motive

ESCAPE OF GIL ROBLES

Madrid, July 14.

Women predominated in the huge crowd that thronged the streets of Madrid this afternoon to watch the funeral of Senor Calvo Sotelo, the Monarchist leader, whose assassination had raised political passions to boiling-point. Senor Sotelo's body was handed over to the city mortuary by men who were after identified as members of the Shock Police.

Fears of riots during the funeral were not realised though

7

a small but rowdy band of Madrid Fascists created a demonstration. The majority of militant members of the Right were in gaol following widespread arrests all over the country. The number of those held has not yet been established but in Madrid alone 135 Fascists have been rounded up by the police as a precaution against reprisals for the murder of Sotelo.

Four people were killed to-day in a collision between Right and Left forces at Orense (Galicia), Senor Sotelo's native city.

CORTES ADJOURNED

So many people assembled in Madrid to see the funeral that the ceremony was postponed for an hour. The Parliament (the Cortes) is to have a week's recess in order to allow passions to cool after a closing session to-day.

Senor Gil Robles, the Conservative leader, was away on holiday when he heard the news of the murder and hurried back to the capital. Many people think he has done so at the risk of his own life, as he is one of the most unpopular men in Spain at present. It was learned to-day that a band of men similar to that which decoyed Senor Sotelo to his doom visited Senor Robles's home on the same night, but he had not returned to the capital.

For the time being the murder has had the effect of consolidating a disintegrating Government. They intended to resign yesterday following their failure to deal with the 100,000 striking building trade operatives who have defied repeated orders to resume work. The new situation has put the Cabinet on its mettle.

NO POLICE ARRESTED

It is known definitely that the murder of Sotelo was carried out by members of the police force in revenge for the killing of Police Lieutenant de Castillo by Fascist gunmen on Sunday night. The man who is alleged to have been in charge of the 'execution squad' that murdered Senor Sotelo was a personal friend of the murdered policeman and had sworn to avenge him if he were killed.

Contrary to last night's announcement that four lieutenants and one captain of police had been arrested for the crime, the Government now states that no arrests have been made yet. Two Madrid evening papers of Conservative–Catholic tendencies have been suppressed indefinitely for printing uncensored reports of yesterday's murder.

Rioting broke out to-day in a working-class district in the north of Madrid between building strikers and police. One striker was killed and many wounded, three seriously.–Reuter.

MORE FASCISTS ARRESTED
Barcelona Affray

Madrid, July 16.

Civil guards in Barcelona were fired on this afternoon while dispersing groups in the district of Pueblo Nuevo. A captain, two guards, and several civilians were seriously wounded.

The Chief of Police of Madrid announced early to-day that throughout Spain 185 leaders and minor officials of the Spanish Fascist party had been arrested during the night, and that numerous arrests of their followers had been made in Madrid and other big towns. 'These men had definite instructions to begin a subversive movement in a few days' time,' he said.

The Permanent Commission of the Cortes has decided to prolong the state of alarm for an indefinite period, and there are many who believe that Parliament will not meet again next week as it is supposed to, but will postpone its next session until the autumn. All the parties of the Right – Fascists, Monarchists, and Catholics – have decided to boycott the Parliamentary system from now on.–Reuter.

SUSPECT SENT OVER FRONTIER?

Hendaye (Spanish Frontier), July 16.

Hints at Government complicity in the escape of the murderer of Senor Calbo Sotelo, the Spanish Fascist leader, are contained in an unconfirmed report from Spain that the lieutenant of the 'shock police', who is generally understood to have been 'the executioner', has been quietly put over to the French side of the frontier with all his papers in order and plenty of money in his pocket. The lieutenant was a personal friend of Lieutenant Castillo, the police officer who was murdered on Sunday, and is understood to have sworn that he would avenge his friend's death.–Reuter.

At the same time that the monarchists and Carlists were stating their intention to withdraw from the Cortes, because of the state of anarchy existing in Spain, the government ordered the closing of Falangist, Carlist and monarchist headquarters in Madrid and 24 hours later suspended the right-wing newspapers, 'Ya' and 'Epoca', for publishing sensational accounts of Sotelo's murder. The communists, socialists and leaders of the Union General del Trabajodes (UGT), the largest socialist trade union, demanded that Quiroga distribute arms to the

9

workers' organisations so that they could play their part in defending the government and the Republic.

It is true that Captain Conde escaped capture but whether he fled to France or simply remained hidden in Spain is an open question; as is the matter of government complicity in his escape.

Saturday July 18 1936   *p.13*

NEW TROUBLE IN SPAIN?
Telephoning Stopped

Reuter learnt early this morning that, owing to what are believed to be 'serious political reasons', Spain is cut off from telephonic communications with the rest of the world.

A cryptic message has been received in Paris from Spain (says Reuter this morning) stating that 'there have been incidents at Cuenca, the number [of] victims is not yet known'. Cuenca is the capital of the province of Cuenca, situated about ninety miles south-east of Madrid.

Monday July 20 1936   *p.9*

SPANISH REPUBLIC FIGHTING GRAVE REVOLT
'The Situation in Control' – GOVERNMENT CLAIM

REBELS STILL HOLD SEVILLE WIRELESS STATION
British Destroyers Stand By

A military, Monarchist, and Fascist revolt on a large scale began in Spanish Morocco during the night of Friday–Saturday, and in a number of towns in Spain itself, as well as in the Canaries and the Balearic Islands.

News from Spain is heavily censored, but it is evident from the messages that were being allowed to come through last night that the threat to the Republic has been – and may still be – very grave.

The Left Government still rules in Madrid – though in fifteen hours it was twice reconstructed – and the capital's wireless station announced last night that it holds the upper hand both in Morocco and in Spain itself.

Among the centres involved in Spain are Malaga, Seville,

Barcelona, Bilbao, and Cadiz. A French air liner from North Africa which refuelled at Barcelona reported that the city had been bombed by aeroplanes.

The Seville wireless station, which is in the hands of the rebels, and has been sending out rebel propaganda of varying degrees of credibility, broadcast yesterday a report that General Franco, at the head of rebel troops, had landed at Cadiz from Morocco and was to march on Madrid.

What proportion of the army is behind the rising is uncertain, but the Civil Guards seem to be faithful to the Government.

The Government claims that the navy remains loyal and that a number of ships have been sent to Morocco to help in quelling the revolt, but a rebel destroyer yesterday bombarded the barracks at La Linea, near Gibraltar, where loyal troops had refused to follow Fascist officers. A Melilla message reports that three warships have joined the rebels.

As for the Air Force, there are frontier reports supporting the Government's claims that its planes have bombed Ceuta, Melilla, and other strongholds seized by the rebels in Morocco.

In a statement broadcast yesterday the new Cabinet, headed by Senor Giral, declared that it would arm the Spanish people with the object of crushing the revolutionary movement. Arms have been issued to civilians in Madrid and other centres for the defence of the Republic.

There has apparently been no serious trouble in Madrid itself.

p.9.

ARMS ISSUED TO CIVILIANS
(Censored.)

Madrid, July 19.

The Republic has survived a well-planned detailed plot against its life. At present the Left is still in command. Senor Jose Giral, who has been Minister of Marine in previous Governments since the victory of the Left in the last elections, became Premier this afternoon. General Pozas is the new Minister of the Interior in Senor Giral's Cabinet.

The Government formed by Senor Martinez Barrios (Radical Democrat) early this morning in succession to Senor Quiroga's Cabinet fell before midday.

The situation in Madrid was still critical to-night. Many soldiers have taken advantage of the Government's offer to abandon their regiments if they are not in sympathy with the attitude of the officers, and some hundreds in Madrid have offered themselves to the Government to carry out any duties that may be imposed on them.

The authorities in Madrid have armed the people, and throughout the streets can be seen taxi-loads of the Milieta Roja (Red Militia) with rifles, revolvers, and daggers.

Several lorry loads of miners from the north west of Spain arrived in the capital to-day and placed themselves at the disposition of the authorities.

JAMMING THE REBELS' WIRELESS

The Seville broadcasting station and telephone building is in the hands of the rebels, and the Madrid station has taken over the Seville wavelength so that it can jam any broadcast from the latter station.

From time to time the Government broadcasts news of the situation throughout the country, from which it appears that the authorities have everything well in hand. Many of the mutinous officers in Morocco are reported to have fled over the French frontier from Melilla. The navy is firmly stated to be on the side of authorities.

In Barcelona, Seville, and Malaga the Government claims to be now controlling the situation.

The importance of the navy's loyalty is emphasised here because of reports that rebels are coming over from Morocco to the home country and that some have actually landed. There is no reliable information here regarding reports that some of the warships sent to Morocco immediately the revolt became widespread have fraternised with the rebels. To all appearances the military rising has been overcome by those sections of the forces of the Republic which remain loyal.

REBEL GARRISONS BOMBED

Airmen have bombed several towns where the garrisons had rebelled including Seville, Ceuta, and Melilla. Six generals have been degraded from their ranks.

The U.G.T. (General Workers' Union) announced that wherever martial law or a 'state of alarm' might be imposed in Spain by the rebels a general strike would be immediately declared by the workmen.

The Minister of the Interior broadcast this afternoon that arms would be distributed to villagers who wished to organise themselves against the rebels. This is in keeping with the policy adopted in Madrid.

The Minister also announced on the air that the rebels at Melilla, a fortified city and one of the most important centres in Spanish Morocco, had been completely routed. Many of them were, he said, fleeing to French territory, where they were being held at the disposal of the authorities.

He also declared that the rebels at Barcelona and Malaga had surrendered. No forces, he asserted, were marching on Madrid.

'The state of siege illegally proclaimed by anti-Government elements in a certain number of towns on the Peninsula and in Morocco, the Balearic Islands, and the Canaries, is rescinded by the Spanish Government,' it is officially announced. Behind this statement lies the first official admission in Spain that the rebel movement is not confined to Morocco and Seville, but has spread to other towns on the mainland as well as to the Balearic Islands and Canaries.

Decrees ordering the dismissal of troops which have taken part in the 'illegal movement against the Republic', and the dissolution of all units of the army which took part in the 'insurrectionist movement' are also announced.

In the troubled areas 'heads of military forces are relieved of their duties of obedience towards any of their superiors who may have turned rebel'.–Reuter.

Tuesday July 21 1936   *p.11*

CHECKS TO THE REBELS
A Short-Lived Revolt in the Capital

GOVERNMENT MAKES HEADWAY
Control of Seville Radio Station Regained

Though all news from Spain is severely censored and a mass of conflicting rumours is pouring in from the frontier towns, it seemed clear last night that the Left Government is more than holding its own against its rebel military and Fascist assailants.

Except in Spanish Morocco, which the rebels hold, and in some centres of Southern Spain the revolutionary movement appears to have made no headway.

The Spanish Government, in an official broadcast from Madrid at 9.50 last evening claimed that the rebellion has been completely crushed.

The official broadcast announcement, made in French, English, German, and Spanish, says the Government has suc-ceeded in restoring order with the help of the Civil Guard, Storm Troops, the Army, and the Militia under the direction of the Popular Front.

MONARCHIST GENERAL KILLED

'The Government dominates the situation in all Spain,' said the Spanish Ambassador in London after a telephone conversation with the capital.

It was added at the Embassy that

There is still fighting in Seville, Valencia, and Saragoassa.

In Madrid forces loyal to the Government have taken one of the barracks that was in the power of the rebels. The situation in Madrid is now quiet.

The navy and the Air Force are with the Government. The navy is taking steps to prevent troops from Morocco crossing to Spain. Rebel forces who have landed in the South of Spain near Gibraltar have been defeated.

It is denied that General Mola (the rebel leader in Spain) is marching on Madrid. General Fanjul and General Goded have been arrested. General Sanjurgo (the Monarchist leader), who was trying to reach Spain by air from Lisbon, has been killed in an accident.

At ten o'clock last night the Seville Radio Station, which for two days has been radiating rebel communiques, began issuing Government statements. It had been announced earlier in the evening from Madrid that an attack on the parts of the city held by the rebels was under way.

The troops in Seville have given assurance, a Government communique stated last evening, that they were able to hold the town for the Government.

The rebels yesterday claimed that they were in possession of Andalusia, Castille (excepting Madrid), Aragon, and Navarre.

BRITISH PARTY RESCUED

Malaga, part of which is reported to be in flames, is still in the Government's hands. A number of British officers and their wives who had gone there from Gibraltar on leave were brought safely back to Gibraltar yesterday afternoon by the dockyard tug Noel Birch, which had picked them up at Marbella, on the road from Malaga to Gibraltar. With them were other British visitors, the party numbering forty all told. No one in the party had been injured.

A British warship has gone to the help of other visitors at Malaga, and R.A.F. planes are standing by at Gibraltar should their services be needed to rescue British subjects.

A Reuter telegram from Tangier reports that two bombs were dropped by a Spanish plane in the vicinity of the British Bland Line steamer Gibel Dersa yesterday afternoon when she was in the Straits on her way from Gibraltar to Tangier. There were no hits. Whether the plane was a Government or a rebel one is not stated.

Fears of bombing by rebel planes from Morocco have led to a rush of refugees from frontier towns into Gibraltar, which is packed with refugees.

Although there were again reports that rebel strong points in Barcelona were bombed yesterday by Government planes, the wireless station there last night broadcast that all was then quiet.

WORKERS' DEFENCE OF REPUBLIC

Madrid, July 21.

Facing the threat of rebel armies on three fronts, the Republic is hastily organising its forces. An improvised army of 5,000 peasants and workmen is marching towards Saragossa to the north-east, having been supplied with arms by the Civil Guard. Madrid taxis and private cars have been requisitioned for transport.

From Saragossa the rebels may be able to aim a blow at the capital. In the mountain roads that stretch between the two places a battle is thought likely. The Government forces have blown up a bridge to stop the rebel advance. Forces of the People's Militia are now occupying the northern road from the capital. All motor-cars travelling towards Madrid are strictly searched.

Government aeroplanes flying northward to-day sighted a convoy of fourteen lorries coming down the road from Segovia (about forty miles north of Madrid) and dropped bombs on them.

17 OFFICERS SHOOT THEMSELVES

In Madrid itself the forces of Red Militia are estimated at about 10,000 men. They are commanded by two officers who remained loyal to the Republic. The militia are supplied with rifles, automatic pistols, and in some cases steel helmets taken from the barracks which were captured yesterday. It has not yet been possible to estimate the number killed in the fighting, which went on almost all day yesterday.

To-day has been quiet and the Government claims to be in full control of the situation here. Mutinous troops in Madrid Barracks have surrendered. Their leader, General Fanjul, is in prison. When the Montana Barracks fell yesterday the bodies

15

of seventeen officers were found in an inner room. They had committed suicide when they saw that the end had come.

Fighting broke out this morning on the Prado, the wide avenue not far from the centre of Madrid. Soldiers and engineers attacked the civilian militia but after a short encounter were put to flight. The Minister of the Interior announced that several hundred rebel officers are being held prisoner.

Two battles were fought near Madrid to-day between rebellious troops and Government forces composed of shock police, Civil Guards, and Red Militia. It is stated here that in both cases the rebels were defeated. ·

For the first time since the beginning of the rebellion troops and sailors have appeared in the streets of Madrid in requisitioned cars. They wore red armlets to show that they are not on the side of the rebels, but otherwise they had regular service uniforms.

CAPTURE OF SAN SEBASTIAN

Rebels have captured San Sebastian.

The rebels, who had marched in force from Pamplona, proclaimed martial law throughout the province of Navarre and gathered up a mass of young men from the countryside, many of whom are stated to have been impressed at the point of the revolver. The authorities gave orders to blow up a bridge on the road to San Sebastian to stop them, but the rebels then took to smugglers' paths through the hills, over which they made their way to the town.

A Government aeroplane was sent up from San Sebastian to watch the progress of the enemy troops as they wound their way over the mountain tracks. Gendarmes and Customs officers stationed at Irun went out fully armed to face the rebels. All the local male population from the age of 17 upwards was called up by the Popular Front to defend the town. Most of them brandished sporting rifles, shot-guns, and old pistols.–Reuter.

Thursday July 23 1936   *p.11*

THE BARCELONA FIGHTING

Perpignan (Southern France), July 22.

A first-hand account of the fierce fighting in Barcelona, in which 500 are stated to have been killed and 3,000 wounded, is given in messages sent over the frontier to-day by Reuter's Barcelona correspondent. The fighting resolved itself into a

16

series of the most bloody street battles, in which loyal troops, assisted by armed civilians, fought hand to hand with the rebels, who attacked repeatedly.

'The worst day was Sunday,' says the message. 'By dusk that evening at least 300 lay dead. At one time bodies were lying piled on the steps of an underground railway station. The firing was continuous from early morning. Machine-guns and artillery were used. The Colon Hotel in Catalonia Square was shelled in an attempt to dislodge the rebels, who were in force there. The noise was tremendous. Besides the firing, aeroplanes roared continuously overhead. Taxis and private cars were commandeered to transport the wounded to hospital. There was a continuous stream of such improvised ambulances. The hospitals were full to overflowing, and an appeal was sent to all private doctors to come and attend patients.'

BURNING OF CHURCHES

The correspondent goes on to describe the scenes that followed the victory of the Government forces.

'Bands of anarchists and Communists raged through the town sacking, looting and setting fire to every church and convent and other religious buildings. No fewer than twenty convents and churches were razed to the ground or seriously damaged, and only the famous cathedral remains intact. In one religious seminary, it is stated, many priests were put to death. It is believed that the clergy were able to get away most of the church treasures before the looters arrived. The mob, drunk with victory, afterwards paraded the streets of the town attired in the robes of ecclesiastical authorities and other officials.

'After the fighting on Sunday and Monday the streets were littered with the dead bodies of men and horses. It was only after the rebels had suffered tremendous losses that General Goded, their commander, surrendered, and fighting continued spasmodically in the streets for some time afterwards. Police, however, mounted guns on the stone setts of the squares and gradually secured command of the situation.'

Saturday July 25 1936   *p.12*

SPAIN AND THE POWERS

The international significance of the Spanish Civil War is far greater than it seemed to be at first. There is reticence on the subject here, and official quarters still profess to know nothing about things that are becoming common knowledge.

The Spanish Government has appealed to the British Government asking it to use its influence with Portugal to prevent the rebels from being supplied with arms through Portugal. The Spanish Government has also tried to buy fuel at Gibraltar for its warships, but so far it has only met with refusal. It has not yet got France to sell it aeroplanes.

The Spanish Government is growing uneasy concerning the intentions of Germany and Italy, and fears that real or alleged menace to German or Italian consulates in Spain may lead to interference on the part of these Powers.

This was the first intimation of the wider significance of the Spanish Civil War.

Saturday July 25 1936   p.13

REBELS AIDED BY ITALIANS AND GERMANS
Berlin's Mediterranean Ambitions

From our Diplomatic Correspondent

London, Friday.

A pessimistic view is taken here of events in Spain. There is no indication yet whether the Government or the insurgents are likely to prevail. Everything points to a protracted and sanguinary civil war.

The insurgents have the advantage of getting outside help whereas the Government is getting none. The latter has applied to the French Government for permission to import arms from France, but so far at least permission has not been given. The insurgents, on the other hand, are being assisted by the Italians and Germans.

During the last few weeks large numbers of Italian and German agents have arrived in Morocco and the Balearic Islands. These agents are taking part in military activities and are also exercising a certain political influence.

WEAPONS OF ITALIAN ORIGIN

For the insurgents the belief that they have the support of the two great 'Fascist Powers' is an immense encouragement. But it is also more than an encouragement, for many of the weapons now in their hands are of Italian origin. This is particularly so in Morocco.

18

The German influence is strongest in the Balearic Islands. Germany has a great interest in the victory of the insurgents. Apparently she hopes to secure concession in the Balearic Islands from them when they are in power. These islands play an important part in German plans for the future development of sea-power in the Mediterranean.

The civil war is of particular interest to Germany because the victory of the insurgents would open the prospect (closed by Anglo-French collaboration and by the existence of a pro-British, pro-French, and pro-League Spanish Republic) of action in Western Europe. That is to say, a 'Fascist' Spain would, for Germany, be a means of 'turning the French flank' and of playing a part in the Mediterranean.

On the Spanish mainland Germany disposed of a numerous and extremely well-organised branch of the National Socialist party. This branch has been strongly reinforced by new-comers from Germany during the last few weeks. She also disposes of a powerful organisation for political and military espionage, which works behind a diplomatic and educational facade. Barcelona in particular has a large German population, the greater part of which is at the disposal of the National Socialists.

The fate of Morocco is naturally of the highest interest to Germany, for if the insurgents are victorious she may hope to secure territorial concessions in Morocco and therefore a foothold in Northern Africa.

Tuesday July 28 1936   *p.14*

BRITISH OPINION ON THE SALE OF ARMS TO SPAIN
Observing Strict Neutrality

PROBLEMS OF EXTREMISTS UNDER NO CENTRAL CONTROL

From our Diplomatic Correspondent

London, Monday.

It is admitted here that the sale of arms to a lawful Government does not constitute interference in the internal affairs of the country under that Government. But Spain, so it is urged, is at the moment a special problem. The civil war is one between the lawful Government and a rebel army, but there are, on both sides, large heterogeneous forces under no central control. Much of the fighting is purely local in character.

It is doubted here whether arms could be supplied to the Spanish Government as such, or to troops that are indubitably under its control. The view taken is that the arms would probably pass into the hands of extremists who, although fighting against the insurgents, are under no central authority.

Although the belief here is that the odds are against the insurgents, it is considered possible nevertheless that they may win. And there is every desire here to be on friendly terms with Spain, no matter what the complexion of the Spanish Government may be. It is for these reasons – and one other – that strict neutrality is being observed.

The other reason is that if some Powers, such as France or Great Britain, sells arms to one side, other Powers, such as Germany or Italy, may sell arms to the other. It is considered desirable that there shall be as few arms as possible in Spain and that there shall be no international complications.

LETTERS TO THE EDITOR

REFUSAL OF SUPPLIES TO SPANISH NAVY
A Breach of International Law at Gibraltar?

Sir,–It appears, from reports reaching this country from Gibraltar, that warships of the Spanish navy, acting under the orders of the Spanish Government, have been refused facilities for refuelling and for taking in a supply of provisions by the Gibraltar authorities, who are, presumably, responsible to the British Government. If this is the case, surely a quite indefensible breach of international law has been committed, amounting to an act of hostility towards a friendly Power at present engaged in coping with a serious internal revolt.

As we understand the position, it is wholly contrary to established international law and practice to refuse fuel or food to vessels which put in at a neutral port, especially when the country to which they belong is not in a state of war with any other country.

We are loath to believe that such an act of international discourtesy – or worse – can have received the approval of the Government of this country or that it can indicate any degree of sympathy with the reactionary forces which have taken up arms against the Spanish Republic. The cause of democracy all over Europe is so grievously at stake to-day that it would be disastrous for Great Britain, which professes to uphold democratic principles, even to appear to be on the side of a reactionary and Fascist uprising against the Parliamentary Constitution and Government of the Spanish Republic.

We therefore appeal to the British Government, if, as we hope, the action of the authorities at Gibraltar was taken without their knowledge or approval, promptly to make the appropriate apologies to the Spanish Government and to extend to it in its struggle all such courtesy and assistance as in accordance with international law and custom, the Government of a friendly nation has every right to expect.–Yours, &c.,

G. D. H. COLE.
WINIFRED HORRABIN.
D. N. PRITT.
H. G. WELLS.
KINGSLEY MARTIN.
DAVID LOW.
J. A. HOBSON.
A. SUSAN LAWRENCE.
HASTINGS (Viscount).
ALLEN OF HURTWOOD.
LEAN MANNING.
J. F. HORRABIN.
RICHARD ACLAND.
W. H. THOMPSON.
R. STAFFORD CRIPPS.
GERALD GOULD.
London, July 27.

Wednesday July 29 1936   *p.10*

SPAIN AND SUPPLIES

The Spanish Government which is now being attacked so bitterly by military and Fascist rebels is the recognised Government of the country, duly and constitutionally elected, and it is therefore entitled to all the rights which are accorded to such a Government by international law and custom. It has the further claim on our sympathy that, broadly speaking, it stands for a free system against reaction, and the free systems in these days are already few enough. It is, therefore, of great moment that the Spanish Government should not be hampered in its efforts to procure supplies of war materials from neighbouring countries, and the suggestions that have been made during the last few days that it was being so hampered, that it was being prohibited from obtaining any sort of supplies,

21

have been alarming. A letter in our columns yesterday, for instance, called attention to the remarkable report that Spanish warships at Gibraltar had been refused facilities for obtaining fuel and provisions by the authorities. It is very necessary to know precisely what the position is, what out Government (and the French Government) are doing.

The explanations of the British Government, if taken at their face value, mean that the Spanish Government can freely obtain from private British firms the munitions that it orders: Paris messages say that this represents also the policy of France. Mr. Eden on Monday said:

> I have been asked whether the Government have put a ban on the supply of oil to the Spanish fleet. The answer is 'No.'

Lord Stanhope added yesterday that at Gibraltar the Spanish warships had obtained fresh provisions from the shore, and might have obtained oil fuel also from any private firm, but not from the official oil supply. Mr. Eden had already said that, although no licences to export arms to Spain had been applied for, the 'ordinary regulations' governing the export of arms to foreign countries were applicable to Spain, and that the Government was maintaining the 'normal attitude' appropriate to 'a situation such as this'. Two considerations, neither of which is negligible, make both the British and the French Governments nervous lest they should be thought to be assisting as Governments the Spanish constitutional Government. The first is that the rebels of to-day may be the constituted (and vindictive) Government of to-morrow; the second is that if democratic Governments begin to assist democrats Nazi and Fascist Governments may take to openly assisting those of their own kidney, and unpleasant frictions may result. What is necessary at this moment is that both here and in France no obstacle should be placed in the way of privately produced munitions and materials going to the Spanish Government if it orders them. But will there be, in fact, no obstacle? Our Diplomatic Correspondent yesterday gave an account of the views held among people who are certainly not without authority. They fear, he said, that arms supplied to the Spanish Government might fall into 'extremist' hands, and by them 'it is considered desirable that there "shall be as few arms as possible in Spain"'. If the Spanish Government orders arms in quantity from private firms and if we faithfully carry out the 'ordinary regulations', how shall we secure that there 'shall be as few arms as possible in Spain' – which may be the short route to the establishment of yet another military Fascist dictatorship?

INTERVIEW WITH GEN. FRANCO
Effort to Turn Rebellion into an International Question

General Franco, the rebel Spanish leader, in an interview with a Press Association correspondent at his headquarters in Tetuan, made what appears to be virtually an appeal for international support, and also indicated the possibility of introducing large numbers of Riffs into Spain to fight against the Spanish Government.

He indicated that the revolutionaries had plenty of money, but did not explain where it came from. He adopted the revolutionaries' favourite argument that time is of little consequence to them, and that all they have to do is to hold on until the Government's funds and supplies are exhausted. He said:

'It is not merely a national question, it is international. Surely Great Britain, Germany, and Italy must be in sympathy with our aims. I am absolutely disinterested personally. As long as the uprising benefits Spain by stamping out Communism I am content, but I have no wish to inflict unnecessary hardships. After all they are not all Communists.

'If all goes well I shall establish my first headquarters at Seville. We are not short of money, but the danger lies in what help the Spanish Government may receive from Moscow and the Popular Front Government in France. On that depends how long the Government forces can hold out.

'The Riffs, too, are anxious to help us. They have made representations asking to be allowed to form regiments of their own under my officers and go and fight against the Communists. The Foreign Legion, both Spanish and native, is entirely faithful to me.'

BOMBING AT TANGIER

General Franco admitted his disappointment at the collapse of the rising in the navy, but went on:

'Without the officers the men can do little. They are ignorant and have no idea of navigation. Fuel and food are short. It is only a matter of time until they finally surrender to us.'

The correspondent asked about the bombing of the Spanish warship Jaime I., at the entrance of Tangier harbour, when bombs fell close to a British steamer and caused alarm in Tangier. The General appeared to be upset. 'The pilot responsible', he stated, 'was sent for and I severely reprimanded him. He had been looking for the boat and missed it until it was nearing Tangier harbour. Then he lost his head and dropped his bombs against my express order.'

FRANCO AT SEVILLE

The Seville broadcasting station (which is still in the hands of the insurgents) announces that Franco has moved to Seville and that this city will be his headquarters.

Friday July 31 1936 p.11

ITALIAN HELP FOR SPANISH REBELS
'Planes Crash in Algeria on the Way

CONFIRMATION OF FRENCH SUSPICIONS
Flying Without Identification Marks

From our own Correspondent

Paris, July 30 (Midnight).

Five Italian military aeroplanes were seen flying over Algeria to-day towards Spanish Morocco, and later one of them crashed near Nemours and two others came down in French territory near the frontier of Spanish Morocco. Of the occupants of the wrecked 'plane three were killed and two injured. A number of machine-guns were found among the wreckage.

The incident confirms beyond doubt the complicity of Italy in the Spanish rebellion. It is rather amusing that this afternoon M. Delbos, the French Foreign Minister, should have spoken with much appreciation of the assurances of neutrality received from the Italian Government earlier in the day.

REPORT OF GERMAN 'PLANES

At to-day's session of the Foreign Affairs Committee of the Senate both M. Blum, the Premier, and M. Delbos flatly denied that any arms, aeroplanes, or other war materials have been sent to Spain from France.

There is at the same time an uneasy feeling in France that whereas the Spanish Government forces are receiving no help from outside, the same cannot be said of the rebels. The 'Intransigeant' received yesterday a message from Spanish Morocco saying that the first of a series of twenty German three-engined Junker aeroplanes had reached Tetuan, the rebel base, and that the rest were awaited there shortly. The same message said that twenty Caproni aeroplanes from Italy were also expected there.

In Rome it is officially denied that any Italian 'planes have been sent to Spanish Morocco.

ITALIAN 'PLANE SEEN ON THE SEA

Oran (Algeria), July 30.

One of the Italian airmen who came down stated that they were on a mission to Nador, south of Melilla, in Spanish Morocco, which is held by the insurgents. The machine carried no mark or identification number.

It is also stated the Belgian commercial 'plane of the Sabena Line which left Oran for Marseilles this morning wirelessed back that she saw a disabled tri-engined Savoia machine (an Italian make) at 11 20 a.m. riding the waves fifty miles out of Oran. The machine carried three persons.—Reuter.

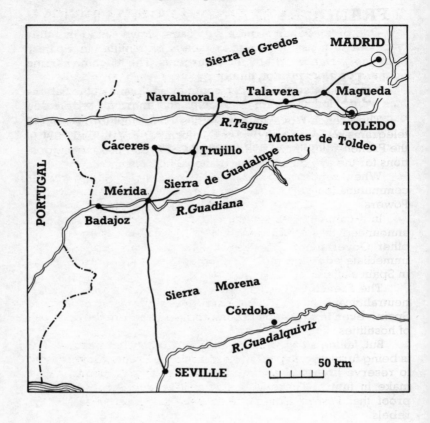

FRANCE APPEALS TO BRITAIN AND ITALY
Pact of Non-Intervention in Spain

DANGER OF FASCIST POWERS SENDING ARMS TO THE REBELS

The French Government on Saturday evening dispatched telegrams to London and Rome, informing Britain and Italy of the French attitude on the Spanish situation and making suggestions for the avoidance of international complications.

When replies are received it is expected that a similar communication will be sent to Germany and other interested Powers.

In a communique issued in Paris the French Government announced that it had decided to address to the British and other Governments principally concerned an appeal for the immediate adoption of a common agreement not to intervene in Spain's affairs.

The French Government has so far observed the strictest neutrality and has not authorised any exportation of arms to Spain – even in execution of contracts made before the outbreak of hostilities.

But, failing an agreement, the fact that foreign war material is being furnished to the rebels obliges the French Government to reserve liberty of action in regard to any decisions it may make in future. There is, it is considered in Paris, sufficient proof that Fascist Governments have furnished arms to the rebels.

It is understood that the British Government is in entire agreement with Paris regarding the necessity of avoiding international complications. No formal reply has yet been sent from London – where Lord Halifax is in Charge of the Foreign Office in the absence of Mr. Eden, – but it is learned that conversations based on the points raised in the French message will be conducted between the Powers concerned through diplomatic channels.

General Denain, former French Air Minister, who has been conducting an investigation in Algeria into the affair of the Italian 'planes – arising from the crashing of two of them on French territory, – returned to Paris yesterday. A statement by the French Government on this matter is forecast for to-day.

27

REBELS AWAIT REINFORCEMENTS BY AIR

A number of minor engagements are reported from Spain during the weekend, but the position is no clearer than it was last week, and a major engagement between the Government forces and the rebels is still to come.

Apparently the rebels are awaiting reinforcements of Spanish Legion and native troops from Morocco, which is completely in the possession of the anti-Government forces. Their transport by air, which has been going on slowly, is to be hastened now that General Franco has at his disposal (according to a report) 18 large Italian 'planes flown from Italy last week, in addition to his other aircraft.

A rain of bombs was poured from the air by Government 'planes on the Balearic island of Majorca, and the Government has captured Cabrera in the Balearic Islands group, some 35 miles from Majorca, which would provide a useful refuelling base for Government aeroplanes in their attacks on Majorca from their present base at Barcelona, more than 150 miles away. Oyarzun, the village near San Sebastian from which the rebels hoped to gain an access to the sea, has been wiped out in another bombardment.

The Government forces are stated to have consolidated their movement closing in on Saragossa, the rebel stronghold in Aragon. The Government claims in addition that a sortie made by the insurgents from Saragossa towards the village of Tardienta was successfully repelled with severe losses inflicted on the rebels.

Two rebel aeroplanes were brought down by Government machines in an engagement not far from Madrid.

Government troops hope to enter Huesca, again bombed yesterday, some time to-day. They also claim to be closing in on Granada.

It is learned from Lisbon that the 'ducal army', 1,500 rebels, mostly exiled aristocrats who have been living in Portugal, who hoped to 'be the first to enter Madrid', were routed yesterday on their way to Salamanca.

In Madrid itself life is beginning to take on a more normal aspect. Letters from England are beginning to arrive again, and in some cases theatres even are opening their doors once more. Messages from press correspondents continue to be heavily censored.

GOVERNMENT CURBING EXTREMISTS

The authorities in Barcelona – the scene, according to refugees' stories, of a 'Red Terror' – as well as in Madrid are taking steps to deal with excesses by extremist adherents.

A proclamation issued in Barcelona at the week-end by the Committee of the Central Anti-Fascist Militia says:

> All are to be shot who pillage unlawfully, carry out searches, or commit injustices.
> The committee has 5,000 militiamen at its disposal to safeguard public order.

'Catalonia', it is added, 'refuses to allow its name to be sullied by acts of terrorism and we shall see that order and revolutionary discipline are maintained.'

The committee has had a similar proclamation dropped by 'planes to all parts of the city in an attempt to stop acts of pillage and assassination which have recently occurred in Barcelona.

In Madrid strict orders have been given by police headquarters that no houses must be burst into unless it is made plain that this is being done under instruction from the authorities. In future the 'Red Militias' will only have the right to indicate their suspicions to the head of the police, but not to carry out any searches themselves.

All householders, in addition, have been given instructions to telephone at once to police headquarters if any attempt is made to enter their houses. Flying squads will, it is promised, at once be sent to prevent such unauthorised visits.

In San Sebastian, too, it was reported last night, the disorders of the first days of the fighting have disappeared and the bands of armed young men and women who paraded the streets have vanished.

Thursday August 6 1936   *p.12*

ITALIAN ARMY 'PLANES FOR THE REBELS
Result of the French Inquiry

Oran, August 5.

The principal results of the inquiry conducted by the French authorities into the forced landing of two Italian 'planes in French Morocco last week are now known. It has been proved that these machines and the three others which accompanied them in the flight to Spanish Morocco were all regular Italian Air Force 'planes.

Documents seized abroad show that the five 'planes, four

of which were Savoia Marchetti machines and one a Savoia
'plane, had up to July 20 belonged to the 56th and 57th and
58th squadrons of the Italian Air Force. The two 'planes which
were seized by the French authorities carried their war equipment with the exception of bombs, and were supplied with
ammunition for machine-guns. The machines had no identification numbers, and the place where the national colours had
been was freshly painted over with white paint.

The results of the inquiry indicated that the expedition was
prepared in great haste both by the organisers and those com-
missioned to carry out the under-taking, and this explained
the lack of precautions taken to conceal the exact identity of
the machines and their pilots. The crews were composed not
only of civilian pilots, both commercial flyers and amateurs,
but also of camouflaged Air Force men whose real identity
was revealed by official papers found on the body of one of
those who were killed as well as by his passport, driving
licence, and military pay-book. . . .

Tuesday August 11 1936   *p.9*

GERMAN 'PLANES SEIZED IN SPAIN
Russia Agrees to Non-Intervention

REBELS CLAIM SUCCESSES NEAR
PORTUGAL AND IN THE NORTH

There was no marked change yesterday in the international
situation created by the Spanish civil war. Germany is expected
to reply to-day to the French proposal for a general non-
intervention pact. Italy is said to have made reservations.
Portugal is also ready to agree in principle but requires
assurances on some points.

It is learned in Paris that the Soviet Government has
informed the French Chargé d'Affaires in Moscow of its
adherence to the text of the French proposals.

A fresh 'incident' has been created by the reported seizure
in Spain of German aeroplanes, which the Germans say were
used for the evacuation of their nationals there.

The State Department at Washington reports that all
Americans have been urged to leave Madrid, as the situation
there is 'increasingly threatening'.

PROGRESS OF CIVIL WAR

The rebels are concentrating for an attack on the Government forces at Badajoz in the south-west sector of Spain. The town was again bombed by aeroplanes yesterday and a column of 500 'buses filled with rebel troops is being sent to join in the attack. The rebels are said to occupy all the hills surrounding Badajoz and hope for its fall at any minute.

If the town falls they hope shortly to gain control of the whole sector west of Madrid, then join with the rebels north and south of the capital, and eventually encircle Madrid.

They also claim to have captured the harbour of Santander and the whole of the province of Santander. If this report is true it will mean that they have at last gained the outlet to the sea and a naval base which they have so long been striving for in this sector to help their transport of supplies and food.

DIFFICULTIES IN WAY OF NON-INTERVENTION AGREEMENT

From our Diplomatic Correspondent

London, Monday.

There would now be no difficulty at all in negotiating an international agreement for non-intervention in the Spanish civil war if it were not for the attitude of Italy and Germany. These two Powers alone prevent the rapid conclusion and application of such an agreement. The difficulties raised by Portugal could easily be overcome. Several interested Powers have now placed an embargo on the export of war material to Spain, and there is no obvious reason why Italy and Germany should not be willing to do the same, as Great Britain and almost all the other Powers are willing.

The Italian suggestion that 'non-intervention' be extended to expressions of sympathy can only be regarded as obstructive, for such expressions could only be suppressed in the dictatorially governed countries. The Italians know perfectly well that their suggestion, to which they appear to cling as though it were an unalterable condition, simply could not be carried out in France and this country. Nor can expressions of sympathy be rightly regarded as being interventionist. And all the time Italy herself gives the Spanish rebels her full moral support, nor does it seem that Italian material support has come to an end.

Germany agrees 'in principle' to the French proposal but asks that it be elaborated and extended without making any concrete suggestions herself. German assurances that no German help will be given to the rebels are very emphatic, but they would carry more conviction if Germany were to accept and carry out non-intervention as proposed by the French Government.

Even a provisional agreement for 'non-intervention' would be welcomed here and in Paris. It is believed that a big, and possibly decisive, battle is impending in the South of Spain, a battle for which the rebels are preparing to take the offensive with Moroccan troops. Any outside help in the form of aeroplanes, arms, or ammunition might decide the issue. With the co-operation of Italy and Germany outside help of this kind could be cut off at once, but without their co-operation this is impossible.

Thursday August 13 1936   *p.9*

NON-INTERVENTION: THE OUTLOOK IMPROVES
Will Italy Follow Germany's New Lead?

From our Diplomatic Correspondent

London, Wednesday.

It is evident that the German Government does not want any more trouble in connection with the Spanish civil war. It seems to believe that further support of the rebels will injure Franco-German and, above all, Anglo-German relations, and, much as it desires a rebel victory and concerned as it is over what it believes to be the spread of so-called 'Bolshevism' in Europe, it prefers, for the moment at least, not to take any risks where no vital interests of its own are involved.

Interference with the internal affairs of other countries is a conscious instrument of German foreign policy, and is for that very reason used only when it is safe to do so, or, if any risks are taken, only when the end in view is regarded as being of vital interest to Germany. It is therefore unlikely that Germany will put any further obstacles in the way of an agreement for non-intervention.

ITALY'S CONDITIONS

The Italian reply to the French proposals is favourable in so far as it accepts the text of these proposals in full, but unfavourable in so far as the Italians wish to add three conditions – that no subsidies be raised on behalf of either Spanish faction, that no subjects of the Powers who sign the agreement join either faction as volunteers, and that an International Committee superintend the working of the agreement.

It is difficult, if not impossible, in a democratic country to stop subscriptions for any cause that is not illegal. As for volunteers, the French are prepared to forbid organised recruiting, but they have no means of preventing French subjects from going to Spain as ordinary visitors and then joining either faction. It does not appear that many volunteers have taken part in the civil war except that a certain number of German emigrés who are trained pilots or machinegunners have offered their services to the loyalists. The French do not think that subscriptions or volunteers for ambulance work in Spain ought to be prohibited. To the Italian proposal for a committee of control the French raise no objection.

RUSSIA STOPS SUBSCRIPTIONS

According to information received here, Russia has already stopped subscription on behalf of the Spanish 'loyalists'. The difficulties raised by Portugal are being met by Anglo-French assurances that she need feel no anxiety lest her territory be violated. Germany, it seems, is no longer an obstacle to an agreement. Italy, therefore, stands alone as the one obstructive Power. But it is believed that the difficulties raised by the conditions she has made will be overcome.

It is therefore possible that the international crisis produced by the Spanish civil war is coming to an end.

TWO DANGERS

Two dangers still remain – that Italy may continue to give clandestine aid to the rebels (it seems unlikely that Germany will do so any more), in which case every agreement for non-intervention will be vitiated, for France at least would resume liberty of action; and that the growing xenophobia of the Spaniards will lead to assaults on foreigners in Spain, especially on Germans and Italians. Such assaults, if at all murderous, might rouse the Germans and Italians to renewed action – and it must be admitted that no Power would stand aside to see its own subjects murdered – only, in the case of Italy at least, the occasion for further delaying tactics might be welcome.

But, 'incidents' apart, the chances now are that an agreement for non-intervention will be negotiated. Such an agreement is being considered in a new light as establishing a precedent and a principle. Internal strife is possible in countries other than Spain – in Central and Eastern Europe, for example. The temptation felt by so-called 'dissatisfied' Powers to intervene with a view to their own advantage might be considerable. Indeed, rival factions in Central and Eastern Europe are receiving support from outside even now. It is believed that non-intervention, if established as a principle, may be of value not only in Spain but in other regions as well.

33

THE SPANISH PRESIDENT
A Special Interview

Senor Azana, in a statement made yesterday exclusively to the 'Depéche', Toulouse, and the 'Manchester Guardian', warned France, of the Right, Centre, and Left, and England, 'liberal and generous', of the gravity of the conflict now in progress in Spain.

France and England must think of the grave reaction which a Fascist victory in Spain would have upon their own countries.

'Your frontier, Frenchmen, is at this moment at Guadarrama' (the battle line north of Madrid). If Fascism conquered there would be a new tyrannous Power. France must think of the Mediterranean, of her African communications, of Algeria, Morocco, of the Balearic Islands – formidable naval bases that might fall into the hands of Germany or Italy. And what of Gibraltar?'

Of France and Britain, without distinction of party, the Spanish Government asked that they should reflect and weigh the pros and cons of the situation. A pacific nation like Spain would suffer, if Fascism won, the same fate as Ethiopia.

Thursday August 13 1936   *p.12*

THE FIGHTING ROUND MADRID
A Survey of the Present Position

In spite of various rebel claims on the wireless there does not appear to be any immediate danger of Madrid's falling to the rebels. Pressure in the north has been relaxed and in the south the rebel forces are concentrating against Malaga and Badajoz.

Madrid is protected upon the north by two mountain ranges, the Sierra de Guadarrama and the Sierra de Gredos, each rising to some six thousand feet. The principal pass in the gap between the two ranges is the Leon Pass, through which runs the railway line from Segovia. At the other end of the range is the Somosierra Pass, through which runs the line from Siguenza. The third important pass is the Navacerrada Pass, through which runs a road from La Granja.

At the beginning of the war the rebel advance guards belonging to General Mola's forces occupied both the Leon and the Somosierra passes, but after continual fighting they were pushed back, although at one time the rebels were at the north end of the Leon tunnel and the Government forces at the south end. On August 7 the loyalists inflicted a defeat on the rebels near Siguenza, and on August 11 the loyalists occupied the village of Leon, which commands the Leon Pass.

There has been fierce fighting at the village of San Rafael, which is the meeting-point of the roads from Avila and Segovia, both towns in the rebel hands. The rebels north of Madrid are still in the neighbourhood of San Rafael and of Siguenza, but Government forces command the three passes and are hoping to push back General Mola's forces so as to prevent them from making contact with General Franco's forces from the south.

To the west of Madrid at an early stage in the civil war the loyalists took San Martin and thereby threw open a road leading across the Sierra de Gredos. To the south of Madrid the loyalists control the country as far as Toledo, and they also control the town of Ciudad Real, farther south. If they could take Toledo they would have further geographical protection from the west and south-west in the mountain range of Toledo. To the south-east they have been in full control as far as Albacete from the beginning, and they took Albacete on July 25, thereby throwing open their communication with the coast.

The main threat to Madrid seems to be less from the mountains to the north than from the roads through Toledo and Ciudad Real, along which General Franco's Moorish troops may advance once they have secured their rear. The rebels' much-boasted plan of starving out Madrid would seem difficult of realisation unless they can cut off the loyalist communications with the sea on the south-east.

Monday August 17 1936   *p.9*

SLAUGHTER AFTER CAPTURE OF BADAJOZ
Native Troops' Part in the Attack

GENERAL'S WARNING OF DANGER FROM EXCITED MOORS
A Non-Intervention Agreement

The Spanish civil war goes on with ever-growing ruthlessness. After the capture of Badajoz by men of the Spanish Legion and by Moors a great slaughter of the defenders took place. The rebel general thought that 2,000 was perhaps an excessive estimate of the number murdered, but he stressed to a journalist the danger of entering the town as the 'Moors are excited'. A very gallant defence of the town was put up against these long-service and highly trained soldiers.

Following the capture of Badajoz it is reported that a column of foreign legionaries and Moorish troops is pressing by forced marches towards Merida, about 30 miles east of Badajoz. A strong column of Government troops is stated to have arrived at Merida with the intention of marching on Badajoz.

Government forces at Olivenza, about ten miles south of Badajoz, are reported to have surrendered.

SAN SEBASTIAN FIGHT

Efforts on Saturday to capture San Sebastian failed, but yesterday the rebels attacked again. It is said that they are trying to avoid damage to the property of their wealthy supporters in the town and that the Government supporters threaten to blow the buildings up if the town is bombarded.

In the district round Gibraltar the rebels claimed to have routed a Government force near La Linea with the loss of 170 men. The transport of troops from Morocco is reported to be continuing.

NON-INTERVENTION AGREEMENT

It is officially announced by the Foreign Office that full agreement has now been reached between the British and French Governments on the text of the French proposals for the prohibition on the export of arms and munitions of war to Spain. The agreement will come into force as soon as the assent of the German, Italian, Portuguese, and Russian Governments is received.

In another Foreign Office official statement (issued with the personal approval of Mr. Eden) the Government announces that it will take every measure open to it to prevent the supply of civil 'planes to Spain. No licences for export of arms have been issued. British subjects who get into difficulties through taking part in the civil war will, it is stated, not receive any assistance.

The Germans and the Italians who are mainly responsible for holding up the agreement, did not make any new move during the week-end.

Few would deny that the Spanish Civil War was fought with great intensity and that atrocities were a feature of it. The slaughter of the Republican defenders of Badajoz was one of the earliest examples of the ruthless way that the war was to be prosecuted. Later, Guernica was to symbolise for many the character of the conflict.

ITALY'S ACCEPTANCE OF NON-INTERVENTION
A Surprise Decision Last Night

VIOLENT GERMAN ATTACKS ON RUSSIA
Outburst in the Nazi Press

The Italian Government last night unexpectedly announced its adherence to the French non-intervention proposal, Count Ciano, the Foreign Minister, summoned the French Ambassador in Rome and handed him a Note embodying the Italian acceptance.

There is no reference to the expression of public opinion, which Italy previously insisted amounted to intervention.

Our diplomatic correspondent thinks that this decision is almost certainly Mussolini's own, and that it reveals his suspicions that Germany is trying to get a foothold in the western Mediterranean.

Germany is now the only country that refuses to co-operate in a non-intervention agreement.

Not only is she at the moment violently antagonistic to the Spanish Government but yesterday the German press began a violent attack on Russia, which is accused of trying to use the Spanish civil war to promote world revolution.

Germany has protested to Russia and Spain against wireless broadcasts which are said to contain 'slanderous propaganda against Germans'.

The Polish Government has sent a strong protest to Madrid against the shooting of the Polish Consul in Valencia.

GERMANY'S ACCEPTANCE OF NON-INTERVENTION
An International Crisis Avoided?

From our Diplomatic Correspondent

London, Monday.

That Germany has accepted the French proposal for non-intervention in the Spanish civil war has given great satisfaction here. It is not quite clear as yet what the next practical step will be. It is hoped that Germany and Italy will place an effective embargo on the export of all war material (including passenger 'planes) to Spain. All-round non-intervention would then be in practice, and it would be possible to discuss and carry out any further measures that might be necessary.

A FEELING OF RELIEF

It may be premature to say that the international crisis arising out of the Spanish conflict is over, but there is a distinct feeling here that it is, and once non-intervention is really working it may be possible to take international action with a view to alleviating the extreme barbarity of the Spanish conflict and then, perhaps, to promoting a truce.

No doubt there will be further incidents such as happened to the German ship Kamerun and the British ship Gibel Zerjon, but with a reasonable absence of conspicuous ill-will and with non-intervention actually working, such incidents need not, so it is felt, be dangerous.

What was feared above all here was that international partisanship on behalf of the two sides should divide all Europe into two corresponding factions and that the so-called 'Fascist Powers' would be arrayed against the so-called 'democratic Powers'. Such an alignment, which has been aired as though it were a good idea at various times, is regarded here as altogether incompatible with the vital interests of Great Britain and the peace of Europe.

There has, through the crisis, been the closest co-operation between Great Britain and France. Indeed, without this co-operation even the success that has been achieved so far in promoting non-intervention would have been impossible. That Great Britain and France are democratic strengthens the bonds that would, out of vital necessity, exist between them even if one of them were not democratic, and gives the two Powers a special and not exclusively political 'mission' so to speak.

TWO EUROPEAN CAMPS

But any general alignment of the kind that has been suggested would be regarded here as disastrous, indeed it would be looked upon as concealing the danger of a kind of modern holy war. The alignment has been crudely conceived and even recommended as consisting of the 'Fascist' Powers, Germany and Italy on the one hand and the 'Democratic' Powers, Great Britain, France, and Russia on the other. Spain, if the rebels win, belonging to the former, and if the loyalists win, to the latter. The expression 'Democratic' cannot in any sense apply to Russia as yet, though it does not in the least follow that there should be any incompatibility between the foreign policies of Russia and Great Britain. As for Italy the hope and belief entertained here is that her vital interests will be satisfied, not by supporting Pan-German expansion (which would, eventually, threaten her position in the Balkans and in the Mediterranean) but by co-operating with Great Britain and France in preserving the Mediterranean status quo.

THE FIVE-POWER CONFERENCE

As for Germany, the 'German question' is the principal European problem of the day, and it is towards its solution rather than to any other single one that the coming five-Power conference is directed. Had Germany and Italy continued to hold out against non-intervention in Spain the five-Power conference might no longer have been possible and the danger of a general alignment that would have divided Europe into two factions would have become very grave. This danger was, indeed, amongst those the policy of non-intervention was intended to avert.

Special satisfaction is felt here because if non-intervention succeeds the Blum Government will have been preserved against a growing menace. It is fully realised here how strong – and natural – the sympathy for the Spanish loyalists is amongst the supporters of that Government. A French internal crisis is one of the last things that are desired here: indeed it would be looked upon as a European calamity.

When the Blum Government was first formed it encountered a good deal of suspicion and prejudice here. But early opinions of it have been very thoroughly revised and two things are frankly admitted – that it has shown great competence at home and that never since the Great War has co-operation with any French Government been so easy and so profitable as it is with the Blum Government.

Wednesday September 23 1936 *p.9*

REBEL VICTORY
'Key to Madrid' in Their Hands

MOLA'S ULTIMATUMS

From our own Correspondent

Paris, September 22.

With the exception of the Aragon front, where the Catalan militia has been making some slight progress in the Huesca district, the rebels, heavily armed and well organised, are advancing on all the other fronts.

Advancing by the Tagus Valley – Napoleon's route in 1808 – they have captured Maqueda, fifty miles south-west of Madrid and twenty miles north-west of Toledo, where the garrison in the Alcazar still holds out. This point, which is on the main road from Talavera to Madrid, was heavily fortified by the Government with concrete trenches and barbed-wire defences, and the rebels claim that the Government troops who abandoned Maqueda were in a state of demoralisation – which is conceivable when account is taken of the vastly superior equipment of the rebels. Messages from Madrid state that large numbers of new recruits full of enthusiasm are being rushed to this front. Maqueda is described by the rebels as the 'key to Madrid'.

The weather is becoming very cold in Central Spain. Snow is expected to fall in the next few days and large quantities of woollen clothes have been dispatched to the front from Madrid.

According to the rebels their aeroplanes have been showering leaflets over Madrid announcing their early arrival in the suburbs of the capital and summoning the population to surrender.

Bilbao, where large but poorly armed Government forces are concentrated, has received another ultimatum from General Mola threatening the town with destruction unless it surrenders not later than Friday. The Basque Nationalists, anxious to spare the town from destruction, are in favour of surrendering it without battle as they did in the case of San Sebastian.

Monday September 28 1936   *p.9*

PORTUGAL & NON-INTERVENTION
To Join Committee

From our own Correspondent

Geneva, September 27.

The British Delegation to-night announced that as a result of the conversations that Mr. Eden and Mr. W. S. Morrison have had with Dr. Monteiro, the Foreign Minister of Portugal, the Portuguese Government has agreed to join the committee supervising non-intervention measures and has given instructions to its representative in London to that effect.

The Portuguese Government maintains all the reservations that it made when it accepted the non-intervention agreement, but has not made any further reservations as a condition of joining the committee. The original reservations, it will be remembered, were of such a kind as to make the accession of Portugal to the agreement far from complete.

SPANISH ALLEGATIONS

Yesterday Senor Alvarez del Vayo, the Spanish Foreign Minister, sent to the Secretary General of the League documents containing the latest information in regard to alleged violations of the non-intervention agreement by Germany, Italy, and Portugal. It is understood that the documents contained detailed information of a grave nature.

I understand that so many aeroplanes have been supplied to the rebels by Germany and Italy that they now have about three times as many as the Spanish Government whereas at the beginning of the civil war the Spanish Government had about four times as many as the rebels. The rebels themselves are unable to manufacture aeroplanes, so that all these additional aeroplanes must have been supplied by other nations. German and Italian airmen who have been taken prisoner have confessed that they were acting under orders of their Governments.

The documents are understood to contain evidence showing that during the military operations of the rebels in Estremadura the air bases, the supplies, and the movements of the rebel troops were organised on Portuguese territory with the help of the Portuguese military forces. Aeroplanes and other arms that have fallen into the hands of the Government are of a type that has never existed in the Spanish army and reveal their foreign origin.

The Spanish Delegation asked that the documents should be published and should be distributed to the members of the League. They have not yet been distributed, and it is impossible to obtain from the Secretariat any information as to whether they will be published.

Advance on Madrid – October–November 1936

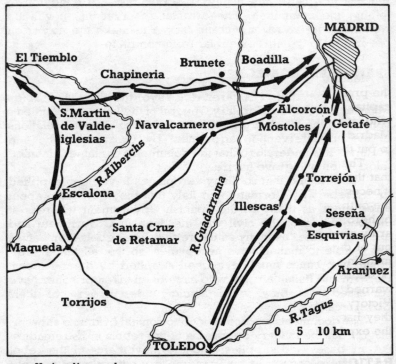

Legend: → Nationalist attacks

Labels on map: MADRID, El Tiemblo, Brunete, Boadilla, Chapineria, S.Martin de Valdeiglesias, Navalcarnero, Alcorcón, Móstoles, Getafe, R.Alberchs, Escalona, Torrejón, R.Guadarrama, Illescas, Seseña, Santa Cruz de Retamar, Esquivias, Maqueda, Aranjuez, Torrijos, R.Tagus, TOLEDO

Scale: 0 5 10 km

PREPARATIONS FOR THE DEFENCE OF MADRID
Review of the Military Situation

Madrid, September 30.

Madrid is making serious preparations for a siege and the press is urging the 'imperative necessity' of defending the capital. A call has been made for five thousand 'brave men', who, it is declared, are worth more than '25,000 deserters'. Madrid has these men, it is declared. All that is needed is to put them on a fighting basis without delay.

The influential morning newspaper 'Socialista', declaring that the 'culminating point of the war' has been reached, finds it necessary to repeat the warning it has given continually since the outbreak of the revolt. It writes: 'It is not isolated examples of heroism, either by individuals or by groups, that make an army an object of fear to its enemy. It is the collective carrying out of duty, which begins with faithful obedience to the commanding officers and ends with the passionate defence of the positions held. The soldier who runs away from the front is warned that he does not ensure his personal safety by so doing.' Victory, says the 'Socialista', will be won by those who knew they had a stern fight before them, not those who enlisted in the expectation of an easy victory and plenty of booty.

RATIONING SYSTEM

The Government has decided to introduce a system of ration cards for food as from the middle of October. So far, in order to obtain even the most ordinary necessaries of life people have been obliged to queue up for hours in the hope of obtaining about half of what they want. Another significant development is the proclamation of the U.G.T. (General Workers' Union) to the effect that certain groups of militia have been collecting from shops quantities of food far in excess of their own personal requirements, paying for them with chits drawn on the Government, which undertakes to repay the sums involved. This, the proclamation declares, must cease at once, as the purchases of the militia, being out of all proportion of their needs, prevent other people from obtaining food.

THE MILITARY POSITION

The military position as seen here is summed up more or less as follows: The Government still holds the important railway junction of Albacete, on the Madrid–Valencia–Alicante line, which gives them an outlet to the sea and the control of the eastern provinces of the country, but the rebels from Toledo now threaten the line at Aranjuez.

To the north of Madrid the Government forces have held up the rebel advance at a distance of some fifty miles from the capital.

Apart from the rebel move against the capital, the position appears to be wholly indecisive on many fronts. The Government troops have held besieged – almost since the beginning of the civil war – the towns of Cordova, Huesca, Oviedo, Granada, Saragossa, and other important provincial capitals. If they have not been able to capture these towns, it is pointed out that the rebels have been unable to relieve them.

BASQUE AUTONOMY

Autonomy for the Basque Provinces has been almost granted. Bilbao is to be selected as the capital and the deputy Senor Aquirre will be the head of the Government.

Four hundred and seventy deputies have been summoned to attend the autumn session of the Cortes, which opens tomorrow under the presidency of Senor Martinez Barrio, but it is estimated that not more than 100 will be there. The rest have been killed, taken prisoner, or joined the rebel cause.– Reuter.

Saturday October 3 1936 p.13

THE 'NEW SPAIN'
Corporate State Planned

FRANCO'S POLICY
Fighting North of Madrid

In a proclamation addressed to the Spanish people General Franco, the rebel commander-in-chief, announced that the 'New Spain' would be ruled by a corporative system similar to that in force in Portugal. The proclamation declared:

Work for all is absolutely assured and will no longer be subject to capitalism. A table of minimum wages will be established, all workers' rights previously obtained will be respected, and social parasites will be destroyed.

Taxation will bear an equitable relation to profits. We will help the peasants to obtain independent work on their own land.

A concordat will be made with the Roman Catholic

Church. We will maintain the best relations with all countries of the world except Soviet lands, of which the new Spain will be the enemy.

BREACHES OF NON-INTERVENTION AGREEMENT
Unofficial Committee's Findings

Breaches of the non-intervention pact relating to the Spanish civil war, enabling the rebels to obtain arms denied to the Government, have placed the Government forces in a disadvantageous military position according to the finding of the unofficial committee of inquiry into breaches of international law relating to intervention in Spain, whose report was published yesterday. . . .

SERIOUS BREACHES

The Committee states that since it issued a short interim report on September 27 it has heard further evidence and examined a number of other statements which confirmed its former findings that assistance in the form of the supply of munitions and expert personnel, together with other forms of collaboration, have been furnished to the rebels by Italy and Portugal since the date of the non-intervention pact. The report adds:

In respect to the German action, although the evidence before us subsequent to the date at which non-intervention was supposed to become general is less abundant some of it is of a most serious character.

We have received, moreover, a large amount of evidence showing German assistance both before and after August 8, 1936, the date upon which the German Government informed the French Government that no war material had been sent or would be sent to the Spanish rebels.

An additional circumstance which raises a grave issue is that the British Government has, according to our information, been made aware by persons in its own employ of the breaches of the non-intervention agreement.

Even from the limited evidence which has been before us it appears to our view that certain of the nations contributing to the international agreement have without question been guilty of bad faith. Other Governments, among them the British Government, possess infinitely more facilities for

45

obtaining information than can possibly be at the disposal of such an inquiry as our own and these Governments must have been able to ascertain that bad faith and breach of agreement which in our opinion have been indubitably established by the evidence which we have been able to examine.

EVIDENCE OF INTERVENTION

In a detailed examination of evidence relating to the alleged supply of assistance to the rebels by various countries the committee reports:

It was evident to us from the photographs of documents found in Barcelona at the headquarters of the National Socialist party that for some time previous to the outbreak of the revolt German subjects in Spain had been pursuing illegal activities and had had in this the support of the German diplomatic and consular representatives. There is some evidence to show that the supply of war material carried by Germany did not cease with the non-intervention agreement. We have before us considerable evidence of Italian intervention.

Owing to its pecular geographic position Portugal must play an important part in the control of the supply of arms to the rebels. All the evidence which we have had before us has gone to show that Portugal has abused this position and has openly supported the rebels and is still continuing to do so. It is quite certain that both before and after the non-intervention pact Portugal has allowed her territories to be used as a base from which the rebels can attack the Spanish Government. . . .

Monday October 12 1936   *p.12*

RUSSIA AND NON-INTERVENTION
Press Attacks

'MANOEUVRING' BY FASCIST STATES

From our Correspondent

Moscow, October 11.

Comments in the Soviet press reflect the Soviet belief that Italy, Germany, and Portugal have achieved their principal aim at Friday's meeting in London of the Non-Intervention Committee in delaying any definite measures against the alleged breaches of the non-intervention agreement.

The Russian allegation is that Italy, Germany, and Portugal manoeuvred for this delay so that further help could be sent to the rebels for the decisive push against Madrid.

'Pravda', the organ or the Communist party, repeats the Government's demands for effective measures by the Committee to end the violation of the agreement.

'CRIMINALS CAUGHT RED-HANDED'

The article in 'Pravda' as quoted by Reuter says:

The non-intervention agreement would produce an immediate effect if it were observed, but in practice the rebels have continued to receive still greater aid from Fascist helpers. The policy of taking no measures against the violation of the agreement is tantamount to a policy of abetting the rebels.

By its declaration on October 7 the Soviet Government tore the mask off the 'neutrality' of the interventionists and evoked a frenzy of anger in their camp. The provocative behaviour of the delegates from the three Fascist countries, when placed in the situation of criminals caught red-handed, confirmed that the accusations put forward against them were fully founded. They have unfortunately not received the rebuff which is their due from the Committee.

The Committee must not hang on to the tail of the interventionists: it must call to order the violators of the agreement.

PORTUGAL'S 'NOBLE' ATTITUDE

Lisbon, October 10.

The attitude taken by the Portuguese delegate at the meeting of the Non-Intervention Committee in London is warmly applauded by the Portuguese press to-day as 'most noble and dignified'.–Reuter.

(The Portuguese representative left the meeting after reference had been made to a Soviet proposal that a committee should be sent to the Spanish–Portuguese frontier to investigate alleged violation of the non-intervention agreement by the Portuguese Government.)

REBELS LESS THAN 20 MILES FROM MADRID

'We Will Enter in a Few Days' – General Mola

General Mola, the rebel general, growing confident by the unchecked rebel advance on Madrid, yesterday declared, 'I affirm that in a few days we will enter Madrid.'

The advance continues most strongly from the south, and the rebels are now several miles beyond Illescas, a Government stronghold which fell into their hands on Sunday almost without a struggle. This brings them within less than twenty miles of Madrid.

In the south-west Valmojado, on the Talavera–Madrid main road, is likely to fall soon to the rebels advancing from Santa Cruz.

In the north-west the collapse of Government resistance near the Escorial is believed to be imminent. The Government troops are, however, holding desperately to their mountain posts there, in spite of the bitterly cold weather, for they are of great importance in the capital's defence. The rebel advance in progress from the south and south-west may drive a wedge between them and Madrid, which would at last end the stalemate on this front.

NEW OFFENSIVE AT OVIEDO

The Government still does not admit the relief of Oviedo. The Madrid account is that a part of the relieving force has entered Oviedo and that a ring has been formed round the town to prevent the entry of the main body. A vigorous offensive is said to have been begun by the Asturian miners against the relieving force.

The rebels, however, are celebrating the fall of the town with great rejoicing. A broadcast from the rebel wireless station at Corunna yesterday stated that there was tremendous enthusiasm in the town. The whole population was short of food, and the arrival of lorries filled with provisions, including 1,000 hams, was hailed with great excitement. According to the special correspondent of the Havas Agency there, over 3,000 bombs were dropped by Government 'planes during the daily bombardments and over 2,000 shells were fired at the town.

Colonel Aranda, commander of the rebel force in Oviedo during the three months' siege, has been promoted, it is stated, General and Commander of Asturias.

SHELTER OF REFUGEES

Senor Castillo, the Argentine Acting Foreign Minister, has proposed that the foreign legations in Madrid should be used to shelter refugees.

Explaining his proposal in Buenos Ayres yesterday, he said: 'Our one aim is to prevent useless waste of life. We maintain the principle of an impartial guarantee for the future for all, whatever their political views.' The Spanish Ambassador has been informed of the result of Senor Castillo's talks with other diplomats in Buenos Ayres on the subject.

Radio Seville, in rebel hands, yesterday stated that a collection among German workmen amounted to 2,000,000 pesetas (roughly £60,000), which will be used to buy winter clothes for the rebel troops. Heavier clothing is much needed by the Moors, who are already suffering from the cold in the mountains around Madrid.

Further food supplies for Madrid arrived at Alicante yesterday by the Russian steamer Neva, amidst cheers for the Soviets. The Neva has now made her second voyage to Spain, carrying food supplies for Government supporters.

'THIS THE HOUR OF CRISIS'
Madrid's Admission

REBELS ONLY 12 MILES AWAY
Two Big Offensives

The rebel advance on Madrid continues swiftly: an announcer broadcasting from the wireless station at Madrid last night said, 'This is the hour of crisis.'

Two big offensives were begun yesterday – on the southern front from Illescas (which the Government on Tuesday had failed to retake in a counter-attack) and on the south-western front from Valmojado.

Last night's broadcast from Madrid admitted that the enemy was exerting 'enormous pressure', but said that the Government troops were fighting valiantly.

The broadcast, however, mentioned an engagement yesterday at Moraleja. A town of that name lies twelve miles south-west of Madrid and eight miles east of Navalcarnero. If a rebel army has reached this point it would represent an advance of some ten miles from Tuesday's position.

Further, Moraleja lies on a road joining the Illescas–Madrid road and the Navalcarnero–Madrid road, and there is a danger that Government troops defending Navalcarnero will now be cut off.

NON-INTERVENTION CONFLICT
Russian Supplies

HOPES OF AVERTING COMPLICATIONS

From our Diplomatic Correspondent

London, Monday.

Some rather ugly prospects are opened by the conflict within the Non-Intervention Committee, though it is believed here that the conflict will not be allowed to go much farther. It is no doubt true that the help given to the Spanish rebels by Germany and Italy has hastened their victory, and may even have been decisive, but according to the evidence available here the help given to the rebels by Italy has been small since the Italian embargo was declared. What help has been given by Germany since her embargo is uncertain, but it does not appear to have been considerable. Non-intervention has not stopped German and Italian intervention altogether but has reduced it substantially.

On the other hand it is argued here that the help given, in the form of war material, to the loyalists by Russia since the embargoes have been in force has been much greater than the help given by Germany and Italy to the rebels. Had there been no Russian intervention the Russian case would have been strong, while the German and Italian case would have been weak. The Russian action – which has not appreciably helped the loyalists – is much regretted here, and there is a good deal of mystification as to the reasons behind it.

If supplies of Russian war material continue to arrive at Spanish ports it is feared by some that the Spanish rebels will take naval action. That is to say, Russian ships will be held up and, possibly, sunk by ships flying the Spanish flag. Whether they will really be Spanish is another matter that suggests ugly complications. But it is hoped and believed that Russia does not wish to see things go that far and that the chief purpose of the Non-Intervention Committee – namely, to prevent the Spanish civil war from precipitating a general European crisis – will be achieved.

LETTERS TO THE EDITOR

THE POWERS AND THE SPANISH WAR
One-Sided Neutrality and Its Results

To the Editor of the Manchester Guardian

Sir,–The sponsors of neutrality are trying to make the world believe that they are acting with the best intentions; they are trying to stave off a new world carnage. One might, by a considerable stretch of imagination, grant them the benefit of the doubt had their embargo on arms included both sides in this frightful civil war. But it is their one-sidedness which makes one question the integrity as well as the logic of the men proclaiming neutrality. It is not only the height of folly, it is also the height of inhumanity to sacrifice the larger part of the Spanish people to a small minority of Spanish adventurers armed with every modern device of war.

Moreover, the statesmen and political leaders of Europe know only too well that it is not out of love that Hitler and Mussolini have been supplying Franco and Mola with war material and money. Unless the men at the helm of the European Governments utterly lack clear thinking they must realise, as the rest of the thinking world already has, that there is a definite pact between the Spanish Fascists and their Italian and German confreres in the unholy alliance of Fascism. It is an open secret that the imperial ambitions of Hitler and Mussolini are not easily satisfied. If, then, they show such limitless generosity to their Spanish friends, it must be because of the colonial and strategic advantages definitely agreed to by Franco and Mola. It hardly requires much prophetic vision to predict that this arrangement would put all of Europe in the palm of Hitler and Mussolini.

Now the question is, Will France go back on her glorious revolutionary past by her tacit consent to such designs? Will England, with her liberal traditions, submit to such a degrading position? And, if not, will that not mean a new world carnage? In other words, the disaster neutrality is to prevent is going to follow in its wake. Quite another thing would happen if the anti-Fascist forces were helped to cope with the Fascist epidemic that is poisoning all the springs of life and health in Spain. For Fascism annihilated in Spain would also mean the cleansing of Europe from the black pest. And the end of Fascism in the rest of the world would also do away with the cause of war.

It is with neutrality as it is with people who can stand by a burning building with women and children calling for help

51

or see a drowning man desperately trying to gain shore. No words can express the contempt all decent people would feel for such abject cowardice. Fortunately, there are not many such creatures in the world. In time of fire, floods, storm at sea, or at the sight of a fellow-being in distress human nature is at its best. Men, in danger to their own life and limb, rush into burning houses, throw themselves into the sea, and bravely carry their brothers to safety. Well, Spain is in flames. The Fascist conflagration is spreading. Is it possible that the liberal world outside Spain will stand by and see the country laid in ashes by the Fascist hordes? Or will they muster up enough courage to break through the bars of neutrality and come to the rescue of the Spanish people?

The main effect of neutrality so far has been the bitter disillusionment of the Spanish masses about France and England, whom until now they had valued and respected as democratic countries. They cannot grasp the obvious contradiction on the part of those who shout to the heavens that democracy must be preserved at all costs yet remain blind to the grave danger to democracy in the growth of Fascism. They insist that the latter is making ready to stab democracy in the back. The Spanish people quite logically have come to the conclusion that France and England are betraying their own past and that they have turned them over to the Fascist block like sheep for slaughter.

However, the Fascist conspiracy and the criminal indifferences of the so-called democratic countries will never bring the defenders of Spanish liberty to their knees. The callousness of the outside world has merely succeeded in steeling the will to freedom of the anti-Fascist forces. And it has raised their courage to the point of utter disregard of the worst tribulations. Everywhere one goes one is impressed by the iron determination to fight until the last man and the last drop of blood. For well the Spanish workers know that peace and wellbeing will be impossible until Fascism has been driven off their fruitful soil.

–Yours,
EMMA GOLDMAN.
Barcelona, October 18.

Emma Goldman has been acclaimed as 'America's greatest anarchist' and this letter would appear to be very much in keeping with her oft-stated political preferences.

IN SIGHT OF MADRID
Rebel 'Offer'

PREMIER'S APPEAL FOR RESISTANCE
'Not a Pace Backward'

With the rebels to the south of Madrid in sight of the capital (according to Radio Seville), General Franco is reported to have given Madrid its 'last chance' to surrender. A time-limit of 45 hours is said to have been fixed.

According to a Cordova broadcast last night General Varela has informed the population of Madrid that all those who present themselves without arms in the rebel lines when Madrid is attacked will not be harmed.

The Prime Minister, Senor Caballero, last night, however, issued a strong appeal to the Government's supporters calling upon them 'not only to stand up against the enemy but to throw him out of his present position once and for all and to free Madrid from the Fascists' claws which are powerless to grab our city.' He adds:

Iron discipline. Not a pace backward. Forward always. And let prisoners who fall into our hands, and whose lives I command you to respect, be the best proof of on which side are barbarism and destruction and on which the heroism of those who, because they are defending the people's cause, can submit themselves to the greatness which inspires the popular masses.

Attack. For the decisive liberation of Madrid, supreme fortress of the world's fight against Fascism, your Prime Minister and Minister for War awaits the reports of your victory.

Preparations for the defence of the capital continue and the Cabinet has ordered the conscription of all men between the ages of 20 and 45.

In Toledo, states Reuter, it is said that General Franco intends the colonial troops to be the first to enter Madrid, as, it is suggested, they are less likely to be carried away by political passion than the rebel volunteers.

Attack on Madrid – November 1936

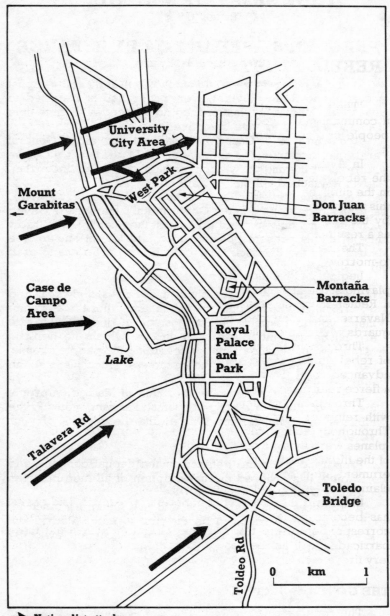

University City Area

Mount Garabitas

West Park

Don Juan Barracks

Case de Campo Area

Montaña Barracks

Lake

Royal Palace and Park

Talavera Rd

Toledo Bridge

Toldeo Rd

0   km   1

Nationalist attacks

'THE ENEMY IS AT THE GATES OF MADRID'
Government's Appeal to People

REBELS FIGHTING IN CITY'S SUBURBS
Streets Barricaded in Capital

'The enemy is at the gates of Madrid.' The phrase is from a communique issued yesterday by the Government, but the people of Madrid would, without the warning, have realised it.

In Avila, General Varela's head-quarters, it is stated that the rebels had fought a fierce battle throughout the afternoon in the suburbs of the capital, and a message from Lisbon early this morning says that the outer districts of the city are occupied by the rebels. Big fires are said to be burning in the streets as a result of rebel bombardment.

The claim in Avila last night was: 'We will be in Madrid to-morrow.'

Legions of Phalangists (Fascists) with flags flying and bands playing started to march on to Madrid at dawn yesterday, states a Reuter message from Avila. They had come from Seville, Navarre, and Leon, and their duty is to act as police and civil guards when the capital is taken.

Throughout the night and yesterday the unbroken sound of rebel gunfire could be heard in the capital as the rebels advanced from Getafe and Leganes, with the militia fighting a fierce rearguard action.

Throughout the day the roads to the capital were filled with refugees leaving their villages as the rebels advanced. Throughout the day, too, Madrid was in fear of air raids: rebel 'planes were flying over the city at frequent intervals, but most of the flights seem to have been for reconnaissance. The Government anti-aircraft guns were busy all the time, and it is claimed that five rebel 'planes were brought down.

In Madrid the bitterest fighting is in prospect. The capital has become a city of barricades, and the Press Association correspondent there telegraphing last night states that these barricades 'will not be easy to take unless destroyed by artillery fire, which is almost impossible, or by mass tank attack'.

THE GOVERNMENT'S APPEAL

The communique issued by the Government contained an appeal not only to the citizens of Madrid but to the whole of Spain to defend the Republic. All parts of Spain are called upon 'to attack the enemy at all points in obedience to the plans of the general order issued by the Government'. The example is being set in the South, where the Government forces have launched an offensive on the Estepona front. It is believed that there are few rebel troops at present in that region (most of them having been diverted to the Madrid fronts), and they are reported to be retreating.

Monday November 9 1936   *p.9*

REBEL ARMY HELD UP BEFORE MADRID
Government Forces Gain Ground

DEFENCE OF BRIDGES BY REINFORCED MILITIA
Long-Range Guns Fire at Centre of City

In spite of a welter of reports, false claims by the rebels, and celebrations of victory, Madrid has not only not been entered but the Government forces have gained ground.

The African army has not been able to cross any of the river bridges – the Government forces, in fact, hold both banks of the river – and reports of fighting in the centre of Madrid are purely imaginary. Street fighting has not yet begun. The militiamen have received reinforcements and their bravery has even aroused the admiration of their enemies.

The militia seem to have gained ground in two places, in the Casa del Campo, a park to the west of the river, and also at Carabanchel, a village to the south of the park. Having failed to get across the bridges Franco's forces began yesterday afternoon to bomb the centre of the city and to shell it with long-range guns.

GOVERNMENT AND THE GOLD REMOVED

The Government has been moved to Valencia, on the coast, which is regarded as a better centre than Barcelona. The Bank of Spain has also been moved to the coast. The Spanish Ambassador in Paris said on Saturday that not one grain of gold would be left for the rebels.

A military governor has been left in Madrid.

REBEL FAILURE
Driven Farther from the Capital

MADRID REPORT
Getafe Said to Have Been Recaptured

THREAT TO DESTROY MADRID

Franco's attitude appears to be that if he cannot enter the city he can at least wreck it with his guns and his 'planes. As Madrid is a city with a population of over a million, his gunners and airmen cannot fail to hit it whenever they like.

In an interview yesterday (quoted by Reuter) General Franco is stated to have declared:–

> The bombardment started yesterday will be continued until Madrid surrenders. Madrid will have to be destroyed, district by district, no matter how much I regret it.

The bombardments on Wednesday and yesterday are said to have been the fiercest yet experienced, shells exploding in all parts. The rebels seem determined to hold the Government responsible for the damage to the capital, and yesterday their headquarters at Salamanca issued a statement, in the course of which they said:

> Anarchy is now reigning in the capital. Fires are raging in the centre of the town, thus showing the excesses which anarchist hordes are committing. These excesses are being perpetrated in zones which are not under fire from us, thus making it impossible for us to take the town with the least possible damage.

NEW SUPPLIES OF ARMS FOR GOVERNMENT FORCES

Fascist States and a Rebel Defeat

From our Diplomatic Correspondent

London, Sunday.

A little more than a week ago it was believed here that Madrid was on the point of falling. The view taken now is that Madrid may fall at any time now or not at all. If Madrid holds out there will have been a decisive turn in the Spanish civil war. The victory of the loyalists no longer seems as unlikely as it did.

At no time – not even when Madrid seemed about to fall – was there any question of British recognition for a rebel Government that might be established in the capital (or anywhere else for that matter). There is complete agreement between London and Paris that the policy of 'non-intervention' must go on whatever happens. Some misunderstanding seems to have been caused because the French Chargé d'Affaires was recalled from Madrid; it was suggested that this step was taken preparatory to withdrawing diplomatic recognition from the Spanish Government, which, although partly transferred to Valencia, still has in Madrid representative Ministers. But the real reason for this step was that the French Government, believing that the fall of Madrid was a matter of hours, did not want a diplomatic representative in a city occupied by the rebels. In other words, the step was taken in conformity with the French (and British) resolve to withhold diplomatic recognition from the rebel 'government'.

ARMS FOR THE GOVERNMENT

It is believed here that the determination of the loyalists to prosecute the war has increased considerably since a week ago, when there were signs of demoralisation in their ranks. It is known here that the loyalists have a far heavier armament than they had. Most of this armament has been rushed to Madrid from Catalonia. It consists of tanks, armoured cars, aeroplanes, and other contrivances of the most modern types.

A large number of military experts, technicians, and experienced officers are co-operating in the defence of Madrid. Some of them are Spanish and have completed their training in Catalonia during the last few weeks. The others are of various nationalities. Of the modern war material now at the disposal of the loyalists most is not Spanish. A good deal – but by no means all – is of Russian origin.

The political situation in Madrid would seem to be less favourable to the Government than the military situation. Groups of 'ultra-anarchists' are trying by various methods, including terrorism and assassination, to hinder the political unity which the Government is imposing on the population. Unless the Government succeeds in suppressing them political disunion may react unfavourably on the actual defenders of the capital.

For Germany and Italy the defeat of the Spanish rebels would be a serious matter. As pointed out in the 'Manchester Guardian' some time ago, the German Government was determined 'not to allow' a loyalist victory, and the same is no doubt true of the Italian Government. Had there been no intervention in Spain a loyalist victory would not have been so serious a matter for Hitler and Mussolini, but since both dictators have identified themselves with the rebel cause it becomes a very serious matter indeed – a rebel defeat is, in fact, their defeat.

There has again been an increase in the supply of war material which the rebels are receiving from Germany and Italy. German and Italian officers, pilots, and experts are playing a more prominent part in the actual military operations. It is no overstatement to speak of an 'Italian occupation' of the Balearic Islands. Italian aeroplanes have operated directly from Italian aircraft-carriers stationed in the vicinity of the islands.

DANGER OF NEW VIOLATIONS

If it seems that the rebels are going to be defeated, will there not be a further increase in the German and Italian violations of the embargoes placed on the export of war material to Spain? And will not further violations by Russia – and perhaps by one or two other Powers as well – be the result?

The view taken here is that the work of the Non-Intervention Committee is more necessary than ever. It has, so it is believed, averted an open rivalry amongst the partisan Powers in supplying the two Spanish factions, and has imposed those limits that are exacted by relative secrecy. In any open inrush of war material Germany and Italy would have an enormous advantage. The need for relative secrecy (imposed by the embargoes and the Non-Intervention Committee) has reduced that advantage. If the Non-Intervention Committee is able to exercise an even closer control by keeping its observers at Spanish ports it may still be possible to avert what has been feared all along both here and in Paris – namely, an open and unlimited (as distinct from a semi-clandestine, limited) competition amongst the partisan Powers in supplying the Spanish factions with war material, a competition which, if it were to gather intensity would make the Spanish civil war lose its purely national character and become an international conflict even if it were confined to Spanish territory.

GERMANY AND ITALY RECOGNISE REBEL GOVERNMENT
Simultaneous Announcement Last Night

MADRID FIRES STARTED BY INCENDIARY BOMBS
Great Damage and Many Casualties

It was officially announced last night almost simultaneously in Berlin and Rome that Signor Mussolini and Herr Hitler had recognised the Government of General Franco, the rebel leader in Spain. The German announcement was sent out by wireless and was picked up in Paris while the official statement was being made in Berlin.

The following semi-official communiqué was issued in Berlin:–

Following the taking possession by General Franco of the greater part of Spanish territory and now that the developments of the past weeks have shown with increasing clarity that there can be no longer any talk of a responsible Government in the other portions of Spain, the Reich Government has decided to recognise the Government of General Franco and to appoint a Chargé d'Affaires for the opening of diplomatic relations.

The new German Chargé d'Affaires will proceed in due course ('alsbald') to the seat of government of General Franco.

The German Chargé d'Affaires, who up to now has been in Alicante, has been recalled. The Chargé d'Affaires of the former Spanish Government left Berlin by his own decision at the beginning of November.

The official Rome communiqué, couched almost in the same words as the German statement announces:

Now that the Government of General Franco has taken possession of the greater part of Spain and the development of the situation makes it continually more evident that in the remaining part of Spain it is impossible to speak of a responsible Government exercising power, the Fascist Government has decided to recognise the Government of General Franco and to send to him a Chargé d'Affaires to open diplomatic relations.

A SURPRISE FOR BERLIN

In Berlin the announcement came as a complete surprise, for officials of the Foreign Office and the Propaganda Ministry, in reply to questions about the possibility of recognition for Franco, had been saying that no move was likely from Germany before Franco had formally installed himself in Madrid.

There is no doubt that the step has been taken by agreement between Germany and Italy.

In Paris the announcement was said to have come 'sooner than we thought', and it is thought that Germany and Italy may now openly supply the rebels with war material.

In London it was declared that the British Government had not the slightest intention of departing from the policy of non-intervention. The German Ambassador, Herr von Ribbentrop, called at the Foreign Office last night to see Mr. Eden.

The suddenness of the recognition announcement is believed in some quarters in London to be due to a desire to give General Franco moral support after the ruthless bombardment of Madrid.

It is four months since the revolt began in Morocco. General Franco, who was given powers of a virtual dictator by the 'Provisional Government' set up by the rebels at Burgos, has announced that he will organise a corporate state on the Italian model in Spain.

Up to last night the Burgos Junta had been recognised as the Government of Spain by nobody except one or two small Latin-American republics.

HUNDREDS OF WOMEN AND CHILDREN KILLED

Tremendous damage is being done to Madrid by Franco's airmen and gunners. Streets are in ruins, palaces damaged, and there are great numbers of killed and wounded. As the results of Tuesday's bombing and shelling it is semi-officially estimated that 200 people were killed and 500 wounded. Yesterday the rebel airmen set buildings on fire with incendiary bombs.

This bring the civilian casualties in Madrid in the last week up to about 500 killed and 1,200 wounded, the majority being women and children. The attacks on Tuesday night were preceded by the dropping of pamphlets telling the people that the worst air raids they had experienced were to come.

THE FIGHTING

Exceedingly heavy fighting continues near the Bridge of the French and round University City. The outcome is still uncertain, but the rebels claim to be advancing.

Friday November 20 1936   *p.11*

HOW GERMANS SEND SUPPLIES TO SPANISH REBELS
Night Flights Across France

From our Diplomatic Correspondent

London, Thursday.

It is the intention of the German and Italian Governments to keep their representatives in the Committee of Non-Intervention, for the time being at least. For these Governments the question is: 'To what extent will the committee serve to conceal rather than to prevent deliveries of war material to the Spanish rebels?' To some extent it has done this already, only during the last few weeks the loyalists have profited by this circumstance as well as the rebels.

Can the committee remain in existence if deliveries to the rebels far exceed those to the loyalists and attain such a volume that even the semi-concealment that has existed hitherto becomes impossible? The committee is not altogether a farce; semi-concealment has limited the aid given to the rebels, although their victories have, no doubt, helped to reduce the effort made on their behalf by Germany and Italy, just as their recent failure has intensified that effort.

A good deal of time elapses between the day when deliveries of war material arrive in a Spanish port and the day when they are notified to the committee – and a good deal more time passes before their existence is recognised by the committee as a whole. Thus there is no reason why Germany and Italy should leave the committee at present. While giving assurances that they are respecting the embargoes placed on the export of war material to Spain, they can increase – indeed, they are increasing – their own deliveries.

A RADIO INDISCRETION

When this method becomes too transparent – or when the committee seriously attempts an effective supervision at Spanish ports – Germany and Italy can always withdraw their representatives from the committee and declare that it is Russia who is making the work of the committee impossible by persistent violations of the embargo, although there can be no doubt that the German and Italian deliveries that for a time (when the rebels were advancing victoriously) lagged behind the Russian deliveries are now far exceeding them once more.

According to information received here big shipments of war material are leaving, or are about to leave, Hamburg. All German war material is sent to Spain by sea (chiefly from Hamburg), except the German aeroplanes, which start off from Boblingen, near Stuttgart, and fly either directly to Spain (passing over France by night) or by way of Austria to Italy, and then to Spain from there.

Great precautions are taken in Germany to impose secrecy. Some time ago a non-German radio station announced that aeroplane engines had been delivered to the Spanish rebels by a certain German firm (the name of which is in the possession of your correspondent). The firm was there-upon occupied by agents of the Gestapo, who made numerous arrests. Amongst the arrested persons are several Nazis. The prisoners are still being detained.

German aeroplane motors destined for the Spanish rebels are first sent to Doberitz (the great military training ground and arms depot near Berlin) and then to Hamburg.

TRAINING-GROUND FOR GERMAN AIRMEN

During the last few weeks Germany has been sending more and more men to Spain as well as material. Volunteers are asked for. Two squadrons in a German tank regiment volunteered for service in Spain on request the other day. The service is popular, for, quite apart from the adventure it promises, volunteers are very well paid. A German private soldier who is accepted for service in Spain gets 500 marks a month and an N.C.O. gets 700 marks.

For German airmen, Spain at war is regarded as an excellent training-ground.

'MADRID ALMOST CAPTURED'
General Varela's View

Lisbon, November 24.

'Madrid is virtually captured,' General Varela, who is in command of the attack on Madrid, told the correspondent of the 'Diario de Lisbon' to-day. 'The capital', he explained, 'is like an old castle with a moat – the Manzanares. In the old days when armies crossed the moat of a castle it had almost fallen. The nationalist army has already crossed the Manzanares, and Madrid has fallen too.

'There is no longer a military problem,' he continued. 'It is now only a police affair for the welfare of humanity. I will do my utmost to cause a minimum of casualties and damage. I shall therefore carry on my tactics quietly to involve the Government forces in defence works until they surrender.

'The army is strong enough to capture the capital immediately if it cared to employ every means it has, but the highest leaders of the nationalist movement think it inadvisable, for obvious reasons, to destroy Madrid.'–Reuter.

Corunna Road and Jarama Battles – December 1936–January
1937; February 1937

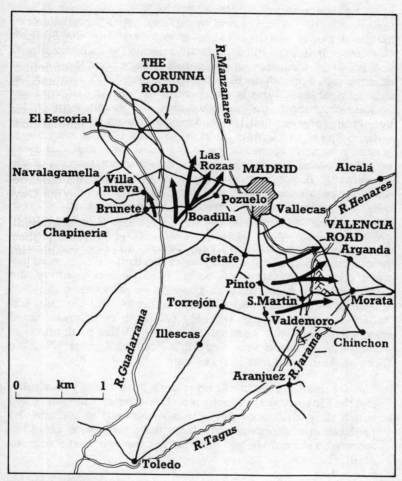

THE
CORUNNA
ROAD

R.Manzanares

El Escorial

Navalagamella

Villa
nueva

Brunete

Chapineria

Las
Rozas

MADRID

Alcalá

Pozuelo

R.Henares

Vallecas

Boadilla

VALENCIA
ROAD

Getafe

Arganda

Pinto

Torrejón

S.Martin

Morata

Valdemoro

Illescas

R.Guadarrama

Chinchon

R.Jarama

0   km   1

Aranjuez

R.Tagus

Toledo

➤ Nationalist attacks

THE 'VOLUNTEERS'

The communiqué published by the Non-Intervention Committee, which met in London yesterday, is so far satisfactory in that it has at last been agreed to forward to the Spanish Government and the rebel junta the scheme for an international and impartial Commission of Control to supervise the passage of arms into Spain. The British representative also raised the serious problem of the large number of 'volunteers' who are fighting or going to fight on each side. Obviously a non-intervention agreement that allows foreign Powers to send volunteers to Spain, or permits them to go there if it can stop them, is pretty farcical. Moreover, who can doubt that many of these volunteers take arms with them in direct contravention of the agreement? A competitive supply of volunteers from Russia and France on one side and from Germany and Italy on the other can only create an extremely dangerous situation. From the very beginning of the civil war German and Italian airmen have been helping the Spanish rebels, and it is hard to blame France and Russia for supplying similar aid. A general European application of the principles of the British Foreign Enlistment Act would therefore be a valuable extension of the agreement if it is to serve its purpose in preventing the civil war from developing into a European crisis. The German and Italian Governments can scarcely refuse to co-operate, since they were long ago nominal advocates of the prohibition of volunteers. In Baron von Neurath's Note of August 17 to the German Ambassador in Paris he said:

> The German Government considers it extremely desirable that the Governments concerned should extend the measures which they shall take (for non-intervention) to include the prohibition of the departure from their territories of volunteers who should wish to take part in the war in the regions under dispute.

The Italian Foreign Minister, in a similar Note of August 21, said that his Government interpreted indirect intervention as including 'the enrolment of volunteers to fight on either 'side' and considered that such indirect intervention was 'inadmissible'. The German and Italian Governments should, therefore, if they were sincere, have no objection to a joint prohibition of volunteers, whilst the Powers friendly to the Spanish Government may realise that it is to the best interest of that Government that it should be left to fight out its own salvation.

At a meeting of the Non-Intervention Committee on December 2 a scheme was agreed for suspending the importation of war materials into Spain and for the establishment of observers at Spanish ports. Details of the scheme were forwarded to both the Republic and Franco.

Monday December 7 1936 *p.12*

BLACKSHIRTS TO HELP REBELS
2,500 Land in Spain

Gibraltar, December 6.

Two thousand five hundred Italian Blackshirts disembarked yesterday at Algeciras on their way to join the rebels, according to reliable information reaching here. They landed from a ship which flew no flag and which was escorted by a gunboat.– Reuter.

Saturday December 12 1936 *p.13*

SPAIN 'INFORMS' THE LEAGUE
No Move Asked For

NON-INTERVENTION VIOLATIONS
British Criticism

Senor del Vayo, the Spanish Foreign Minister, yesterday laid his Government's case before the League Council that had been called at Spain's request, but he did no more. He did not ask for League intervention in the Spanish war (or, as he called it, 'the international war on Spanish soil'). The meeting had been asked for to show the Council the danger to international peace in the Spanish situation.

He spoke of the Fascist intervention in Spain, warning the other democracies of the serious danger of the extension to them of these Fascist methods. He envisaged the time when there might be a Europe 'wholly pacified because all problems will have been settled, thanks to the decisive action of international Fascism' – this said with great irony. . . .

GERMAN VOLUNTEERS DESERT

Of the fighting in Spain there is again little news. Activity seems to be confined to the front south of Bilbao, where the

67

Basque Government claims some successes. Its communiqué states that a number of rebel deserters newly arrived from Morocco passed over to the Government side.

Our Valencia correspondent cables that many of the German volunteers who arrived in Spain recently have gone over to the Government, 400 changing sides in a block earlier this week. He adds that General Franco is thus unable to trust them.

On December 4 the British and French governments had called upon the governments of Germany, Italy, Portugal and the Soviet Union to join with them in renouncing both direct and indirect intervention in Spain.

Monday December 14 1936   *p.9*

GERMAN TROOPS IN SPAIN
With the Rebels at Seville and Salamanca

FRANCO RULED BY HIS ADVISERS

From a Correspondent lately in Spain

Lisbon, December 4.

Seville, the future capital of Spain according to the rebel authorities, is full of life. The factories are working day and night. General Queipo de Llano, who spends half an hour before the microphone every night passing judgement on international politics and advising Great Britain and France to follow the example of Italy and Germany, is one of the principal diversions of the people of Seville, educated and uneducated alike. I sought in vain for a room in any of the splendid modern hotels of Seville. They are all full of Germans and Italians – diplomats, aviators, press agents, and, above all, future soldiers in Franco's army. Hitler and Mussolini have sent to Seville and Salamanca their best technicians in the field of propaganda. The Fascist emissaries from Rome are giving instructions to the Spanish 'Falangistas' on the organisation of syndicates and on the technique of the conquest of power. They say that neither Hitler nor Mussolini was satisfied with the Spanish Fascist movement, which is too revolutionary, too violent, too much inclined to the elimination of political enemies by death.

'THE MORE, THE MERRIER'

I made the journey from Seville to Salamanca by motor-car with the war correspondent of a Seville newspaper. This paper, like all the papers published in the territory controlled by Franco, is militarist. My journalist companion was a talkative man: we talked of the avalanche of Germans who have come to Seville – rigid and rubicund, robots who salute with the raised palm of the hand and a dutiful 'Heil, Hitler'.

'The more Germans, the merrier,' said the journalist. 'Germans and Spaniards have always been good friends. During the Great War the true feelings of the ordinary Spaniard were pro-German; only a clique of intellectuals and aged politicians stood up for the Allies, and to-day there are no intellectuals of that type in Spain. They do not dare to come here, and any who do pay for their sins of the past. They have been the enemies of Spain.'

When we reached Salamanca the journalist invited me to lunch in the leading hotel in the venerable Castilian town. The dining-room was full of Germans and Spanish soldiers. General Millan Astray, who had just been appointed head of the Press and Propaganda Department, a physical ruin with only one arm and one eye, went to and fro, greeting the Germans in the hall and the dining-room. He is scarred all over with shot wounds received in the Moroccan war, when he commanded the Foreign Legion. After an hour's waiting the Spanish journalist lost patience and sent for the manager. 'Can we not have anything yet?' he asked.

'I am sorry, sir. We have to serve these German gentlemen; they are very particular and object if they do not get quick service.' We got nothing to eat until, at about 3 p.m., the dining-room had become empty of Germans, and the poor Spaniards who had been waiting began to enter.

BLOND YOUNG MEN

'Deutschland über Alles,' 'Giovinezza,' and the Spanish Falangist 'hymn' are given on the wireless. The children whistle the first two in the streets. The Plaza Mayor, the principal square of Salamanca, is full of blond young men who have come to fight. I was told that Madrid is being defended by a Russian army of 30,000 men. 'What do we care?' said a young Falangist. 'Germany is ready to send 60,000 if necessary. The Germans will never allow the Russians to be masters of Spain.'

All the press and propaganda machinery is in the hands of German experts. French and American journalists are being expelled, for no apparent reason except that they are objected to by the Germans. The press agency which sends news to the French papers is German, with German editors and staff.

General Mola's chief adviser is a German; they call him Don Walter. A general staff is at work at Salamanca in collaboration with the Spanish military authorities; it is said to be the real author of the new plan for the conquest of Madrid.

Thus we are now witnessing the Germanisation of Spain. It was reported that five thousand Germans had arrived: the truth is that German 'volunteers' have been arriving at Cadiz and Vigo from Germany every week for a month past. It is impossible to give the actual number. Many of them are already on the outskirts of Madrid as legionaries, with their own officers, forming independent units. An approximate calculation made by a Spanish 'Nationalist' put the number of the Germans at 20,000. The Italians are much fewer. Italy is contenting herself with sending her best war material, mobile tanks, and her technicians.

A GERMAN 'TERROR'

For more than a month past there has been incarcerated in Valladolid a journalist, Aznar, who is accused of having been the author of a violent anti-German campaign during the World War. There is talk of a 'Tcheka' directed by agents of Hitler. A Spaniard, who complained in my presence in the Restaurant Frailo of the excessive number of persons who have been executed in the 'Nationalist' cities, was hotly criticised by a German who was also present. The German gave vent to this opinion: 'Communism needs to be nipped in the bud, and all Spaniards who protest ought to be shot.'

Almost every day groups of Germans march through the Plaza Mayor in Salamanca and down the broad avenues of Seville singing their national anthem and the 'hymn' of the Spanish Foreign Legion. Some of them wear the uniform of the Foreign Legion, but most wear the blue shirt of the Falangists, though without the insignia of that Spanish Fascist group – five arrows and a yoke. Two months ago Moors were to be seen strolling through the streets of Seville. They are disappearing, and their place has been taken by the blond men of the North. In order to conquer Madrid General Franco has been obliged to Germanise his cities, relegating to the background the many Fascist and traditionalist Spanish volunteers who have shown so much enthusiasm until lately. The colonial war which Franco has been carrying on victoriously since July 19 has given place to a different tactic. Madrid is not to be conquered by columns of infantry nor by light cavalry. Franco's volunteers have disappeared, because neither Franco nor the German and Italian experts consider them sufficiently hardened to fight the powerful Russian army which we are told is defending Madrid.

'NATURAL ALLIES'

The Spaniard is an individualist, and rebels against any foreign interference. He has always rejected the rule of foreign races. He has shaken off the yoke of superior forces. What is the explanation, then, of the presence of Germans and Italians in Seville and Salamanca as specially privileged inhabitants? The Spaniard feels humiliated by their presence. The Spanish soldiers are being thrust aside and are obeying the orders of foreigners. To explain this fact, they tell you in Seville that the Germans are the natural allies of Spain, and that they are only fighting as legionaries. The original Foreign Legion has disappeared. New recruits rallied to it. But the legionaries of to-day are not so efficient or so daring as those who captured Badajoz and Toledo. It is precisely for this reason that the Germans are there, to infuse new vitality into the exhausted Legion.

Germany's support, the Spaniards tell you, is going to grow considerably. But what sort of sacrifices will Germany demand of Franco if, thanks to Germany, Franco wins and yet continually denies that there has been any mortgaging of national territory? Is it not possible that Germany's excess population may come in the future to fill the Spanish cities and countryside? Will not Spain be converted into a country of fields and factories worked by Germans, into a sort of German industrial colony, from which Germany may draw the raw materials she needs?

DESTRUCTION OF MADRID

Until Franco's disaster at the gates of Madrid foreign intervention was limited to the material of war with which the Germans and Italians were ready to experiment on Spanish soil. But since Franco's failure in his attempt to conquer Madrid he has found himself obliged to accept Italy and Germany as advisers and to admit soldiers from those countries. Now no military move is made without the prior approval of Germany and Italy. The destruction of Madrid is the result of the advice of the Germans and Italians, who considered it to be a military necessity to destroy a capital in the power of Communism — a capital, moreover, for which they, unlike the Spaniards, have no love. It is said that Franco had always refused to destroy Madrid, and that it is only in face of German and Italian insistence that he has found himself obliged to take that painful course.

Germany and Italy had arranged to recognise Franco's Government when Madrid had been conquered; but in face of the failure at Madrid and in their eagerness for direct political and military intervention in Spain's internal affairs they precipitated the recognition. This is the explanation that is heard to-day

71

all over Spain. I heard the same explanation in Portugal. The rebels are delighted now with the intervention of Germany and Italy – as saviours, they think: and they make no secret from anyone, not even from a foreigner like myself, of the fact that they 'will win the war, because Germany, Spain's natural ally, will fight to the end against Spanish Communism'.

SWASTIKA AND FASCES

The newspapers are concealing the fact of the dispatch of German soldiers, but every day they have articles extolling Hitler and Mussolini. In the shops, alongside portraits of Franco, Mola, and Jose Antonio Primo de Rivera are those of Hitler and Mussolini. The Nazi and Fascist 'hymns' are being sold in a Spanish translation alongside those of the Falange Espanola (Spanish Fascist group) and the Foreign Legion. Many people are wearing the Swastika and the fasces on the lapels of their coats. In almost all the shops badges are for sale with the Italian, German, and Spanish colours – the Spanish colours of the time of the monarchy. The Nazi salute is the same as that of the Falangists, and is used when passing a group of Germans. The Germans, who know only their own tongue, address the waiters in it, assuming that everyone in Spain speaks German.

The only journalists permitted to see Franco's generals are the Portuguese, the Italian, and the German ones. For them the censorship is less severe, and for them there is no risk of expulsion or imprisonment. Every journalist who is neither Spanish nor Portuguese nor Italian nor German is regarded as an enemy and a possible spy. If one wants to know what is happening in Spain one must go there as a tourist, and on no account should one admit having anything to do with foreign newspapers or news agencies.

This is clearly a subjective and impressionistic account, the validity of which cannot be ascertained.

Málaga Campaign – January–February 1937

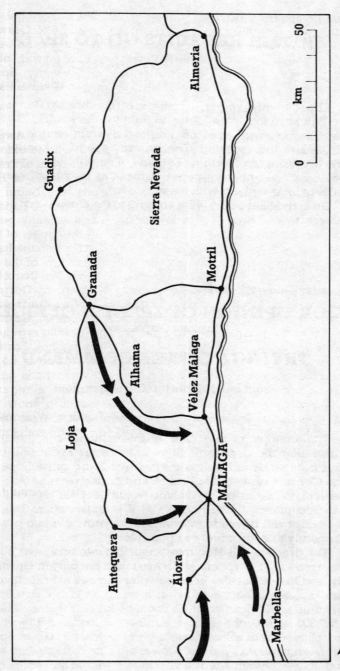

Nationalist attacks

BRITISH RECRUITS GO TO SPAIN
A Party of 80

Paris, January 3.

About eighty young members of the British Communist party left here for Spain to-day to fight for the Madrid Government. They arrived here from England by train-ferry via Dover and Dunkirk this morning. The majority are from London, but some are from the North of England. The only luggage some of them had were brown-paper parcels, as they had been told to take little or nothing with them.

On arrival here they went straight to the Communist party's headquarters.–Reuter.

POOR OPINION OF SPANISH OFFICERS
Germans Displeased

TRYING TO TAKE COMMAND

From our Diplomatic Correspondent

London, Wednesday.

The attempts to negotiate an international agreement for suppressing the departure of volunteers for Spain will in no event be abandoned unless they prove to be quite hopeless. If the German reply to the French and British request that 'non-intervention' be made to include volunteers for the civil war is an acceptance 'in principle', as it is expected to be, then the attempt will be made to translate the principle into practice as speedily and effectively as possible.

The practice will of course, mean that measures – or further measures – to stop volunteering are taken not only in Germany, Italy, and Russia but also in France (the number of French volunteers in Spain is estimated as at least 10,000), in Great Britain (the number of British volunteers on the loyalist side is believed to be 300 or 600, though the number of British subjects who have shown their willingness to go is at least 3,000) in Poland (where exceptionally drastic measures to enforce non-intervention are contemplated) and also in Portugal and some other countries.

BLOCKADE QUESTION

Practical measures to suppress volunteering and to enforce non-intervention as a whole more effectively might include a blockade of Spain, but it would have to be one in which all the naval Powers represented on the Committee of Non-Intervention, would co-operate. It is believed here that both Germany and Italy will, once there has been agreement 'in principle on the suppression of volunteering', violate that principle only by the dispatch of small batches of troops to Spain and by clandestine deliveries of war material.

Germany, it is believed here, has a special interest in not tying up too many men in Spain. Whether she will move in Central Europe or not cannot be foreseen as yet, though that she has contemplated moving in Central Europe is certain. To have a small army in Spain would be an asset to her in so far as it would help to distract both France and Great Britain (and Italy for that matter) from Central European preoccupations.

GERMAN AND ITALIAN TANKS DAMAGED

The Germans are now trying to secure a bigger influence over the actual military operations conducted by the rebels. They are thoroughly dissatisfied both with Franco and with his officers as a whole. The rebel commanders have been unable to deal with a difficulty that has caused the Germans the greatest exasperation.

This is that the tanks supplied by the Germans and Italians are constantly being damaged by the men in charge of them, chiefly, it would seem, because these men do not like serving in the tanks detachments, though it may be that some of them are hostile to the Germans or even have secret sympathies with the loyalists.

Even on the loyalist side there has been some dissatisfaction amongst the Russian officers over the way in which the Spaniards seem able to mishandle or damage their tanks, though on the rebel side this phenomenon has been like an epidemic that has seriously affected the fighting power of the rebel army, indeed, only a fraction of the German and Italian tanks have been able to go into action at all, and where these have had newly trained Spanish crews they have often turned back as soon as the action has begun.

Hitherto the Germans on the rebel side have not gone into action – except in the air – but have remained at the bases as instructors, mechanics, experts, anti-aircraft gunners, and so on. Apparently they will henceforth, without necessarily receiving any considerable reinforcements from home, play a bigger part in the firing-line as well as at the bases.

MORE GERMAN 'VOLUNTEERS'
2,000 Blackshirts

GERMANY HEARING OF CASUALTIES

From our Diplomatic Correspondent

London, Friday.

Two thousand 'S.S.' (Blackshirts) have been assembled at Munich and are about to leave for Spain. The assembled 'military division' of the 'S.S.' are a fully trained and equipped military formation, 30,000 or 60,000 strong, and have the value of a Regular Army. Their function in case of war is chiefly the maintenance of order at home – this, as the German authorities conceive it, is a military task, for the menace of rebellion at home is reckoned with as the accompaniment of war abroad.

The reason why 'S.S.' and not Regulars (Reichswehr) are being sent to Spain would seem to be, partly at least, that they are to gain experience in street fighting. The 2,000 men have been withdrawn from various 'divisions' of the 'S.S.' and tanks have been assigned to them. They are to go via Austria to Italy, and will embark for Spain at an Italian port.

There is some discontent in the 'S.S.' because their men are being sent to Spain as 'volunteers'. A good deal of grumbling is heard, and some 'S.S.' men have been saying that the Regulars ought to go to Spain because 'that is what they are there for'.

The fact that German troops are fighting on the side of the Spanish rebels is becoming more and more widely known in Germany, in spite of the recent official German denial that there is a single German soldier in Spain. Reports of German casualties are spreading and have, no doubt, influenced the attitude of the 'S.S.'.

4,000 VOLUNTEERS FROM ITALY
A Reported Landing

A report has reached Gibraltar of the landing of a further large contingent of Italian volunteers at the southern rebel port of Cadiz. According to a reliable eye-witness who has just returned from that city (says Reuter) the volunteers disembarked last Tuesday night from a large transport which bore neither name nor flag. He estimated their number at over 4,000. Italians and Moors far outnumbered Spanish troops in Seville, Jerez, and Cadiz, the traveller reported. . . .

REBEL ADVANCE ON MALAGA
Shelling of Madrid

HEAVY WEEK-END BOMBARDMENT

The news from Spain over the week-end shows, briefly, that Madrid has suffered the most severe bombardment of the war on Saturday, and a further bombardment yesterday, and that the rebels are now advancing on Malaga from two directions.

Of the advance along the coast from the west there is no news – there has, in fact, been little since the rebels took Marbella, – but it is now claimed that rebel forces have advanced 21 miles in the province of Granada, north of Malaga, towards the coast. Radio Seville claims that a Government relief column from Carthagena was defeated and 100 Government forces were killed.

From Valencia last night it was reported by Reuter that all was quiet on the Malaga front.

The British Consulate at Malaga has been closed in view of the rebel advance, and the British Vice-Consul there arrived in Gibraltar on Saturday on board the destroyer Antelope. Forty-eight refugees were also on board.

BOMBARDMENT OF MADRID

The bombardment of Madrid on Saturday began at ten o'clock in the morning when shells fell on the working-class quarter of Wallecas, South-east Madrid. Later the bombardment grew more fierce and spread to other parts of the city. In the end the central streets and almost all the suburbs and outlying districts of the city had suffered.

Six-inch shells fell in the centre of the city. Fire broke out in one quarter, but was extinguished. The streets presented a scene of desolation; they were strewn with pieces of stone, glass, wood, and tiles. Cars were covered in a white dust from falling masonry.

The shelling led to a sudden exodus, many people hastily packing their few belongings into bundles and fleeing from the city. The calm with which the falling of the first shells was greeted soon gave place to general alarm when it was seen that the bombardment was something more than the usual daily dropping of a few shells.

Five dead and 37 injured, many of them seriously, are the official casualty figures of the bombardment, but it is probable that further casualties will be discovered.

CENTRE OF CITY SHELLED

The centre of Madrid was again shelled by rebel artillery yesterday afternoon. The bombardment lasted over an hour, and the firing was remarkably accurate. The Telephone Building in the centre of the city was hit, but telephone communications were not interrupted. Eight people are reported to have been killed and thirty injured.

On February 8 1937 the Republican Government issued a statement that Malaga had fallen. It was alleged that German naval vessels, including the battleship, Graf Spee, had bombarded the city before a rebel force, aided by large numbers of Italian and German troops and with support from Italian tanks, completed the capture.

Tuesday January 26 1937   *p.10*

THE TWO NOTES

The German and Italian replies to the British Note on 'volunteers' to Spain are a great deal more reasonable than anything that had been expected. Both proclaim a wish to make non-intervention work: both seem agreed that the stopping of 'volunteers' is one of the first necessities; neither makes this dependent on other conditions which are less urgent but more difficult to attain. And both, one may add, are noticeably more polite. Indeed, were it not for previous experience one would be inclined to accept them without hesitation as a sincere and genuine step towards true non-intervention. Unfortunately this is hardly possible. If, for instance, the German Government really noted 'with satisfaction' that the British Government believed in 'the necessity for immediate measures for preventing the influx of volunteers to Spain', why did it wait fifteen days before answering? In order to consult with the Italian Government? But the Italian Government 'is happy to be able to reconfirm that these are among the principal objects which it desires to attain'. Then why have the two Powers so long delayed? The first Anglo-French appeal was made on December 4 last year; Berlin did not answer until December

78

12 and Rome until December 24, and Berlin and Rome did not reply until January 7. On January 10 the final British appeal, to which these replies have now come, was sent, and since then Portugal, France, and Russia have all answered, and France has passed the necessary Bill through both Chamber and Senate. We know, of course, that Germany and Italy have delayed so that they could send more troops to Spain and so that they might watch the course of the war. This does not necessarily mean the two Notes are insincere, but it justifies some caution in accepting them.

On close consideration the German and Italian proposals offer opportunities of further delay should these States desire to take them. The German Government, for instance, links the question of stopping 'volunteers' with that of establishing an international control. The plans for this control are well advanced, but there is still room for much 'negotiation' in the London Non-Intervention Committee before they are completed. Again, the German Government still 'attaches special value' to its proposals that all volunteers now in Spain, 'including political agitators and propagandists' should be removed from Spain. Fortunately it does not make this a strict condition of stopping more volunteers from going, but if it did the chances of success would be remote. For how are the democratic countries to bring back their 'volunteers' and, if they found a way, how are they to convince Germany that they have done so? The Italian Note also hints at the same question, but perhaps it is unwise to make difficulties in advance. On their face value the two Notes may be considered satisfactory. Their principal proposal, that the London Committee should fix a date on which each of the Powers concerned should put into force its measures for preventing volunteers (or troops) leaving their countries, is thoroughly sensible and, incidentally, illustrates how futile it was for the British Government to have taken single-handed action in advance. On the basis of this the Committee should move at once, co-ordinate the various replies, and agree upon a date. But it is for the French and British Governments to show that they cannot brook indefinite delay and that one universal measure in practice is worth half a dozen accepted 'in principle'.

LETTERS TO THE EDITOR

'NON-INTERVENTION' IN SPAIN
The Tedious Farce Goes On

To the Editor of the Manchester Guardian

Sir,–Malaga has been taken mainly, it appears, by the efforts of Italian 'volunteers'; Rome chooses that moment to deny all official participation in Spain immediately afterwards an Italian warship lands 1,000 more 'volunteers' at Malaga itself. What purpose can this cynical impudence be still supposed to serve? Whom is it still hoped to deceive? We are to imagine that in a country where a kitten can hardly mew without a permit the paternal head of the Duce cannot restrain thousands of prodigal sons rushing 'adventurously' to the slaughter. In fact, we know that the youth of Italy and Germany alike is being bribed, bullied, or 'shanghaied' into Spain. And then the Non-Intervention Committee holds another meeting.

Surely it is time that Lord Plymouth was instructed to address to that body a little plain English of the kind that in the past was understood quickly enough throughout Europe. We know that Italy and Germany are short of money, yet are pouring it like water into Spain, we should know that they will take their own repayment and that it will not be only at the expense of Spain. But to-day only when the lion's own tail is trodden on does he even turn in his sleep.

As over Ethiopia, our policy is palsied by one fundamental thing. More and more it stands out above every other factor. A large selection of English opinion is obsessed with a delirium tremens which sees everywhere the red rat of Bolshevism gnawing its way into its bank cellars. Hitler may arm to the teeth, bestride our trade routes, yell for colonies; no matter, this agony about their beloved bank balances blinds these people to all else. Hitler, they think, may save them from being plundered by 'the Reds'; he well may – to do it twice as effectively himself.

Nothing will get done till we are cured of this ignoble paranoia. The Fascist International is not merely odious in its practice, as, unhappily, the Soviet Union also sometimes is, its whole theory is, for all who value intellectual liberty and individual happiness, a second Black Death hanging over Europe. Yet still we are crippled by this faction which cries out for pacts with Germany and, to gain a brief respite, would fling Eastern Europe to the Nazi wolf.

Surely the only way to secure non-intervention in Spain

is to make it clear in plain words that we mean to have it, if necessary, by an Anglo-French blockade of the Spanish seaboard. Failing that, it would be more dignified to have done with this tedious farce of the Non-Intervention Committee, compared with which a conference of crooks and gangsters in a Chicago back street would be ennobling. For among thieves there is, at least sometimes, some sort of honour—Yours,&c.

F. L. LUCAS,
20 West Road, Cambridge, February 12.

CLOSING FRENCH FRONTIER TO VOLUNTEERS
Has Diplomatic Victory Come Too Late?

REMOVAL OF FOREIGNERS FROM SPAIN
Committee's Next Task – The French View

From our own Correspondent

Paris, February 16.

At the Cabinet meeting this morning a decree was signed by the President of the Republic prohibiting

1. Volunteers to leave for Spain or Spanish Morocco.
2. All recruiting activities in France.
3. The transit through France of foreigners intending to enlist in Spain.

No railway, steamer, or aeroplane tickets for Spain, can be delivered without a special permit. No aeroplane may fly within a six-mile zone of the Pyrenees. The decree comes into force at midnight on Saturday.

Another decree reinforces the French air police along the Spanish frontier. The frontier will thus be virtually closed except to the very few persons with a special visa. Whether the French the French frontier is also to be submitted to international control will depend on whether Portugal will ultimately agree to a similar control being exercised along her frontier with Spain, though in all probability France will also agree to this control if an effective naval control is imposed on Portugal in the absence of frontier supervision.

The latest non-intervention decision continues to be criticised in a number of Left-wing quarters where it is felt that the diplomatic victory of M. Corbin, the French Ambassador, has come too late. If it had come before the landing of thousands of Germans and Italians in Spain it would have been a more genuine diplomatic victory and more in keeping with the spirit of the non-intervention idea – the essence of which was to let the Spaniards fight it out among themselves.

With a huge Spanish 'National' army composed of thousands of Germans and Italians ravaging Spain, non-intervention, it is felt, will remain a mockery, and it is strongly felt that the Non-Intervention Committee should not consider its main task at an end but make every effort to have all foreign troops withdrawn from Spain as quickly and as completely as possible.

Germany's apparent reluctance to send more troops to Spain – apart from considerations of a general diplomatic kind – is attributed here to a number of concrete facts. Among these is the heavy casualties – about 1,500 – suffered by the German troops in the last few weeks, and also to the numerous cases of desertion, including that of eight officers, among the German troops around Madrid.

It is believed that the reports of serious discontent in Germany over the dispatch of troops to Spain are not unfounded, and that this discontent has had a certain influence on the German Government.

Saturday February 20 1937   *p.17*

POSITIONS IN THE VALENCIA ROAD BATTLE
Rebel Claims of Air Raid Successes

GOVERNMENT OFFENSIVE IN ESCORIAL SECTOR

The battle for the Valencia road begun by rebels almost a fortnight ago had yesterday come to a standstill. The attack began from Piato and some ground has been gained, but the rebels have been pushed back from the positions they held at the beginning of the week.

It was made clear by a Government communiqué yesterday that the Jarama River has been crossed and that a small force of rebels, said to be 'German troops', are holding fortified positions in the Morata sector, north of Chincon. But the main rebel forces appear never to have been across the Jarama, and in the Government's counter-attack of Wednesday were pushed back. According to the Government's claims the Repub-

licans advanced on a front of five miles, the greatest advance
– of three miles – being from San Martin.

On Thursday the rebels again attacked in La Maranosa
sector, south-west of Vaciamadrid. Of this engagement the Government communiqué said yesterday:

> On the Jarama front the rebels, in reply to the Government
> offensive, launched a vigorous counter-attack in the La
> Maranosa sector. After five hours' fighting the rebel on-
> slaught weakened and the Government troops maintained
> their positions.
>
> The Government troops carried out a particularly bril-
> liant operation in the Marata sector, where they stormed forti-
> fied positions held by German troops.
>
> A diversion was staged by the rebels in the University
> City sector with the double object of distracting attention
> from the Jarama front and re-establishing communication
> between the rebel positions at the Bridge of the French
> (across the Manranares) and the advance guard holding the
> Clinical Hospital. The attack, however, completely failed.

REBEL CLAIMS

At the rebel headquarters at Avila yesterday it was stated
that no ground has been gained by the Madrid Command in
the last three days and instead it has suffered heavy losses.

Sixteeen Government 'planes were brought down in Thursday's fighting, it was also stated. Five were brought down in
the Aragon front and eleven on the Madrid front. There were
two engagements round Madrid, one in the morning, the other
late in the afternoon. In the morning battle some forty chaser
'planes, fighting at a height of two and a half miles, took part.
Within half an hour of the beginning of the battle nine Government machines had fallen to the ground in flames.

There were about a score of 'planes taking part in the
afternoon battle, but the Government machines refused to fight,
it is stated. Two, however, were brought down. The official
communiqué proudly claims that no rebel 'plane was brought
down and that only one rebel pilot was wounded.

Taking advantage of a brilliant moonlight night, rebel
'planes also harried Government concentrations in the valleys
near Arganda and a great air battle ensued between the rebel
bombers and the Government fighters. The bombing raid
began at 11p.m. and was repeated every quarter of an hour.
The rebel 'planes dropped their bombs and then came down
low to machine-gun the bivouacs and convoys. After a machine-
gun battle with Government 'planes one Russian 'plane fell
in flames and another fell in the Government lines.

It is also stated in Avila that heavy traffic has been observed on the secondary roads by which Madrid is supplied with food and munitions. Rebel aircraft bombed troop concentrations and convoys at Guadalajara, a town on the roundabout route linking Madrid with Valencia at Cuenca.

The Battle of Jarama ensured that the Republic maintained control of the Madrid–Valencia road which was of paramount importance for the defence of Madrid itself.

Monday February 22 1937   *p.9*

PROHIBITION OF VOLUNTEERS
Decrees in Force

FRANCE & PORTUGAL ACT
No Transit Allowed

As from midnight on Saturday volunteers were prevented from crossing into Spain. The French frontier has been closed. No form of international control will come into force for a fortnight.

A decree preventing the enlistment of volunteers in accordance with the decision of the London Non-Intervention Committee has been issued in Moscow. A similar decree has been issued in Portugal, which also prohibits foreign volunteers from travelling across Portugal. Most of the other countries have also issued decrees including Germany. There was no last minute rush on the French frontier.

DISCUSSIONS WITH PORTUGAL

Negotiations with Portugal will be resumed to-day to overcome the Portuguese objections to foreign supervision of her frontiers. It is understood that Britain has been invited to undertake this by officers attached to our Legation at Lisbon.

Naval supervision will be by zones but no agreement on the zones has been reached.

Reuter's correspondent at the rebel headquarters at Salamanca says it is felt there that the prohibition is to the advantage of General Franco, as the Government forces have come up against crushing military superiority.

FOREIGN HELP FOR FRANCO
Nearly 100,000 Men

10,000 ITALIANS IN LAST RUSH
A Hundred Bombers

From our Diplomatic Correspondent

London, Wednesday.

Further detachments of Italian troops arrived last week in Spain just before the prohibition of volunteers came into force. Their total strength is estimated at about 10,000, so that there are now at least 70,000 Italian troops in Spain. Some 5,000 French volunteers also succeeded in reaching Spain just before closing time.

Amongst the war material shipped to Spain from Italy this month was a consignment of 100 Caproni bombers, which arrived in an aircraft-carrier. It does not seem that any Russian volunteers or war material have reached Spain during the last few weeks. Instead, it would seem that Russia has given up her intervention altogether.

All figures relating to numbers of troops – whether Spanish or foreign – in Spain are conjectural, but as far as can be judged at the moment there would seem to be between 30,000 and 60,000 volunteers on the Government side and between 80,000 and 100,000 on the rebel side, the latter, of course, bring supplies with an incomparably superior armament.

Battle of Guadalajara – March 1937

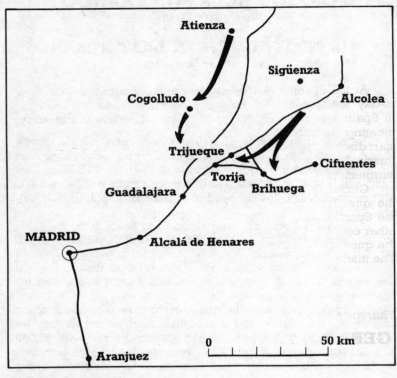

'VOLUNTEERS'
Fascist Opposition to Withdrawal

From our London Correspondent

London, Monday Night.

At the Spanish Non-Intervention Sub-committee's meeting to-day the question of withdrawing the 'volunteers' already in Spain was brought up for the first time. It was put to the meeting by Lord Plymouth whether the time was not ripe to start discussing the withdrawal of 'volunteers'. France, Belgium, Russia, Sweden, and Czechoslovakia, I gather, favoured the suggestion.

Germany, Italy, and Portugal, however, would not consider the question by itself. They took the view that if the case of the Spanish gold which the Government of Spain had sent to other countries was also taken up they would consider whether the question of withdrawal of 'volunteers' should be gone into. The matter was left there till Friday.

GERMAN TANKS FOR SPANISH REBELS
A Fresh Consignment Just Sent

NAZIS TOLD THAT THE VATICAN IS SUPPORTING THE GOVERNMENT
From our Diplomatic Correspondent

London, Wednesday.

German intervention in Spain continued until quite recently and may be going on still. The supervision of the Spanish coasts and frontiers will hardly be complete before the 20th of this month, so that there is still plenty of time for Germany and Italy to supply the Spanish rebels with further auxiliaries and war-material.

At the end of February a consignment of twenty tanks left Germany for Spain. Presumably the men to man these tanks have also been sent, for the German experience is that tanks entrusted to Spaniards suffer more damage from those who are inside them than from those who try to destroy them from outside. Indeed, very few tanks manned by Spaniards have reached the firing-line at all.

Although all figures relating to numbers of men engaged in the Spanish civil war are conjectural, estimates of the numbers of Germans serving under General Franco diverge most of all. The Italians fighting on the rebel side certainly number no less than 70,000, as stated in this correspondence recently. The figures stated in the House of Commons yesterday show that the strength of the Italian contingents is greatly under-estimated in this country. As for the Germans, estimates vary between 15,000 and 30,000.

THE VATICAN AND THE SPANISH GOVERNMENT

The Spanish civil war has one aspect that makes it a little awkward for Germany. The conflict between National Socialism and Roman Catholicism is getting severer day by day. The most ardent champions of the rebel cause in Germany are also the most ardent anti-Catholics, and for them to support a cause that can be identified with that of Roman Catholicism is only one degree less insufferable than to support Communism itself. Indeed, the extreme anti-Catholics in Germany treat Catholicism as being akin to Communism.

Most of the German troops in Spain belong to the S.S. (Blackshirts), and the organ of the S.S., the 'Schwarze Korps', of February 27 gets over the difficulty by explaining that the Vatican is really on the side of the Spanish Government. It writes:

The Vatican allows priests and monks to fight arms in hand on the side of Communism even in Spain. We hesitated for a long time before stating this fact, although from the beginning of the Spanish conflict the newspapers of the world announced that while thousands of Catholic priests and members of Catholic orders died the death of martyrs . . . Catholic priests were fighting against the national rising.

That Romish doctrine combats all nationalism as a matter of principle has been shown a thousand times, but that Catholics can appear with arms as allies of the gangs of Communist murderers seemed unbelievable in view of the atrocities committed against priests and nuns. But even this infamy has become a terrible fact.

SPAIN FOR THE SPANIARDS

It is satisfactory to learn that if there are no more unforeseen obstacles the international naval cordon should now be definitely drawn around Spain on Saturday. Although owing to the opposition of the Fascist Powers there is no form of air control, it should henceforward be extremely difficult for any Power to smuggle munitions or men into Spain in defiance of its pledged word. But Signor Mussolini has made certain that before he allowed the control to come into being a large Italian Fascist army of between seventy and a hundred thousand men should be in Spain ready to help the rebels. Eight days after the Italian Government decreed that no more 'volunteers' should go to Spain 10,000 Italians landed there. On Saturday, according to reports from Gibraltar, yet another Italian shipload reached Cadiz. The Spanish militia has yet to contend with this highly trained army of foreign invaders. Mussolini is thus investing handsomely in the future. For General Franco has assured him that the rebels 'would not forget the friendly Italian hand which in dangerous moments shook their own nor the heart which throbbed next to theirs during the hard days of war'.

However, the Non-Intervention Committee has also promised to consider 'as soon as possible' the question of the withdrawal of all non-Spanish nationals engaged directly or indirectly in the war. This proposal was first put forward by Italy herself and by Germany. Yet when the question was first raised in the Non-Intervention Committee a week ago those Powers announced that the question could not be raised unless the question of the Spanish gold sent abroad by the Spanish Government was also considered. The gold question is, of course, a separate problem which on the face of it has little to do with non-intervention. Nothing, it may be noted, was said about the Spanish gold when the proposal for the withdrawal of non-Spaniards was last raised by these Powers. In the Italian and German Notes of January 25, for example, no mention whatever was made of Spanish gold in relation to the withdrawal of foreigners. There was, and is, no connection. The German Government, on the contrary, 'attached special value' to the proposals for withdrawing all soldiers and 'agitators' already there, which it had described earlier as 'the best solution'. The Italian Government thought that 'an effective policy of non-intervention' required that 'the situation of last August' (when there were few or no Italian infantrymen in Spain) should 'be restored'. The British Government must take the first opportunity to remind the Fascist Powers of their own proposals and, encouraged by the willingness of the Valencia Government to allow the genuine volunteers on their side to go home, press for a speedy agreement on the withdrawal of all non-Spaniards taking part in the war. A non-intervention control scheme which leaves a hundred thousand Italians to fight in Spain would be as big a farce as non-intervention has hitherto been without a control scheme to enforce it.

Friday March 12 1937   *p.13*

THREE REBEL ARMIES TRYING TO ENCIRCLE MADRID
The Capital Facing Isolation

The great rebel army marching on Madrid from Siguenza made a further advance yesterday and took the important centre of Brihuega. It was to Brihuega that the Government had sent strong reinforcements after the setbacks on this front early in the week. With the fall of the town the first Government attempt to hold up the rebel advance has failed.

THREE SEPARATE THRUSTS

From Brihuega the rebels are now advancing in three directions. Each force will be formidable, for the rebel army in this region numbers 32,000 men – 15,000 of them, it is alleged, Italians.

One column set out to the north-west with the idea of joining the rebels who have been held in the Guadarrama mountains since the autumn. Another column is advancing down the road that runs parallel to the left bank of the River Tajuna. The immediate objective of this column is Armuna, a village lying at the point at which the Guadalajara–Valencia road crosses the Tajuna.

The eventual aim is to join the rebel forces who for the past month have been fighting, as yet unsuccessfully, for the possession of the direct Madrid–Valencia road.

A direct advance down the Saragossa road is also being made, and the rebels last night claimed that they had reached the neighbourhood of Torija, twelve miles from Guadalajara.

THE LAST ROADS

Of the seven main roads that lead from the capital five are already completely cut – those to the west and south on the outskirts of the city and that to the north at a distance of 50 miles. The main Valencia road remains precariously open, and much of the traffic has been diverted by way of Guadalajara or by the loop round Alcala.

Those roads are most seriously threatened by the present rebel offensive; if it succeeds Madrid is isolated.

The Battle of Guadalajara, following so soon after the Republican success in halting the nationalist advance at the Battle of Jarama, served to prevent the encirclement of Madrid.

NO RESUMPTION OF SPANISH REBELS' OFFENSIVE
Exhausted by Last Week's Fighting

Madrid, March 15.

In spite of warm and sunny weather, which usually brings heavy fighting, relative quiet prevailed to-day on all fronts round Madrid. Both sides needed rest after the strong attacks and counter-attacks which have taken place daily throughout the last week in the Guadalajara battle and were fortifying their positions. Government artillery has been active on both the Guadalajara (north-east) and Jarama (south) fronts with the object of preventing rebel concentrations.

The cloudless sky was ideal for war in the air. It is reported that loyalist 'planes bombed and machine-gunned rebel positions on the Guadalajara front, while rebel machines raided Government lines on the Aranjuez sector of the south front.

Reports from Oviedo are meagre. Storms and snowfalls are hindering communications between Madrid and Asturias. It appears, however, that fighting in that city has been limited to artillery fire in consequence of the extreme cold prevailing.

The rebel forces on the Guadalajara front now appear to be re-forming behind the lines to which they fell back on Saturday. It is expected that they will lose no time counter-attacking to try to regain the initiative, and to-day the Government airmen tried to prevent this.

Further details of to-day's operations on the Jarama river indicate that the rebels carried out local attacks and were driven back to their original positions by Government counter-attacks. The main sectors involved were about three miles west of the main Madrid–Valencia road.

PRICE OF ITALIAN HELP

A communiqué issued by the Madrid Defence Committee gives details of an 'Italian plan of campaign' alleged to have been drawn up by General Bergonzoli, who is said to be the commander-in-chief of the Italian forces attacking the Guadalajara front. Rebel headquarters scoff at reports of a Government victory on the Saragossa road, and the claim that Trijueque has been captured by the loyalists has been denied many times by their wireless stations.

But a point-for-point reply to the rebel denial has in its turn been broadcast from Madrid. The Government says it can prove the capture of Trijueque by photographs, and if necessary by the Italians captured there.

The Government forces on the Madrid front captured 59 Italian prisoners this evening, according to a communiqué issued in Madrid and quoted by the Spanish Press Agency. New documents throwing further light on the activities of the Italian army in Spain were obtained, it is added.

Another communiqué says that 'with the complicity of Spanish traitors probably more than 100,000 Italians are invading Spain, and you know the price that has had to be paid for that help – sale of Spanish territory and the material interests of the country. Spaniards throughout the world should know that Spain has been invaded.'–Reuter.

ITALY'S SECOND 'CAPORETTO'
Retreat Goes On

ITALIANS 'USELESS IN SPAIN'

Spanish Government troops continue to advance north-east of Madrid and the collapse of the Italian army is now fully confirmed. Vast quantities of equipment and munitions were thrown away or left behind.

It is thought that the Italians have not suffered heavy losses as they appear in the main to have kept out of the reach of the Government troops.

A special correspondent of the Press Association who has visited the front described it as a 'second Caporetto'.

The correspondent says that the country is ideal for mechanised units, but the cold has destroyed the morale of the rebels. He says that the Italians are useless in such a climate.

The Italian forces in Spain were heavily committed at the Battle of Guadalajara and met with a severe reverse when confronted largely by Republican troops of the International Brigades. Not since the Battle of Caporetto in the First World War had Italian troops experienced a comparable setback.

Wednesday March 24 1937   p.11

NO ITALIAN TO LEAVE SPAIN TILL THE WAR ENDS
Signor Grandi's Startling Stand

A NEW CRISIS IN NON-INTERVENTION'S TARDY PROGRESS

From our London Correspondent

Fleet Street, Tuesday.

What was defined by the chairman, I understand, as 'a situation of extreme gravity' was revealed to-day in the proceedings of the Spanish Non-Intervention Sub-Committee. It seems that Signor Grandi announced that the Italian Government was not ready or willing at present to begin discussing the question of the withdrawal of volunteers from Spain.

The Chairman, Lord Plymouth, asked if Signor Grandi would give a reason why, and received the answer that the Italian representative had nothing to explain or to add. That was the position of the Italian Government on this question.

The Russian Ambassador asked if the Italian Government was withdrawing its own proposal of January for the committee to discuss the withdrawal of volunteers.

A STARTLED COMMITTEE

Signor Grandi then said that not a single Italian volunteer would leave Spain until the end of the civil war in Spain. This statement created a startling impression on the committee.

The French Ambassador pointed out that this was in sharp contradiction to the position taken up previously by the Italian Government and to what Signor Grandi himself had repeatedly said at the committee. The question of the withdrawal or non-withdrawal of volunteers from Spain would decide the fate of the Committee of Non-Intervention.

Lord Plymouth, the chairman of the committee, seemed greatly surprised and said that Signor Grandi's announcement had created a situation of extreme gravity. He associated himself with what the French Ambassador had said. He would refer this question to his Government. The Swedish Minister, according to my information, spoke in support of the French and British view.

HERR VON RIBBENTROP'S CHARGE

Then Herr von Ribbentrop spoke. He reserved his opinion on the question of volunteers for the present. He sought to meet the Russian point by accusing the committee of having previously delayed the discussion of this question. The chairman energetically protested against this charge of delay, pointing out that the committee had to deal with first questions first, particularly the prohibition of volunteers and the supervision scheme, before reaching the discussion of getting the volunteers out of Spain.

This fateful meeting ended by Mr. Maisky's hoping that the Italian Government would not persist in this attitude. It imperilled the peace of Europe, and while the committee had tried all the time to confine the Spanish conflict to Spain, this attitude of the Italian Government would defeat the ends of the committee.

Earlier in the meeting the Russian Government had shown its desire for the progress of the committee by withdrawing from its previous position and agreeing to the discussion of questions of Spanish capital assets, including gold. It was agreed that this question could now go to a committee of experts to consider and report. The meeting, I gather, broke up with feelings of apprehension and disappointment. To-night these happenings are the talk of London.

Monday March 29 1937   *p.13*

BRITISH VOLUNTEERS IN SPAIN
'Not Gulled into Coming by Promises of Big Money'

The following resolution has been passed at a meeting of the British Battalion in Spain – the 16th Battalion of the International Brigade. It is signed by J. W. Cunningham, for battalion commander, W. S. Harrington, battalion secretary, and G. S. Aitken, battalion political commissar:–

We the members of the British working class in the British Battalion of the International Brigade now fighting in Spain in defence of democracy, protest against statements appearing in certain British papers to the effect that there is little or no interference in the civil war in Spain by foreign Fascist Powers.

We have seen with our own eyes frightful slaughter of men, women, and children in Spain. We have witnessed the destruction of many of its towns and villages. We have seen whole areas which have been devastated. And we know beyond a shadow of doubt that these frightful deeds have been done mainly by German and Italian nationals, using German and Italian aeroplanes, tanks, bombs, shells, and guns.

We ourselves have been in action repeatedly against thousands of German and Italian troops, and have lost many splendid and heroic comrades in these battles.

We protest against this disgraceful and unjustifiable invasion of Spain by Fascist Germany and Italy; an invasion in our opinion only made possible by the pro-Franco policy of the Baldwin Government in Britain. We believe that all lovers of freedom and democracy in Britain should now unite in a sustained effort to put an end to this invasion of Spain and to force the Baldwin Government to give to the people of Spain and their legal Government the right to buy arms in Britain to defend their freedom and democracy against Fascist barbarianism. We therefore call upon the General Council of the T.U.C. and the National Executive Committee of the Labour party to organise a great united campaign in Britain for the achievement of the above objects.

We denounce the attempts being made in Britain by the Fascist elements to make people believe that we British and other volunteers fighting on behalf of Spanish democracy are no different from the scores of thousands of conscript troops sent into Spain by Hitler and Mussolini. There can be no comparison between free volunteers and these conscript armies of Germany and Italy in Spain.

Finally, we desire it to be known in Britain that we came here of our own free will after full consideration of all that this step involved. We came to Spain not for money, but solely to assist the heroic Spanish people to defend their country's freedom and democracy. We were not gulled into coming to Spain by promises of big money. We never even asked for money when we volunteered. We are perfectly satisfied with our treatment by the Spanish Government; and we still are proud to be fighting for the cause of freedom in Spain. Any statements to the contrary are foul lies.

The British citizens who fought for the Republic jealously guarded their claim to being volunteers in the cause of democracy and not even their most committed opponents could have accused them of being lured to Spain by the prospect of personal reward.

Capture of Bilbao – March–June 1937

→ Nationalist attacks

NEW WARNING TO BASQUES
Call to Surrender

'DESTRUCTION' THE ALTERNATIVE

A second manifesto was sent to Bilbao yesterday by the
rebel High Command again threatening the population of Biscay
Province with destruction unless they surrender. An earlier
manifesto – then said to be the 'final warning' – invited the
citizens of Bilbao to surrender under guarantee that their lives
would be spared and under threat that if their submission were
not immediate Biscay Province would be destroyed. This did
not produce any effect.

In spite of official denials by the Basque Government
rumours of negotiations between the rebels and the Basques
continues. The latest unconfirmed report from Bayonne is that
Cardinal Goma, Primate of Spain, has gone from Rome to attempt to open negotiations between the two Basque Catholic
sections, the Basque loyalists and the Carlists, who support
Franco.

The Basque communiqué yesterday stated that the rebel
offensive in the North of Spain had failed; the rebel communiqué
stated, 'The bad weather in Biscay is preventing us from continuing military operations on that front.' According to General
Queipo de Llano an army of 50,000 men from Asturias is on
its way to Bilbao to reinforce the defence of that city. He also
declared that contrary to the claims in the Government's communiqués the enemy had not gained one inch of ground in
the recent attacks. They had on the other hand lost 18,000 men,
of whom 5,000 were killed.

p.20

LETTERS TO THE EDITOR

SPAIN'S STRUGGLE AGAINST FASCISM
A Protest from British Members of the International Brigade

To the Editor of the Manchester Guardian

Sir,–We staunch trade unionists in the front line were
astounded by the attitude adopted by Transport House at the
International Labour Conference, and are of the opinion that
the official leaders of the Labour party and Trades Union Congress, in pursuing their present policy, are ignorant of what
is going on out here. They believe that Fascism can be isolated

by ignoring it and place their trust in a useless Non-Intervention Committee.

As we sit here in our dugout writing, Italian trench bombs are whizzing overhead and explosive bullets are cracking like a multitude of whips. While M.P.s are saying that the number of the 'volunteers' from the Fascist States is minute, we know definitely that we have to face thousands of them, trained soldiers beyond a doubt, machine-gunners who play a tune on our parapets and strip the bark of a tree covering one of our fellows without wasting a shot.

We were not dupes in coming to Spain; we quitted sound jobs and good homes; we were not lured by promises of big money, but came to fight with the knowledge that a defeat for international Fascism meant a halt to its brutal aggression throughout Europe and would give time to the democratic countries of the world to unite and preserve world peace and democracy.

We have been out here since November with the International Brigade, and from our experiences on several different fronts are convinced that despite the aid given by the Fascist Powers to Franco, helped again by the indirect aid of England's foreign policy, the great cause of democracy will triumph in Spain.–Yours, &c.

M. LEVINE,
National Union of Tailors and Garment Workers (Manchester)
D. W. C. MOWATT,
Railway Clerks' Association (London).
16th Battalion, 15th Brigade International Column, Somewhere in Spain, April 1.

Many of the British volunteers in Spain were members of the Communist Party or had been members of organisations connected with it such as the National Unemployed Workers' Movement. Throughout the 1920s and 1930s friction had existed between the Labour and Communist Parties over both domestic and foreign policy. The Communist Party sought radical solutions to the evil of unemployment at home and the rise of fascism abroad whilst the Labour Party shied away from radicalism and sought political respectability through more moderate policy pronouncements.

On April 16 the Chairman's Sub-committee of the Non-Intervention Committee set the date for the introduction of the control scheme to monitor the importation of war materials into Spain at midnight, April 19 and recommended consideration of the question of foreign volunteers.

'FURIOUS FIGHTING'

Madrid, April 23.

Latest reports from the Basque front speak of 'furious fighting' by both sides. Tremendous efforts are being made by the Government forces to dislodge General Mola's troops from Elorrio, Elgueta, and other small villages south-east of Durango, in which the General is mustering all available strength to proceed on Durango. Numbers of rebel aeroplanes for their part have bombed the villages nearer their objective, including Kibar. In order to stop the rebel advance and to prevent their obtaining access to the San Sebastian–Bilbao main road the Basque forces have withdrawn to a few miles east of Elorrio, taking up better positions there. At Eibar the Government troops are now offering strong resistance, in spite of heavy rebel bombing.–Central News.

BASQUE TOWN WIPED OUT BY REBEL 'PLANES
Three Hours' Massacre from the Air

GERMAN PILOTS ALLEGED TO HAVE TAKEN PART

Guernica, till 1876 capital of the Basque country, has been reduced to ruins by rebel 'planes of German make. The bombardment, which lasted for three and a half hours on Monday afternoon, killed hundreds of the 10,000 inhabitants, and yesterday only a few of the buildings remained standing. Many of the ruins were still burning.

General Mola, who is in charge of the rebel offensive on the Basque front, is apparently trying to carry out his threat 'to destroy the whole of Biscay Province' if the Basques do not immediately surrender. When he made the threat early in April he added, 'We have the means of carrying out our intentions.' Yesterday the Basque Government alleged that Germans were piloting the German bombers that carried out the raid.

NO SURRENDER

It is reported that General Mola has now warned the Basque

Government that he will raze Bilbao to the ground unless the town surrenders. But the Government states that after the destruction of Guernica surrender of the Basque capital is less than ever possible. A report that the Argentine Ambassador at Hendaye had been asked to act as intermediary to arrange for the surrender is denied.

REBELS REPULSED?

It seems, in fact, that the vicious bombing of Guernica will stiffen the Basque resistance. The Basques were last night claiming that the rebel offensive in the region of Durango had been 'brilliantly repulsed' and that the rebels were being held back from the Eibar sector to the coast.

On the other hand, the rebels spoke of a Basque 'rout', and declared that Marquina and Lequeitio had been taken and that Guernica, or what remains of it, is their new objective.

Senor Aguirre, the Basque President, last night published a decree reorganising the regular army into battalions, brigades, and divisions under a new commander-in-chief. Under another decree all industries catering for the needs of war are militarised and mobilised.

Thursday April 29 1937 *p.11*

FALSE STATEMENTS
Foreign Journalists as Witnesses

Bilbao, April 29.

The accusations of Radio Salamanca – which, well-informed Govermental quarters claim, is controlled and directed by Italians – that Kibar was burned by the Asturians and Guernica destroyed by the Anarchists have aroused great indignation here.

The allegations can, if necessary, be refuted not only by the inhabitants of these Basque towns, who for three and a half hours were subjected to possibly the worst bombardment in the history of modern warfare, but also by all foreign journalists who visited the scene the same night.–Press Association's Special Correspondent.

BASQUES APPEAL TO BRITAIN AND FRANCE

Help in Evacuation of Women

'WE ARE AT WAR NOT WITH FRANCO, BUT WITH GERMANY'

From our own Correspondent

Paris, April 29

That the Basques have asked the British and French Governments to help them to evacuate the women and children of Bilbao was disclosed by Senor Picavea, the representative of the Basque Government in Paris, at the Spanish Embassy this evening. He had just come from the Quai d'Orsay, where he had seen M. Delbos, the Foreign Minister. He said:

We have enough ships lying at Bilbao and all we want is that France and Britain should see that ships full of women and children be not sunk by the rebels.

He estimated the number of women and children to be evacuated at 150,000 to 200,000. Almost with tears in his eyes he added:

We hope to God that no diplomatic manoeuvres will interfere with what is a task of elementary humanity. We are more frightened of diplomatic manoeuvres than even of Hitler's aeroplanes. We are not even asking France and Britain to send ships to Bilbao to take our women and children away: all we ask is to have them protected against destruction.

AT WAR WITH GERMANY

The Basque people, he continued, were in terrible danger, and though the situation was not desperate it was serious. He added:

We are at war not with Franco – what would that matter? – but with Germany. The German General Staff at Deva (some sixteen miles due east of Guernica) with a few Italians attached to it, are conducting against us the most hideous and monstrous war of destruction that history has ever known.
They have concentrated with 100 aeroplanes against us, and their plan is to exterminate the civilian population of

101

the Basque provinces so as to terrify Bilbao into surrendering to them. For they do not want to destroy Bilbao: they want to receive its industry – the most flourishing in Spain – intact, and for this purpose German aeroplanes fly over our peaceful open town sowing death and destruction.

They fly sixty feet above the ground, drop incendiary bombs, and mow down the people with their machine-guns not only in the streets but even across country. There is no escape from this horrible massacre. At Guernica, now a heap of ruins, they have destroyed the hospital, and all the wounded have been burned to death. The Red Cross itself is helpless – anyone picking up the wounded in the streets is shot down from above.

WARNING OF GUERNICA SIX WEEKS AGO

Senor Picavea disclosed that the Basque authorities in Paris had received warning six weeks ago from persons claiming to be in close contact with the German Government of what exactly would happen to the Basques. They were even warned that Guernica would be destroyed – if they did not make a separate peace with the rebels. These people said that the hundred aeroplanes would be sent over the Basque country. He continued:

We have no aeroplanes left to defend ourselves. We had twelve, and they did heroic work. We had a pilot who brought down four German machines. In his fifth battle he was burned to death.

We are retreating. We may be obliged to retreat to the last trench, and there we may all die: but we shall not surrender to Germany. The oldest people in Europe is being ruthlessly destroyed, the people with the most ancient democratic traditions and with deep religious faith.

ANGER IN PARIS

The horrible destruction of Guernica has aroused the greatest feeling of anger in Paris. The French pro-Fascist press, it is true, including some so-called 'Catholic' papers like the 'Echo de Paris', are either ignoring Guernica or minimising it. One of them has the bad taste to speak of Guernica as 'the capital of Basque Separatism' and to speak of its destruction almost with approval.

ONE REASON FOR BOMBING
Italian Reluctance

From a Diplomatic Correspondent

London, Wednesday.

Information from the Basque front is that the many air raids on Bilbao have been carried out by German bombers only. Up to three days ago the rebels had at their disposal thirty heavy Junker bombing 'planes, which raided Bilbao regularly and on April 24 dropped more than 700 bombs on various parts of the town, each of the thirty 'planes making six flights and dropping four 500lb. bombs each time.

The rebel commanders have given instructions that towns in Government hands should be destroyed regardless of the presence of women and children, the reason being that the Italian troops are reluctant to fight until all resistance has been wiped out.

On the Madrid front the next big operation of the Government troops is expected to be against the University City, in which during the past ten days the Government have surrounded a force of 4,000 rebels, whose position is now serious.

Many arrests of rebel officers and members of the Falangists took place in Salamanca on and about April 13 after the discovery of a plot against the Falangist leader Hadilia, and many of them have since been shot.

Saturday May 1 1937   *p.17*

TOTALITARIAN WAR METHODS
Guernica Tactics Explained in Advance in Germany

EVIDENCE OF AIRMAN'S PASSPORT

From our own Correspondent

Paris, April 30.

Whether Franco was informed or not in advance of the air raid on Guernica and whether Germans alone were responsible are considered here to be questions of secondary importance. What is considered to be important is that Guernica may be regarded as the most glaring example – more glaring even than the Italian methods in Abyssinia – of the full application of the 'totalitarian war' principle in so far as such a war must take no humanitarian considerations of any kind into account. It is also regarded as an experiment in future German warfare, and Guernica is aptly described by a French observer as 'Göring's air manoeuvres' – at the expense of innocent Spaniards.

The passport of a German airman, Hans Sobotka, who crashed at Bilbao a few days ago, and photographs of which were reproduced in the 'Soir', provides additional confirmation of the concentration of an important German air force in the North of Spain within the past few weeks. The passport was issued in Berlin as recently as April 5 and stamped in Rome on the following day.

GERMAN FOREKNOWLEDGE

Attention is also drawn here to a particularly significant article from the special correspondent of the 'Frankfurter Zeitung' with the rebel troops in the North of Spain, in which he said that the rebel authorities have concentrated between 'twelve or fifteen dozen bombers and pursuit-'planes on the Viscaya front, and with only a dozen "Red" aeroplanes to oppose them they can fly over the whole Basque country practically undisturbed'. He also admits that the rebels are ten times better equipped with material than the Basques.

Further, a particularly sinister episode is contained in the dispatch in which the system of demoralising the unprotected 'Reds' by bombarding them first and then firing down on them from machine-guns – a system fully applied at Guernica – is described in every detail. The article appeared in the 'Frankfurter Zeitung' on April 22 – that is, three days before the Guernica massacre, – and its author had obviously been in contact with the German air authorities in the North of Spain.

The attitude of certain French papers of the Right is now even more extraordinary than it was during their subsidised campaign in favour of Mussolini during the Abyssinian conflict. They now actually proclaim even without question-marks that Guernica was burned by the Basques themselves.

BASQUE WOMAN'S ACCOUNT

And yet a Havas message from Bilbao, which is naturally not used by the papers in question, but is extensively quoted by other more responsible papers like the 'Petit Parisien' (though not hitherto unsympathetic to Franco), gives the following account of the bombardment of Guernica by a woman refugee, Maria Goitia, who escaped after the destruction of the town:–

'Monday was market day,' she said, 'and the villagers of the neighbourhood were assembled at Guernica. At four o'clock in the afternoon, when the crowd was largest, an aeroplane appeared and dropped a few bombs, causing the first victims. The people fled from the marketplace to hide in the houses. New aeroplanes then appeared and bombarded the houses and churches. People were dying under the ruins of the demolished houses.

'The houses were burning as a result of the incendiary bombs. The people were obliged to run out of the houses, and then they were fired on from machine-guns. I saw all this from the house where I had taken refuge. Many people remained lying in the street dead or wounded. In the houses you heard the wounded howling with pain. Many were burned alive under the ruins.

'When the house to which I had fled began to burn I ran like mad. Machine-gun bullets continued to whistle round me, but I did not stop. When I got into a field I hid under a bush. People were running across the field trying to escape the bombs and bullets, which continued to pursue them. I remained under the bush till eight o'clock at night until it grew dark and the aeroplanes departed. Guernica by that time was nothing but a horrible bonfire.'

EXAMPLE OF REBEL PROPAGANDA

Spanish messages show that the rebels are still actively explaining away the destruction of Guernica and Eibar by German 'planes by saying that they were destroyed by 'Reds'. A communiqué issued by the rebel G.H.Q. at Salamanca, received by Reuter in London yesterday, said:

'The destruction of the richer part of Guernica, as of Eibar, by the retreating Reds has aroused indignation among our troops and is spurring them on to save the Basque people from the Communists who are destroying their property.'

Monday May 3 1937   *p.6*

DESTRUCTION OF GUERNICA
Priest's Account

'SKY BLACK WITH 'PLANES'

A message has been received by the London delegate of the Basque Government stating that Father Alberto Onaindia, Dean of the Cathedral at Valladolid, is on his way to lay before the Pope a statement on the recent aerial bombardment of

Guernica. The following details of his report were received in London yesterday:–

'I was in Bilbao when the Basque Government decided to evacuate Guernica, where I had friends and relations. I arrived at Guernica on April 26 at 4.40 p.m. I had hardly left the car when the bombardment began. The people were terrified. They fled, abandoning their livestock in the market-place. The bombardment lasted until 7.45 p.m. During that time five minutes did not elapse without the sky being black with German aeroplanes.

METHOD OF ATTACK

'The method of attack was always the same. First there was machine-gun fire, then ordinary bombs, and finally incendiary. The 'planes descended very low, the machine-gun fire tearing up the woods and roads, in whose gutters, huddled together, lay old men, women, and children. Before long it was impossible to see as far as 500 metres owing to the heavy smoke occasioned by the bombardment.

'Fire enveloped the whole city. Screams of lamentation were heard everywhere and the people, filled with terror, knelt, lifting their hands to heaven as if to implore divine protection.

'The 'planes descended to 200 metres, letting loose a terrible machine-gun fire. I reached my car and just had time to take refuge in a small group of oaks. I have not heard of any inhabitants who survived among the ill and wounded in the hospitals.

'The first hours of the night presented a terrible spectacle of men and women in the woods outside the city searching for their families and friends. Most of the corpses were riddled with bullets.

'OUTRAGE ON RELIGION'

'As a Catholic priest, I state that no worse outrage could be inflicted on religion than the Te Deums to be sung to the glory of Franco and Mola in the Santa Maria Church at Guernica, which was miraculously saved by the heroism of firemen from Bilbao.

'The rebels have destroyed the following towns and villages in the Basque country:– Marquina, Elorrio, Durango, Ceanuri, Dima, Yurre, Ceberio, Ochandiano, Abadiano, Villarreal, Guernica, Bolivar, Eibar. In the last few days the Moors have violated 24 women in the town of Ceanuri, three belonging to the same family. The Basque authorities possess incontestable evidence to this question.–(Signed) Alberto Onaindia.'

IRISH BRIGADE'S RETURN
Gen. O'Duffy Explains

THE CONDITIONS IN SPAIN
Typhoid Peril

A remarkable message from General O'Duffy on the reasons for the return of the Irish Brigade from Spain is published by the 'Irish Independent'.

General O'Duffy, in a message sent from Caceres, says of his men:

'They have now been in the front line trenches without a break since February 19, on which date they received their baptism of fire. Since then they have been subjected to almost unceasing shell fire and bombing day after day and night after night.

'We have left seven dead on the field, we have many seriously wounded, some maimed for life, and many others suffering from shell shock, pulmonary diseases, rheumatic fever, &c., developed in the trenches during the incessant heavy rains of February and March, from which complaints, I fear, some of the men may never fully recover. By the end of March we had 150 in hospital.

'The greatest trial of war will undoubtedly be the danger of typhoid and other fevers from now on, but the climatic conditions during the past few months, and the almost complete absence of water for either drinking or sanitary purposes, have had serious effects on the health of the Irish troops already.

'Nevertheless, neither the sick nor wounded ever made any complaints and returned to the front cheerfully immediately on their discharge from hospital.

THE SIX MONTHS' PERIOD

'As our brigade is composed entirely of volunteers General Franco has been concerned about the safety of minors – those under 21 years of age – and has made representations to me from time to time in regard to their repatriation. The number of volunteers under 21 is upwards of 106.

'Owing to the understanding in regard to the six months' period of service, a large number of volunteers arranged with their employers to engage substitutes during their absence, and about the middle of April I received requests from upwards of 200 officers, N.C.O.s, and men to make arrangements for their return to Ireland. All expressed, however, their loyal acceptance of my decision and signified their willingness to remain here if I so desired.

'The transport of volunteers from Ireland to Spain always presented difficulties, but now, with the Free State Non-Intervention Act and the activities of the international observers on the frontiers, we are confronted with the position that no further support from Ireland will be forthcoming. The Irish post offices have even refused to accept parcels addressed to members of the brigade in Spain since the passing of the Act.

THE ABSENCE OF RESERVES

'Without a reserve, or any hope of a reserve, it is a very serious responsibility for any commander or leader to order men into action in modern warfare where one or two activities might result in the complete annihilation of a little band of men like this which constitutes the Irish Brigade.

'No one knows better than I do the high morale, the spirit, and the bravery of the men, and I know that no danger, not even the certainty of death itself, would daunt them, but such an ending of the brigade, however, glorious, would be as bad for Spain as it would be for Ireland.

'Taking all these facts into consideration, I considered it my duty as leader of the brigade to give each member an opportunity of deciding for himself as to whether he should return to Ireland now or continue on here for the duration of the war.

'With the exception of a few who have made up their minds to remain in Spain, the unanimous decision has been to return to Ireland now, our obligations having been fulfilled.

'Accordingly the brigade will return to Ireland as soon as its place in the front line has been filled and the men have had a rest in Caceres. Meanwhile travelling arrangements will be made.'

General O'Duffy quotes a warmly expressed letter from General Franco expressing gratitude to him for his help.

In practice, very few citizens of Britain or the Irish Republic served with the Nationalists in Spain: the figures given in O'Duffy's message for the number of volunteers under his command appear to be wildly inflated and should be treated with some scepticism.

REBEL REPLY ON GUERNICA
'Minor Event of Hypothetical Bombardment of Small Town'

An official rebel communiqué replying to the accusations concerning the bombing of Guernica was received by Reuter yesterday from Salamanca. It runs:

With the unanimity which might appear to suggest obedience to orders many English and French newspapers are using a comparatively minor event such as the hypothetical bombardment of a small town as the basis of a campaign designed to present 'Nationalist' Spain as anti-humanitarian and opposed to the principles of the laws of nations, thus serving the ends of the Soviet faction which dominates the Spanish 'Red' zone. These newspapers clamour against the bombardment of open towns, attempting to lay the blame for such outrages upon the 'Nationalists'. 'National' Spain energetically rejects so injurious a campaign and denounces these manoeuvres before the world.

'RED' MURDERS

The newspapers now crying aloud remained silent when in Madrid, under the presidency of the 'Red' Government, thousands of innocent beings were murdered. Over 60,000 died at the hands of the 'Red' hordes without any motive other than the whims of a militiaman or a servant's dislike. In this way perished old people, women, and children, all of them innocent. In the Madrid prisons murders were committed without check under the supervision of the 'Red' Government agents. There fell intellectuals, politicians, many Republicans, Liberals, Democrats, and members of the Right.

At Barcelona also 50,000 or 60,000 horrible murders have been committed, and there have been many thousands more killed in Malaga, Valencia, and other large towns after barbarous tortures. This was not war. It was crime and vengeance. But then the newspapers which are to-day defending so-called humanitarian principles were silent or spoke timidly or even attempted to justify such barbarous crimes. They were silent too when bishops and thousands of priests, monks, and nuns were cruelly done to death and beautiful artistic treasures were burned in the churches of Spain.

'RED HUNS'

The hospitals at Melilla, Cordova, Burgos, Saragossa, and recently the schools at Vallodolid and towns miles from the front have been bombarded by the 'Red' aeroplanes. There were numerous victims among the women and children without any word of protest being heard from the self-appointed champions of humanity. The city of Oviedo has been literally destroyed by the 'Red Huns' and aeroplanes in the same silence.

And now the Basque Soviet allies have blown up Eibar, a hard-working industrial city before the entry of our troops. They used dynamite and liberally sprayed petrol until most of the buildings were destroyed. But those who to-day weep for Guernica remained unmoved and suffered no scandal. Irun suffered a similar fate under the eyes of European journalists and witnesses from Hendaye in the same negligent or culpable silence.

GUERNICA 'A MILITARY OBJECTIVE'

Guernica, less than four miles from the fighting line, was an important crossroads filled with troops retiring towards other defences. At Guernica an important factory has been manufacturing arms and munitions for nine months. It would not have been surprising if the 'National' 'planes had marked Guernica as an objective. The laws of war allowed it, the rights of the people notwithstanding. It was a classical military objective with an importance thoroughly justifying a bombardment. Yet it was not bombarded.

It is possible that a few bombs fell upon Guernica during days when our aeroplanes were operating against objectives of military importance. But the destruction of Guernica, the great fire at Guernica, the explosions which during the whole day occurred at Guernica – these were the work of the same men who at Eibar, Irun, Malaga, and countless towns of Northern and Southern Spain demonstrated their ability as incendiarists.

The Spanish and part of the foreign press duly reported the 'Red' Militia's threats to destroy Madrid before the 'National' troops entered it. The blowing up of great buildings which are to-day still mined has been systematically prepared by the 'Red' Government, which is indirectly served by those now clamouring about Guernica. Let this manoeuvre at the service of 'Red' Spain cease and let the world know that Guernica's case, though clumsily exploited, turns against this Government of incendiarists and assassins, who at Russia's orders pursue the systematic destruction of the national wealth of Spain.

SERIOUS ANARCHIST RISING IN BARCELONA
Street Fighting Causes 100 Deaths

REVOLUTIONARIES SAID TO BE IN CONTROL OF THE SUBURBS

Reports reaching Perpignan, on the Franco-Spanish frontier, state that there was an Anarchist rising in Barcelona yesterday. At least 100 people are reported to have been killed, and by the afternoon the hospitals were filled with wounded.

Telephone communication with Barcelona is cut and the Franco-Spanish frontier is closed, and it is therefore difficult to obtain accurate information. A passenger who arrived at Perpignan yesterday evening by 'plane from Barcelona stated that the Government had regained control of the centre of the city after fierce fighting, but that the Anarchists held the suburbs and the outlying districts. The Government hoped to gain complete control to-day.

The Catalan authorities have installed machine-guns at strategic points in the city, and tanks have also been brought into use. The President of Catalonia, Senor Companys, is understood to have appealed for troops from the Aragon front to deal with the situation.

SEEKING A SETTLEMENT

On the other hand, it is reported that Socialist, Communist, and Anarchist leaders have held a meeting to reach a settlement of the conflict. Representatives of the two big labour organisations, the U.G.T. (Socialist–Communist) and the C.N.T. (Anarchist), broadcast appeals while the fighting was going on calling on their supporters to cease fire and to keep calm.

A warning to the population to stay indoors was also broadcast, apparently by the Government, and this broadcast ended with the words 'These streams of blood must cease to flow.'

CAUSE OF THE RISING

The Anarchists are nominally supporters of the Catalan Government and have, in fact, two seats in the Cabinet. Their ability to collaborate is not strong, however, and they are constantly in dispute with the Socialists and Communists in the Government.

Tension between the authorities and the Anarchists has been acute for some days. The disorders began when the

111

Generalitat (the Catalan Government) ordered the Anarchists to give up any arms they possessed. They refused, and the Generalitat sent police reinforcements to places where the Anarchists were in control.

Some Anarchists installed themselves in the tall telephone building, and it was round this that the most serious fighting took place. At first several Anarchists were made prisoners in the building, but later the police are said to have been beaten off. Then the Anarchists made a large-scale attack on all policemen found in the streets and chased them into the suburbs at the point of the revolver.

An alternative explanation of the cause of the rising is given by the passenger who arrived at Perpignan. He said that the Valencia Government recently proposed the nomination of a general to command the Catalan forces, but the Anarchists refused to accept the appointment. The Valencia Government insisted and fighting broke out.

The French Consulate, states Reuter, is understood to have been cut off by the rioters, and the Consul had to send an appeal for help to a French vessel in the port.

REVOLT IN ANOTHER TOWN

The reported rising in Barcelona is not an isolated instance of disagreement between the Anarchists and the other supporters of the Catalan Government. The Anarchists are also in revolt in the town of Puigcerda, two miles from the French border, to the north-west of Barcelona. The trouble there followed a recent incident in which Antonio Martin, head of the Puigcerda Anarchists, was killed.

The Valencia Government, it appears, asked the Catalan Government that the situation should be got under control, and the Generalitat accordingly sent 400 carabiniers and Civil Guards to occupy strategic points round Puigcerda. They also cut the bridge on the road between Puigcerda and a neighbouring town to prevent the arrival of Anarchist reinforcements.

The Anarchists are described as being well armed and determined not to submit to discipline from the Catalan Government, and have erected barbed-wire entanglements and dug trenches round Puigcerda to prevent an attack.

This was not the first crisis to be faced by the Generalitat. A serious political breach had arisen a month earlier between the socialists and the anarchists. At that time, it was hoped that the two great trade unions represented in the Generalitat, the socialist CNT and the anarchist UGT could work together to produce a strong cabinet. The unwillingness and inability

*of the UGT to give an undertaking to discipline its members
in support of collectively reached cabinet decisions and the
murder of a leading member of the CNT led to the antagonism
spilling over into the streets.*

HOW FIGHTING WAS STOPPED IN BARCELONA
Catalan Government's Deputation

AWAITING ANNOUNCEMENT OF SETTLEMENT TERMS

Perpignan, May 5.

Both sides remained under arms to-day awaiting the publication of the terms of the agreement following yesterday's armistice. The Barcelona wireless announced this morning that an agreement had been reached by the negotiators which, it is hoped, will end the conflict.

The attempt by the Government to requisition arms held by unauthorised elements and to exercise closer control of telephonic communications is believed to be at the bottom of the rising. The Anarchists seized a number of suburbs, in one of which an Anarchist commune was proclaimed.

The central telephone building was also seized by the Anarchists. The Catalan Government sent shock guards against the building. They were met by a salvo of fire and suffered heavy losses. There were also a number of casualties among the dense crowd watching the operations. The police reformed, continued the offensive, and succeeded in penetrating the ground floor. The Anarchists barricaded themselves in the upper storeys.

In the midst of the battle an influential representative of the Catalan Government accompanied by secretaries of the leading trade unions, arrived. They informed the Anarchists of the deplorable effect in Barcelona, where the population was terrified, and begged them to submit. The Anarchists finally consented to abandon the building provided that only technicians were allowed within the walls, which was agreed to.

An agreement has been reached and a provisional Government formed.

The agreement is considered as a defeat for the F.A.I. (International Federation of Anarchists), which was hitherto con-

113

trolled the C.N.T. (Anarcho-Syndicalists), and the broadcast threat by a member of the C.N.T. giving the Anarchists an hour's grace to evacuate the streets is regarded as a first step in the repudiation of F.A.I. domination.–Press Association Foreign Special.

MUSSOLINI AND REBELS
Help Alleged to Have Begun in 1934

From our own Correspondent

Paris, May 5.

That Mussolini had been encouraging the Spanish rebellion for two years before it actually broke out is suggested by a document published to-night by 'Ce Soir', the new Left-wing Paris evening paper.

It publishes a memorandum purported to have been signed in Rome on March 31, 1934, and according to which its authors, Lieutenant General Don Emilio Barrero and three other Spanish reactionary leaders, were received that day by Mussolini, who declared himself willing to help the two Spanish Opposition parties in their attempt to overthrow the Republic and to replace it by a regency pending the final restoration of the monarchy.

To give tangible proof of his intentions Mussolini agreed to provide immediately 20,000 rifles, 20,000 handgrenades, 200 machine-guns, and cash. He added that this aid was only preliminary and would be followed by more substantial help in accordance with the work done and with the necessities of the moment.

Wednesday May 12 1937   *p.15*

ERNEST HEMINGWAY ON HIS STAY IN SPAIN
The Building of a Republican Army

Paris, May 11.

'I had always been against all wars, up to the time I saw on the battlefield of the Guadalajara the defeat of the Italian interventionists,' declared Ernest Hemingway, the American novelist, to a representative of the Spanish Press Agency. Mr. Hemingway has just concluded a long stay in Spain. He continued:

'I believe that the setback to the Italians has done more

114

for the cause of peace in the whole world than all the pacifist campaigns of the last ten years. All civil wars are naturally long. It takes months, sometimes years, to create a war organisation of the front and the rear and to turn thousands of ardent civilians into soldiers. And this transformation can only take place by their going through the living experience of battle. If you neglect this fundamental rule you risk getting a false idea of the character of the Spanish civil war.

'A great number of American newspapers, admittedly in good faith, not very long ago were giving their readers the impression that the Government was losing the war owing to its military inferiority at the outbreak of the conflict. The error of these American newspapers was to mistake the character of the civil war, and not to deduce from it the logical conclusions of the history of the American Civil War.

'The Spanish military situation, following the encouraging days of March, has consistently improved. A new regular army is taking shape which is a model of discipline and courage and which is secretly developing new cadres in the military academy and schools. I sincerely believe that this new army, born of the struggle, will shortly be the admiration of all Europe, despite the fact that hardly two years ago the Spanish army was considered an agglomeration of individuals resembling actors in a comic opera.

'As a war correspondent I must say that in few countries does a journalist find his task facilitated to such a degree as in Republican Spain, where a journalist can really tell the truth and where the censorship helps him in his work, rather than impeding him. While the authorities in the rebel zone do not permit journalists to enter conquered cities until days after, in Republican Spain journalists are asked to be eye-witnesses of events.'

The presence in Spain of writers like Hemingway and Orwell did much to create the false impression of the Spanish Civil War as being the war of poets, artists and scholars.

REBELS DESTROY TWO MORE BASQUE TOWNS
Shelled, Bombed, Machine-Gunned

VILLAGE BURNS ALL DAY AFTER AIR ATTACK
Valencia Political Crisis Ended

Bilbao, May 17.

Two more Basque towns have been destroyed by rebel 'planes. One of them, Amorebieta, ten miles south-east of Bilbao, is a small but important town on the Basque line of defence, but the other, Lemona, is yet, as was Guernica at the time of its destruction, well behind the lines.

The technique of Guernica has now been refined, for in addition to the dropping of high explosives and incendiary bombs, and in addition to machine-gunning from the air, the towns suffered a preparatory artillery bombardment. It is estimated that a thousand shells fell on the two towns.

TOWN BURNS ALL DAY

The bombing took place yesterday, and all day to-day Amorebieta has been burning, although there has been heavy rain. The town is the next objective of the rebel left wing on the main road between Durango and Bilbao. In spite of the raid, and in spite of the fact that five rebel battalions are concentrated on capturing the town, Amorebieta still remains in Basque hands.

The Basques yesterday were forced to give a certain amount of ground in front of the town owing to an unusually violent rebel attack supported by the aeroplanes which later bombed the town. But to-day the weather has prevented the rebel aircraft from taking the air, and the Basques have taken advantage of this lull (a lull only in the air, for the fighting has continued without pause) to dig themselves in in new positions.

Lemona, a village which lies $2\frac{1}{2}$ miles from Amorebieta, had similar treatment, being bombed with high explosives and incendiary bombs and then machine-gunned.

BASQUES RETIRE

At the same time the Basque lines were continuously attacked by bombers and fighter 'planes, supported by artillery. After holding on against these overwhelming odds most of the day, the Basque troops finally withdrew from their positions in the hills and took up a new line slightly farther back.

During the day's fighting the rebel aeroplanes dropped several bombs of an exceedingly large calibre, and it would seem that they have now replenished their supplies which had been depleted by earlier bombardments.

For only the second time since March 31 there was no air raid alarm in Bilbao itself to-day.

Senor Aguirre, President of the Basque Republic, has asked the Catalans to begin an offensive on the Catalan front within eight days' time in order to divert the rebel pressure on Bilbao. This is revealed with the publication here to-day of an exchange of telegrams between Senor Aguirre and Senor Companys, President of Catalonia.

Senor Companys, in reply to the request, states that the General Staff of the Eastern Army is drawing up plans, and that it hopes that it will be able to comply with Senor Aguirre's request.

APPEAL TO SURRENDER – IN BAD ENGLISH

Considerable speculation has been caused here by a number of pamphlets dropped by the rebel aeroplanes over the Basque lines that were printed in bad English and French. They contained an appeal to the Basques to surrender, and declared that their local traditions would be respected. Reading these pamphlets one Basque officer exclaimed, 'If they do not think we can understand Spanish, why don't they use Basque?'

The only foreigners fighting on the Spanish Government side on this front are half-a-dozen political émigrés, who enlisted in Socialist battalions. The rest are 70 per cent Basques and 30 per cent Spaniards.– Press Association Foreign Special.

MORE ITALIAN TANKS SENT NORTH

A Gibraltar telegram from the Spanish Press Agency says that two trainloads of Italian tanks left Algeciras on Sunday for the Bilbao front.

A NEW GOVERNMENT FORMED IN VALENCIA

Valencia, May 18, 1 a.m.

Dr. Negrin, the Finance Minister in the last Government has succeeded, after a day of strenuous effort, in forming a Government in place of Senor Caballero's, which resigned on Saturday owing to internal differences.

Dr. Negrin's Cabinet maintains the same Popular Front formation as that of Senor Largo Caballero, but consists of nine members instead of fifteen. Dr. Negrin had previously stated that he would aim at such a reduction. The new Cabinet has only three Socialists, whereas formerly they had six Ministers. The Communists retain their previous strength of two.

The major changes are the departure of Senor Largo Caballero and the dropping of Senor del Vayo, the Socialist Foreign Minister.

Dr. Negrin has formed his Government without the active collaboration of the two large groups of trade unions the U.G.T. – Socialist and Communist – and the C.N.T. (mainly Anarchists and Socialists). These bodies refused during the afternoon to collaborate in the Government formed by Dr. Juan Negrin. The reason was his intention to cut down the number of Ministers allotted to them.

However, three of the new Ministers are members of the Socialist party, which predominates in the U.G.T. One of the significant features of the new Government is the concentration of the Ministries of War, Air, and Marine in the hands of one Minister of National Defence.

The government headed by Largo Caballero had been formed on September 4, 1936 and resigned on May 15, 1937. Caballero was invited by President Azana to form a new government but failed in his attempts to do so. It would seem that the Barcelona revolt played a part in the fall of Caballero's Government but his real problems arose from the refusal of the Communists to collaborate with him and the unpreparedness of the Socialists to work with him in the absence of the Communists.

118

NEW SPANISH CABINET EXPLAINS ITS POLICY

Unifying Military Operations

APPEAL TO TRADE UNIONS TO JOIN GOVERNMENT

Valencia, May 18.

The particular task of the new Spanish Government (which was formed here late last night by Senor Juan Negrin, Finance Minister in the Caballero Government) will be 'to unify the command of military operations as well as the control of economic life'. The statement of its policy says:

The Government declares that, in view of its political composition, it considers itself the authorised representative of all the parties that are united in the task of crushing the rebellion, assuring the liberty of the people and maintaining the independence of Spain.

At the same time it deplores the absence of representatives of the trade union organisations and hopes that they, in the common interest, will modify their attitude.

It considers that its principal mission is to lead the popular masses to victory over the rebels and invaders, being convinced that peace in Spain is impossible until the rebellion is completely crushed.

WILL MAINTAIN ORDER

Considering that order behind the lines is an essential factor for victory, the Government promises to maintain this inflexibly and will not permit or tolerate that in the unrest caused by the war excesses should be committed which are not justified by any theory or political organisation.

Its particular care will be to unify the command of military operations as well as the control of economic life.

It is determined to maintain the closest contact with Parliament, before which it will shortly present itself.

Its international standpoint will be the following of the path traced by the previous Ministry. In consequence it again raises the most energetic protest against the restrictions which the non-intervention pact imposes on the rights of the legitimate Government.

It expresses its wholehearted gratitude to all those who, during six months' fighting, have generously given their lives for the cause of the popular revolution.

119

The War Council has been abolished, and the change was explained by the new Premier as follows:– 'In view of the small number of Ministers the full Cabinet takes the place of a War Council, which is accordingly dispensed with.'

On paper the new Cabinet lacks the support of the two great trade union organisations – U.G.T. (Socialist–Communist), and C.N.T. (Anarcho-Syndicalists) – but as far as the larger body, the U.G.T., is concerned it is becoming evident that refusal to collaborate is merely a matter of form, as the Cabinet as it stands bears a Socialist complexion, with three Socialist Ministers including the Premier.

Late to-night it is announced that Senor del Vayo, Foreign Minister in the last Cabinet, has been appointed Spain's representative to the League. He will go to Geneva for next week's meeting of the League Council.

Senor Giral, the new Foreign Minister, who was Minister without Portfolio in the old Cabinet, has had a long experience in diplomacy. Further he will have the advice of the new Prime Minister, half of whose adult life has been spent abroad. Senor Negrin speaks fluently three foreign languages and during the civil war has conducted the Government's banking negotiations in England.–Reuter.

MIAJA TO REPORT TO PRIETO

General Miaja, Government commander on the Madrid front, his chief political commissar, and members of the General Staff spent yesterday in visiting the Madrid front, according to a Spanish Press Agency message from Madrid.

The commander-in-chief was expected to leave last night for Valencia for a Consultation with the new Minister of National Defence, Senor Prieto.

Saturday May 22 1937 *p.6*

THE 'IRON RING' ROUND BILBAO

Bilbao, May 21.

Senor Aguirre, President of the Basque Republic, has declared 'They will never take Bilbao', and a visit to the 'iron ring' around Bilbao supports this view.

Men, women, and children have been working feverishly for weeks on this 'iron ring', which is intended to make Bilbao an impregnable city. The men dig the deep, concrete trenches; the women hand them the bricks and mortar; the children lead

120

asses laden with various materials to the trenches. All of them work under the constant threat of raids by hostile aeroplanes. They have only one meal a day.

The 'iron ring' begins at a point situated east of Plencia and extends as far as Laquiniz to the west. From there it goes in a south-easterly direction towards a point which is some distance from Mount Bizkargi. There it makes a semi-circle in a south-westerly direction. Five miles from Bilbao the 'iron ring' cuts the road to Durango and follows the road from Orduna to Miravelles.

If the rebels tried to take this place they would first have to break the ring, which besides its military fortifications here has also natural fortifications such as steep, mountain-slopes and deep valleys. Woods and forests have been cut down so that the enemy can approach only in the open.

The trenches of the ring are very deep and built by the most modern methods. Machine-guns are mounted behind cemented parapets and are skilfully camouflaged against air attacks. It is not too much to say that the 'iron ring' is a miniature Maginot line. From an aeroplane it looks just a narrow ribbon across the Basque country, but a close examination will show its wonderful defensive value.–Spanish Press Agency.

LEAGUE COUNCIL'S RESOLUTION ON SPAIN
Del Vayo Asks for Firm Stand

BITTER ATTACKS ON ITALY AND GERMANY

The extent of foreign intervention in the Spanish civil war and the possibility of withdrawing foreign volunteers from the country were the main subjects raised when the case of Spain came before the League Council yesterday.

Senor del Vayo, the former Spanish Foreign Minister, explained the attitude of his Government and appealed to the League to adopt 'a clear and firm position' – perhaps, he suggested, the League's last chance to do so.

This was a stand the League should take, for the extent of foreign intervention could not be overlooked: there were, he said, from 75,000 to 80,000 Italian troops in Spain. Senor del Vayo also referred to the intervention of Germany, a point on which the Spanish 'White-book' laid before the Council had been silent. Bitterly he spoke of the 'barbarous tactics' of the bombing of Guernica. He said:

> In the peaceful Basque countryside German aircraft selected the town which symbolised the soul of the ideals and the whole of the religious sentiment of a glorious people. The soul of this people has been dealt with in the same manner as the women and children. They are merely objects on which the experiment of totalitarian war is to be tried.

WITHDRAWAL OF VOLUNTEERS

He criticised the working of non-intervention, but pointed out that the Spanish Government had accepted it 'in a spirit of international co-operation', and then went on to speak of the withdrawal of foreign volunteers.

This idea the Spanish Government had accepted, though 'it is pain for the Government to accept the lumping together under the title of volunteers of two categories of men who are worlds apart'. On the one side were men who were not even volunteers in name; on the other men who came to fight because 'they knew full well that on the battlefields of Spain is being decided the future of Europe and the fate of all free men'.

He returned to this theme later in his final appeal to the League – beyond the Spanish question was the question of the League. The League's 'fatal drift' should be ended: the way to do it was never to sacrifice those who were present to those who were absent.

Mr. Eden explained Britain's policy and the reasons for the move to obtain withdrawal of foreign volunteers, now the 'fundamental problem'. He said:

> The object of the approach to the two parties in Spain is intended to be strictly limited to asking them to agree to a temporary cessation of hostilities on all Spanish fronts for a period sufficient to enable these withdrawals (of volunteers) to be arranged.

Mr. Eden made it clear that this approach had not yet been made and would not be made until 'the Governments represented on the Non-Intervention Committee are in agreement, both upon the plan for the withdrawal of volunteers and upon the means for a temporary cessation of hostilities in order that it may be carried out.' He added:

> We have had a number of replies from Governments in response to the soundings which we have made. I am convinced

that it would be wiser not to attempt to analyse these replies at this stage. Suffice it to say that though they may vary in temper and in the cordiality which they offer, the replies so far received by no means preclude the possibility of agreement.

M. Delbos, the French Foreign Minister, and Mr. Litvinoff, the Russian Foreign Minister, also spoke in the debate – M. Delbos defending the working of non-intervention and Mr. Litvinoff roundly attacking it.

THE COUNCIL'S RESOLUTION

After the public meeting a private meeting of the Council was held, at which a resolution was agreed upon. It will be submitted to a public session of the Council to-day. The resolution

1. Takes note with satisfaction of the scheme of control of the Non-Intervention Committee and of the undertakings by the European Governments now in force.
2. Declares that the participation of persons of non-Spanish nationality in the conflict constitutes a danger to the peace and supports the efforts being made to secure their withdrawal from Spain.
3. Expresses the hope that success will attend the efforts to bring about a cessation of the civil war in Spain and to give the Spanish people an opportunity to decide their own destiny.
4. Expresses sympathy with the sufferers from the war, recognises the humanitarian efforts of certain Governments, deplores the bombing of open towns and civilian populations, expressing confidence that early means will be found to bring to an end such practices.

Tuesday June 1 1937   *p.11*

GERMAN WARSHIPS REPRISAL COMPLETED
19 Killed and 55 Wounded at Almeria

FASCIST POWERS LEAVE NON-INTERVENTION SCHEME
50 Dead in Torpedoed Spanish Liner

As a reprisal for the bombing of the German battleship Deutschland, German warships yesterday bombarded the port of Almeria without warning. About 200 shells were fired into the town. The casualties are officially stated to have been 19 killed, of whom five were women and one a child. Fifty-five people were injured and 35 houses are said to have been destroyed.

It is stated by the Spanish Government that the warships appeared to have no special targets, but just fired at any part of the town.

The reprisal for the bombing of the warship is now said to be ended.

The Spanish representative at Geneva yesterday handed a Note to the League asking that the bombardment should be brought to the notice of League members.

WITHDRAWAL FROM NON-INTERVENTION

Germany announces that she has withdrawn from the naval control scheme and from the Non-Intervention Committee until she obtains guarantees against the repetition of the incident.

Italy last night announced that she would adopt an identical attitude.

The long section of the Spanish coast which falls to those two countries under the non-intervention scheme therefore is, in theory, without supervision, and arms can be imported to the Government ports. There is no indication what use the two Governments are going to make of the free hand they have thus assumed.

There is apparently no question of a withdrawal, as fresh ships are to be sent from Germany to Spain, either as reinforcements or to replace those withdrawn. At the moment it is not clear which.

The German Government has also issued orders to its warships to repel by fire any approaching Spanish aircraft or men-of-war. The Spanish representative at Geneva recalls that a similar order was issued before the bombing of the Deutschland and that in fact the Spanish 'planes were fired on by the battle-ship.

A message from Rome indicates that Italy has no intention of allowing armaments to reach 'Red' ports, that more ships will be sent if the Italian Government thinks it desirable, and that they will fire if they consider there is any danger that they may be attacked.

On the evening of May 20 the German battleship Deutschland was attacked by two Republican aircraft while lying at anchor off Ibiza. Twenty-two of her crew were killed and 83 wounded. The Republican Ministry of Defence claimed that its planes had been fired on by the Deutschland and had retaliated by bomb-

ing the ship. No firm evidence exists to determine which of these two versions of the incident is factually correct. Certainly the Deutschland was bombed but whether another German ship, the cruiser Leipzig, was attacked remains dubious (see report of Wednesday, June 23 1937).

In Berlin, on June 23 1937, Baron von Neurath, German Foreign Minister, announced that Germany was withdrawing from the control scheme but not from the Non-Intervention Committee. Italy gave notice of her intention to do likewise. In theory, German and Italian withdrawal from the control scheme would have left a large stretch of the east coast of Spain unsupervised. In practice, German and Italian naval vessels maintained station in their respective zones.

Wednesday June 2 1937   *p.11*

GERMAN REINFORCEMENTS FOR MEDITERRANEAN
Berlin and the London Committee

WILLING TO RETURN, BUT WILL MAKE NO PROPOSALS

From our own Correspondent

Berlin, June 1.

The cruiser Leipzig has been sent to Spanish waters to strengthen the German fleet there, it is officially announced this afternoon. It is added that further units will be sent in the next few days.

Upon the reasons for the strengthening of the German fleet at a time when Germany with Italy has retired from the coastal control scheme little that is definite is to be ascertained here. In some quarters it is suggested that the Government's action is due to fear that unless the naval forces are strengthened they will be in danger of attack from the Valencia Government. This on the face of it seems a remote possibility. It is also explained that technical reasons demand a reinforcement temporarily, since actual technical withdrawal from the control patrol cannot be made overnight.

As to the ultimate purpose of a concentration of a larger German force in the Mediterranean outside Spanish waters, which will ultimately be effected, information is even more scarce.

'IRON RING' BROKEN
Rebel Success

GRAVE DAYS AHEAD FOR BILBAO
All Not Yet Lost

The position of Bilbao is critical, but the city is not yet lost. The rebels have, indeed, at one point broken through the outer fortifications of the 'iron ring', Bilbao's last line of defences, but the salient driven into the Basque lines is at present dangerously exposed.

The rebels were able to break through on Saturday by concentrating most of their forces north of Mount Bizkargi, by most fierce air and artillery bombardment, and by repeated infantry attacks. The fighting was still going on yesterday, but the outcome was not known last night.

The 'iron ring' consists of a line of fortifications running in a rough circle round Bilbao about seven miles distant. There are four lines of trenches, protected with, in places, as much as six lines of barbed-wire entanglements. Communicating-trenches link the whole line.

BILBAO BOMBED

While the fighting was going on on Saturday the centre of Bilbao was heavily bombed and machine-gunned, as on Friday had been the villages between the front line and Bilbao. The bombardment lasted an hour, and many houses were destroyed. The number of dead is not yet known.

Apparently begun with the aim of diverting the rebels from Bilbao, Government offensives are reported from two other fronts. On both these fronts, Cordova and Araga, the Government claims and the rebels deny successes.

BASQUE PRESIDENT'S APPEAL

Senor Aguirre, the Basque President, has addressed to the British and many other Governments a manifesto denouncing the 'Fascist–German–Italian–Moorish invasion of the Euzkadi' (the Basque territory) and the 'attempt to destroy the world's oldest democracy'. The President rebukes the 'countries calling themselves democratic for their supineness and even apparent tacit connivance at this intervention'.

NAVAL CONTROL PLANS
London Agreement

RETURN OF FASCIST STATES

An agreement that will enable Germany and Italy to return to the Non-Intervention Committee was reached in London on Saturday. It contains the following points:

Calls for assurances from the Spanish Government and from General Franco to prevent the recurrence of 'incidents' against the ships of the four Powers operating the control:

Defines what the four countries consider legitimate measures of self-defence:

Provides that no acts of reprisal shall be taken against Spain until there has been consultation between the four naval Powers.

An extension of the safety zones to which the ships operating the patrol may repair for rest and refuelling is also, it is understood, laid down.

When the necessary assurances have been received from the Spaniards – and it is expected that these assurances will be forthcoming – a plenary meeting of the Non-Intervention Committee will be called. It is hoped that this will be this week.

BRITAIN'S SHARE

Throughout the negotiations of the last two weeks the British Government has taken the lead and a successful end was reached, fittingly enough, on Mr. Eden's fortieth birthday.

It was the British Government that devised the draft agreement which has formed the basis of the ten hours' discussions in the last two days between Mr. Eden and the three ambassadors, and it is the British Government which will transmit the agreement to the Spanish authorities in order to receive their assurances.

COMPLIMENT FROM UNUSUAL SOURCE

Probably for the first time for years, Britain is complimented by Signor Gayda in the 'Giornale d'Italia'. As quoted by Reuter, he says:

We will willingly recognise the contribution of goodwill and action which Great Britain has made this time for the restoration of collaboration. But the first contribution of goodwill came from Italy and Germany, who deliberately confined their reaction to criminal aggression within moderate limits.

MUSSOLINI AND THE BATTLE OF GUADALAJARA
Saving Italian Honour at Bilbao

From our Diplomatic Correspondent

London, Thursday.

An article in the 'Popolo d'Italia' (attributed no doubt correctly to Mussolini himself) is the first public admission in Italy that the Italian army serving in Spain was defeated in the battle of Guadalajara. The details given in the article do not quite tally with the information received here from various sources and collated with reports received in other capitals.

It seems very doubtful, for example, whether the so-called 'Reds' lost 'over 5,000 men'. Nor does the 'Popolo d'Italia' mention the fact (which has been established beyond any doubt by the information received here) that the panic which was the principal cause of the Italian defeat was started by Spanish Government aeroplanes (most of them Russian) which, flying very low, bombed the Italian columns, who found themselves in a situation that would have tried the endurance of any army in the world. The attack from the air was followed up by an advance on the part of the International Column, especially of the German and Italian detachments. The Italians serving under the Spanish Government had a big share in winning the victory. This advance turned the Italian rout into a total defeat.

There is much difference of opinion with regard to the details of the battle. Estimates of the numbers engaged as well as of the casualties differ widely.

The 'Popolo d'Italia' article is interpreted here as tending to confirm the belief that the capture of Bilbao will be regarded by Mussolini as avenging the battle of Guadalajara. German 'honour' having been saved at Almeria and Italian 'honour' at Bilbao (if Bilbao really falls – and there seems to be little chance that it can hold out), some, at least, of the difficulties in the way of withdrawing all 'volunteers' from Spain will, perhaps, have been removed.

HOW BILBAO WAS OCCUPIED
Accounts from Rebel Sources of the Taking of the City

FINAL DESCENT FROM THE HILLS

Hendaye, June 20.

Bilbao did not surrender, but was captured by force of arms. This is a point on which all the rebel papers of the North of Spain lay special stress.

The dissension between the Basque Nationalists and the Asturian Anarchist militia in the town which is reported to have broken out into an open conflict on Friday night may have hastened the actual occupation, but there was no official surrender by the authorities.

CAPTURE OF THE CITY

Latest accounts of the capture of the city show that it was at 1.30 yesterday afternoon that the first rebel armoured cars made their appearance, coming up from the south on the Durango road, and entered the old quarter of the city on the east bank of the River Nervion.

At the same time the 4th, 5th, and 6th Brigades of Carlists of Navarre descended from the northern heights. Coming down the slopes of Archanda, north of Bilbao, their arrival finally sealed the fate of the capital. They advanced with their right on the slopes at Deusto and their left on the station of Lezama towards the Paseo del Arenal that lies on the east bank of the river.

As soon as the armoured cars also reached the Paseo del Arenal a pontoon bridge was thrown across to the left bank facing the Gran Via, as the bridge there had been blown up. At the same time a motorised column coming rapidly down the main road of Las Arenas arrived on the Paseo del Arenal.

BRIDGES BLOWN UP

A few machine-guns manned by Anarchists continued to fire up the Gran Via and on the west bank of the river, but they were easily silenced by rebel skirmishers. The Anarchists had carried out their threat to blow up all the bridges, which were reported yesterday to be mined. At least six had been destroyed according to reports reaching here this afternoon.

The railway tunnel at Portugalete in which several hundreds of women and children had taken refuge was also dynamited. Several persons who were unable to escape in time lost their lives, it is stated.

129

ACCOUNT OF THE ENTRY

A Spanish journalist who entered the city with the first companies of Requetes at 4 p.m. says: 'We came down from Archanda into the little streets of old Bilbao. Hardly a soul was to be seen. The houses seemed deserted, though all their windows were opened and many of the interiors were on view. The few spectators seemed stunned, looking out furtively without noticing what was happening.

'Many of them had spent twenty-four hours in the tunnel, where they had fled from extremists who had tried to force the inhabitants to evacuate the town.

'Here and there we saw the bodies of those shot down, the last victims of Anarchist terrorism. In Arenal we found large crowds who gave us a great ovation. Tears were mingled with cheers. A radio van arrived broadcasting the Requetes' and Phalangists' hymns and marching-songs.

'Many gave the Fascist salute, weeping and singing. Some asked for bread. And so we came over the pontoon bridge in the middle of the city.'

By four o'clock the Town Hall, the Presidencia, and the Ministry of the Interior had all been handed over by the Civil Guards without bloodshed, and Bilbao may be said then to have entered into the possession of the army of the rebels.

18,000 PRISONERS IN WHOLE CAMPAIGN

It is not known how many Basque Militia have been taken prisoner in the town itself, but three battalions who had stayed behind all night in order to try to prevent rioting and pillaging by extremists surrendered after a struggle. The total number of prisoners captured since the opening of the offensive is stated to be 18,000, exclusive of several thousands who passed over voluntarily into the rebel lines.

Several battalions of shock troops (stated by Basque quarters here to be Italians, but this is unconfirmed) marched into the town during the evening, accompanied by companies of rebel Civil Guards, who will be responsible for the policing of the town during the period of administrative reconstruction.

Meanwhile the advance by the main rebel army towards the west continues. A force of 4,000 militiamen caught between the rebels to the south of Bilbao and Llodio, which is now in rebel hands, in the Nervion valley has no choice but to surrender. This will facilitate the efforts of General Davila to cut the roads to Santander.

NO REPRISALS

General Franco has issued the strictest orders to avoid all reprisals. Military tribunals have been set up and only those accused of crimes against the common law will be tried and imprisoned. Many civilian prisoners have already been released.

The material damage in Bilbao is far less than might have been expected. Apart from the bridges mined by the Anarchists and a few shops said to have been burned by incendiaries, the urban quarters suffered little during the operations. The rapidity of the Archanda advance prevented the extremist threat of wholesale destruction from being put into execution.–Press Association Foreign Special.

p.6

INTERVENTION IN SPAIN
Del Vayo's Allegations

Albacete, June 20.

Senor del Vayo, General Commissar for War, received the foreign press to-day and answered a number of questions put to him. Senor del Vayo declared that the Germans had 'cleverly used the recent Deutschland–Almeria incident to obtain for themselves and the Italians a mode of control more favourable to them.' 'They have done a wonderful business by it,' he said. 'I suppose they will now bombard another Spanish port.'

He stated that German 'planes were still being sent to Franco's aid and that they were being flown from Italy to the Basque country by way of the Balearics. 'During the last three weeks the rebels' 'planes on the Basque front have been trebled in number,' he said. 'On that front there is an incredible number of machine-guns, and the artillery are manned by Germans.' Italian troops were used for attacking movements.

Senor del Vayo further stated that he had learnt that a new type of German 'plane was being used by the rebels whose top speed was 322 miles an hour. 'Spain is a laboratory now for testing the new materials of war that Germany and Italy acquire,' he said.

Senor del Vayo was not able to make a statement regarding the latest incident of the Leipzig, but in speaking of the naval situation in the war he declared that ever since December the German and Italian fleets had been taking part in the civil war.–Press Association Foreign Special.

GERMANS DEMAND JOINT NAVAL DEMONSTRATION
Refusal by Britain and France

BREAKDOWN OF LONDON FOUR-POWER DISCUSSIONS
Move by Hitler Expected To-day

The Four-Power conversations that began last Saturday on the alleged attempts to torpedo the German cruiser Leipzig broke down yesterday after another meeting in the Foreign Office. The Germans and Italians held that the incident was proved beyond all doubts, and demanded immediate action, including a joint naval demonstration against Valencia.

Great Britain and France, on the other hand, are not convinced that a case has been proved against the Spanish Government, and they ask for an inquiry into all the facts of the case before committing themselves to any action.

Under the recent Four-Power agreement Germany now regains her freedom of action. The situation is very serious. The exact extent of its gravity depends on what action, if any, Germany takes against the Spanish Government. Germany is expected to make this decision to-day.

THE GERMAN ALLEGATIONS

The German evidence that an attack was made is based on the assertion that the noise made by a torpedo was registered on the sound-recording instruments installed on the Leipzig and that a surge of water as the torpedo was released was seen; that the Leipzig then changed her course and that members of the crew then heard a noise which they took to be the warship touching the super-structure of a submarine or a torpedo that did not explode hitting the hull of the ship at an acute angle. The Germans do not claim to have seen a submarine.

The Spanish Government denies that an attack was made or that any Government submarine was anywhere about. It offered facilities to the British Government to investigate the matter.

Last night an official statement was made in Berlin alleging that the presence of two 'Red' submarines in the neighbourhood of the Leipzig on the day of the attack had been proved. It says that on Wednesday, June 16, at noon, 'two "Red" submarines bombarded National Spanish positions on the coast near Calahonda, on the southern coast of Spain, east of Malaga.

The attacks on the Leipzig took place on the 15th and the 18th in the neighbourhood of Oran, which is half a day from Calahonda.'

LETTERS TO THE EDITOR

NON-INTERVENTION IN SPAIN
Its Practical Results

To the Editor of the Manchester Guardian

Sir,–The non-intervention agreement has been presented as an even-handed holding of the scales between two comba-tants. This will not bear a moment's examination. It has through-out worked to the advantage of the rebels, from the days when German and Italian 'planes enabled Franco to win his initial victories to the capture of Bilbao with the aid of Italian Black Arrow legionaries. But for 'non-intervention' the revolt could have been crushed in the early stages. We clapped an arms embargo on the Spanish Government whilst aware that arms were pouring in to the rebels. The long-drawn-out agony of the Spanish people is therefore due to the policy we have pursued. I know it is claimed that we were hoping that Germany and Italy would keep to their word. But we have no right to go on tying the hands of the victim of an assault whilst his opponents continue to belabour him. We have been doing it for ten months, and it is time we dropped it.

Again, non-intervention is put forward as a means of pre-serving the peace of Europe. This claim also will not bear investigation. Put bluntly it means that we should throw Spain to the wolves in order that we may dwell in peace and security ourselves, that the British Empire should shelter behind the ill-equipped Spanish worker. Non-intervention has a nice name, but it stands for a very nasty policy. Nor is it the way to preserve even our own peace. Peace is preserved by the strong and well-armed nations standing in with the rest and forming a united front against attack, not by allowing the aggressor to seize their members one by one. We may decorate this latter policy with the high-sounding name of 'localisation of the con-flict', but it leads straight to world war. The dictators unite for aggression. Cannot the democracies unite for peace? Is our slogan to be 'Divided we stand, united we fall'?

Even if we have not the courage to place an embargo on the aggressor we might at least raise it from the victim.

Best of all would be for the League to reassert its authority, impose an armistice with the withdrawal of all foreign troops, and, with the aid of an international police force drawn from nations that had taken no active part in the fighting, maintain order until conditions were settled, and carry out some of the reconstruction of the country that will be so badly needed.–Yours, &c.,

G. E. LEE,
31, Rydal Road, Streatham, London, S.W.16, June 22.

A BETRAYAL OF DEMOCRACY

To the Editor of the Manchester Guardian

Sir,–It would seem that the people of this country are undergoing a similar betrayal at the hands of the diplomats in connection with the Spanish revolt to the one experienced with regard to Mussolini's campaign of mechanised murder in Abyssinia. Our Government is allowing the farce of the non-intervention talks to continue, in the face of the issuing by the Italian Government of official casualty lists giving the names of many thousands of Italian conscripts killed and wounded in Spain and also in the face of the destruction of Guernica by German aeroplanes.

The 'front line' of democratic civilisation was once in far Manchuria, but through the incompetence of our politicians and the perfidy of the diplomats it shifted to Abyssinia, and again, owing to the democratic countries being betrayed by their Governments, it is now in Spain – nearer and nearer it creeps. Before it is too late democrats must wake up to the danger they are in of being betrayed by those who should be their servants but who have, as far as this country is concerned, ignored the mandate given them – as expressed by the people at the last general election, when a thoroughgoing policy of collective security through the League of Nations was endorsed by the electorate. In engaging in these spurious non-intervention talks our Government is exchanging 'the genuine money of democratic undertakings for the base coin of Fascist promises'.–Yours, &c.,

H. SMALLEY,
Sanctuary, Lissoms Road, Chipstead, Surrey, June 21.

The majority of letters to the editor of the 'Manchester Guardian' were critical of the British Government's policy.

PREMIER'S POINTS

Following are points from Mr. Chamberlain's speech:–

Our policy has been consistently directed to one aim – to maintain the peace of Europe by confining the war to Spain.

Although it is true that intervention has been going on and is going on, in spite of the non-intervention agreement, yet it is also true that we have succeeded in achieving the object at the back of our policy, and we shall continue that object and policy as long as we feel there is reasonable hope of avoiding a spread of the conflict.

I do not believe that it is fantastic to think that we can continue this policy successfully, even to the end. The situation is serious, but it is not hopeless. Although it may be true that various countries or various Governments desire to see one side or the other side in Spain winning, there is not a country or a Government that wants to see a European war.

Since that is so, let us keep cool heads. Neither say nor do anything to precipitate a disaster which everybody really wishes to avoid.

When I think of the experience of German officers, the loss of life and the mutilation of men on the Deutschland, and the natural feelings of indignation and resentment that must have been aroused by such incidents, I must say that I think the German Government in wisely withdrawing their ships and then declaring the incident closed have shown a degree of restraint which we ought to be able to recognise.

I make an earnest appeal to those who hold responsible positions both in this country and abroad to weigh their words very carefully before they utter them on this matter, bearing in mind the consequences that may flow from some rash or thoughtless phrase. By exercising caution and patience and self-restraint we may yet be able to save the peace of Europe.

Mr. Chamberlain's speech was made in the House of Commons on Friday June 25. It was his first statement on the British Government's policy toward the Spanish Civil War since he assumed the premiership.

Brunete – July 1937

'NON-INTERVENTION'

The London Non-Intervention Committee meets to-day to hear the replies of the German and Italian Governments to the Anglo-French proposal to fill temporarily the gap in the naval control scheme created by the withdrawal of the Fascist Powers after the Leipzig episode. The attitude adopted by the German and Italian representatives at the meeting of the Committee on Tuesday held out little prospect of favourable replies. The control scheme in its original form consisted of a corps of observers at various ports near Spain, members of which had to be received on board all European merchant ships proceeding to Spain; their duty was to see that neither munitions of war nor volunteers were being carried in breach of the Non-Intervention Agreement. The warships of the four Powers formed a naval cordon round Spain to ensure that each ship carried an observer. International observers were also placed at Gibraltar and on the Franco-Spanish frontier, and there were British observers on the Portuguese frontier. On Tuesday the Germans and Italians not only announced that they were most reluctant to let British ships take over the zones vacated by their own ships, but also stated that they were withdrawing their observers at the ports and on the frontiers. Finally Portugal, 'our oldest ally', suspended the facilities granted to British observers on her frontier. It is true that Herr von Ribbentrop was understood to say that German merchant ships would continue to receive observers at the 'control' ports. But unless to-day the German and Italian representatives appear with some constructive suggestions the naval control scheme to ensure non-intervention in Spain is as good as dead.

Besides the future of naval control, the Non-Intervention Committee is also to discuss to-day the vital proposal to withdraw all foreign volunteers engaged in the Spanish war. On both these questions the German and Italian Governments have taken a singularly stiff and uncompromising attitude during the past ten days. In an article attributed to Signor Mussolini in yesterday's 'Popolo d'Italia' it was asserted that 'the Italian Government has not the means to recall the volunteers', and Herr von Ribbentrop on Tuesday put the rhetorical question to Lord Plymouth, 'What would you say if we were to propose concentrating the whole naval control under the German and Italian fleets?' The answer to Signor Mussolini is that if democratic Governments think they can withdraw their nationals from Spain, the same action should not be beyond the scope of Fascist Governments; and the answer to Herr von Ribbentrop is, first, that the British and French warships have offered to carry foreign observers as a guarantee of fair play; and, secondly, that if the German and Italian Governments did not want this situation to arise, why did they leave naval control at all? The principal reason given for the Fascist Powers' abandonment of naval control was that their ships were in danger of attack from the Spanish Government. But as since the time of their 'withdrawal' German and Italian warships have not only remained but have been reinforced in the Western Mediterranean, the conduct of those Powers is hard to understand unless it is based on ulterior motives.

To judge by the tone of the German and Italian press, the two Fascist Governments would like naval control to be abandoned altogether, to forget about their own proposal for withdrawing volunteers, to maintain 'non-intervention' in the entirely spurious form under which it existed before the control scheme was established, and also to obtain from the British and French Governments the recognition of General Franco as a belligerent, if not as the legitimate ruler of Spain. Their expectation of thus eating their cake and having it is, of course, fantastic. For us to recognise Franco as a belligerent would be to empower him not only to maintain a blockade (if he possesses the ships to make it effective) but also to search British ships on the high seas for contraband. The suspicion would unavoidably arise that, since the Germans and Italians are outspoken in their desire for Franco to win, their warships might be employed, either directly or indirectly, in assisting Spanish rebel ships to interfere with British and French shipping. For Britain and France to consent to any such solution would be not merely to betray the Spanish Government and leave the path open to wide-scale Fascist intervention, but to submit to a resounding diplomatic defeat. Even for us to recognise Franco as a belligerent in return for the Fascist Powers' agreeing to the resumption of naval control might have the air of yielding to blackmail. Throughout the entire Spanish war the British Government, with major interests in Spain, and the French Government, based on a majority most sympathetic to the Spanish Government, have acted with great moderation and restraint in the face of open and determined interference in Spain by Germany and Italy. They have stifled their own desires and even their respect for the letter of international law in order to try to create a European concert to insulate the Spanish war. They have been prepared to make every reasonable concession to Germany's and Italy's points of view. But there comes a time when patience is exhausted and the cheek can be turned no more. Italy and Germany will have to learn that that time has come.

Saturday July 3 1937 *p.13*

A NON-INTERVENTION LAST HOPE
Deadlock Complete, but Decisions Put Off Till Next Week

FORTHRIGHT REJECTION OF FASCIST PLAN

From our Diplomatic Correspondent

London, Friday Night.

The French and British Governments absolutely reject the German and Italian proposals for a reformed system of carrying out non-intervention in the Spanish civil war. These proposals are regarded as no more than a device for making non-intervention altogether illusory and for helping General Franco to a rapid victory.

As the German and Italian Governments reject the Franco-British naval patrol, there is a complete deadlock.

If any new proposals are thought out during the week-end they will be considered, but there is little hope now that systematic non-intervention can survive. All that is demanded here is that non-intervention be effective; any serious proposal for making it so will be favourably considered.

The question now is: Do Germany and Italy want effective non-intervention or not? There is little doubt about the answer – but for the sake of that little all final judgements are being suspended until the Committee of Non-Intervention re-assembles.

Tuesday July 6 1937 *p.11*

FRANCO IN NEED OF MORE MEN
Appeal to Italy and Germany

SECRET DOCUMENT

From our own Correspondent

Paris, July 5.

The information that has reached me from a very reliable source to-day may help in a large measure to explain the Spanish policy that Germany and Italy have been pursuing since the fall of Bilbao, and also to throw light on their intentions in the immediate future.

139

This information is a summary of a memorandum sent by General Franco to Herr Hitler and Signor Mussolini, and possibly to the Portuguese Government, at the time of the fall of Bilbao. It is divided into three sections – military, political and economic. On the economic section my information is unfortunately scanty, but the information on the first two sections is complete and of the greatest importance.

FRANCO'S MILITARY POSITION

In the military section, General Franco says that as far as the northern front is concerned he believes himself able to 'liquidate' it completely with his present offensive within three months.

He says that he has lost 20,000 men in killed and wounded in the course of the Bilbao campaign and about 20 per cent of his war material. But he believes that the morale of the northern Republican troops has sunk very low after the fall of Bilbao, and says that he can now even afford to send some of his present war material to the other Spanish fronts, particularly to the Madrid front.

General Franco strongly emphasises in his memorandum that it is absolutely necessary to avoid a second winter campaign, which he says he can hardly afford – a statement which, one may well imagine, has produced a particularly strong impression in Rome and Berlin. He therefore proposes simultaneously an offensive against Madrid and one on the Teruel front, the purpose of the latter being to reach the sea at Castellon and Sagunto and thus to cut off Valencia from Barcelona.

MORE MEN AND ARMS ASKED FOR

He declares that such a double offensive cannot succeed unless he receives very considerable reinforcements from outside; and he asks for 125,000 more men, 500 more 'planes (which he says would give him three times the number of 'planes on the Republican side), fifty batteries, and a considerable number of tanks. (I do not know what figure, if any, he gives for the tanks.)

In the political section of the memorandum General Franco expresses the opinion that the time has come for a big political offensive in favour of his recognition by foreign Powers.

He believes that after the fall of Santander his Government will be recognised as the legal Government of Spain by several South American States. As for the countries which are unlikely to recognise his political authority, he hopes that every effort will be made that they, at least, concede him belligerent rights which, he says, is of the most vital importance to his military success.

The main argument against recognising him, he says, is that he has not the support of the Spanish people. He therefore declares himself willing to hold a referendum in that part of Spain held by the rebels and assures Herr Hitler and Signor Mussolini that 'the result will be favourable'.

HEAVY FIGHTING CONTINUES WEST OF MADRID
Militia Claims Another Success

REBEL ACCOUNTS OF ENORMOUS GOVERNMENT LOSSES

Fighting continues fiercely west of Madrid; last night around Brunete the battle had been going on without stop for 24 hours. The main Government claims of successes are in the sector about fifteen miles due west of Madrid.

A Reuter message from Valencia states that early yesterday morning Government troops captured the village of Villanueva del Pardillo. In the official communiqué of the National Defence Ministry it is stated that more than 600 prisoners were taken, including seven officers. The communiqué adds, 'The listing of the war material, which is considerable, is still proceeding.' In Spanish quarters in London it is learned that [among] the captured officers were a number of Germans.

Salamanca claims that the village of Villanueva del Pardillo is still in rebel hands. The communiqué reads: 'On the Madrid front the enemy pressure continued with desperate attacks. The Villanueva del Pardillo garrison has repulsed continuous attacks for three days and has caused the enemy thousands of losses and destroyed ten Russian tanks.'

A Salamanca communiqué received at St Jean de Luz yesterday reports that the Government forces are continuing their attack with great violence west of Madrid. The Government command is stated to be employing larger forces of troops than have been used in any single Government attack since the beginning of the civil war. Forty-five thousand men and 100 'planes was an estimate given. Rebel headquarters at Avila are believed to be organising a counter-attack, but no word of their plans has appeared in official Salamanca communiqués.

Less official rebel sources than Salamanca report enormous losses of Government troops in the Madrid fighting. A rebel claim from Avila, for instance, states that in the last three days of the Government offensive from Madrid the Government losses have totalled 10,000 including 4,000 killed.

The 'destruction' of the International Brigade, fighting in the suburb of Usera, south of Madrid, with losses amounting to no less than 3,000 dead, is claimed by Radio Falange of Valladolid, which also states that the Republican attack on the rebel positions in this suburb has been abandoned. This claim is not repeated from any other rebel source, and the Government communiqués make no mention of any fighting at Usera.

SANTANDER TOLD TO SURRENDER

It is learned in Vitoria that rebel aircraft has dropped leaflets on Santander containing a manifesto in which the inhabitants were called upon to surrender. A message received by wireless at Bayonne from Santander reports that a large-scale counter-offensive on the part of the Government forces east of Santander may be expected shortly. The report of the arrival of two squadrons of aerial reinforcements is confirmed.–Reuter.

The Battle of Brunete was a key element in one of the largest military operations undertaken by the Republic. The underlying strategy was to further ensure the safety of Madrid but it had the added purpose of showing that the Republic was capable of going onto the offensive after having been forced to defend since the beginning of the war. For the Nationalist version of the Battle of Brunete, see the report of Tuesday August 3, 1937.

Wednesday July 14 1937   *p.6*

RESISTING MADRID'S OFFENSIVE
Great Activity by the Rebel Air Force

PRESSURE SAID TO BE SLACKENING

Messages from the rebels' forward headquarters at Avila claim that the pressure of the Government offensive has now slackened following Monday's heavy bombing and machine-gunning of Government gun emplacements by rebel 'planes. It is claimed that the rebels now command the air over a distance of forty miles and that their 'planes are almost perpetually in the air. It is said that thirteen Government 'planes were brought down on Monday.

A message from the rebels' Salamanca G.H.Q. alleges that

the Government troops have now lost 16,000 dead and wounded. As earlier rebel messages placed the Government force engaged at 30,000 it is apparent that they claim to have put more than half of it out of action.

Salamanca claims that a great air battle took place over Brunete between sixteen squadrons of Government machines – their exact number is not given – and 80 insurgent 'planes. The 'squadron of death' commanded by Captain Morato is stated to have appeared on the scene at the moment when the superior Government forces seemed likely to gain the upper hand, and 'hurtling themselves like thunder-bolts against the slower Russian 'planes shot down five of them, as well as three reconnaissance machines, in less than eight minutes.'

25 REBEL 'PLANES BROUGHT DOWN

The Spanish Government claims to have brought down 25 rebel 'planes on the Madrid front during the last 48 hours, according to a Spanish Press Agency message received in London. During the same period the Government admits having lost five 'planes.

REASONS FOR THE OFFENSIVE

Madrid, July 13.

Details of the Republican attack launched on the night of July 5 and which still continues are now available. The advance is ten miles deep and ten wide. Four villages and half a dozen hamlets have been captured, some 1,500 prisoners have been taken, and very important war material, which has not yet been fully listed.

The attack is intended to cut the insurgent lines of communication running up to the Madrid front and has as its final aim the liberation of the capital from the besieging forces.

Following the successes of the first days the Republicans naturally had to contend with a greatly increased resistance. The insurgents have made desperate efforts, particularly in some sectors to the south-west of Brunete, to hold up the Republican advance. They have been greatly assisted in this by reinforcements of artillery and aircraft.

It is now not impossible that in a short time a great part of the Government will be re-established in Madrid. More and more frequently Ministers are leaving Valencia to visit the capital.–Spanish Press Agency.

THE BRITISH PLAN TO END THE SPANISH DEADLOCK
Port Observers to Replace Naval Control

BELLIGERENT RIGHTS UNDER STRICT CONDITIONS
Withdrawal of Volunteers

The British plan to prevent the threatened collapse of non-intervention in Spain was issued last night after its communication to the representatives of the other 26 States on the Non-Intervention Committee.

The British plan for –

1. Land supervision to be reconstructed.
2. Naval patrol system to be abolished.
3. International observers to be placed in Spanish ports to carry out the duties hitherto performed by the naval patrol.
4. Grant of belligerent rights at sea to both parties in Spain on conditions including the withdrawal of all foreign 'volunteers', whether in the fighting or any other war services (such services as ambulance work excepted).
5. A commission to be sent to Spain to arrange and supervise the withdrawal of 'volunteers'.
6. Belligerent rights to be accorded only when arrangements for the withdrawal of foreigners are working satisfactorily and substantial progress is being made.
7. Non-member Powers to be invited to co-operate.

TO-MORROW'S MEETING

A plenary meeting of the Non-Intervention Committee has been summoned at 11 a.m. to-morrow. It is hoped by that time that the various Governments will be in a position to state their attitude towards the plan. The Committee will be asked to pass a unanimous resolution in favour of the withdrawal of 'volunteers'.

It was at its unanimous request that the British Government undertook the difficult task of producing a compromise plan, and in issuing the proposals which are set out textually on another page the British Government says that they can only be successful if accepted in a spirit of compromise.

'Unless a greater spirit of international co-operation is evident than has been shown in the past', says the statement, 'this scheme will fail and the nations of Europe will be faced with a new and infinitely more dangerous situation.'

The British plan was accepted as a basis for discussion by the Non-Intervention Committee on July 16.

Friday July 16 1937 p.8

REPUBLICANS STILL ADVANCING WEST OF MADRID
Rebels Claim Complete Check

ALLEGATIONS OF 24,000 MEN LOST BY THE LOYALISTS

The rebel headquarters at Salamanca now state that the Government offensive west of Madrid has been completely checked. The rebels persist in their denials that the Government has achieved any of its objects, in spite of the fact that half-admissions in the official Salamanca communiqués of the past few days and semi-official messages from rebel sources have to some extent supported the Government claims.

The rebels' latest claim is that in the offensive the Government has so far lost 24,000 men in dead, wounded, and prisoners captured. (Last week the rebel estimate was that 30,000 Government troops were engaged in the offensive.)

According to messages from Madrid last night the fighting is still going on, and the Government forces are advancing northwards towards the Escorial.

REBEL COUNTER-ATTACK FAILS

Madrid, July 15.

The Republican attack west of Madrid continued throughout last night and this morning, it is claimed here. The main theatre of operations has been in the direction of the Escorial, north-west of the capital.

Rebel forces desperately counter-attacked in mass formation the Government positions defending the newly won village of Villanueva del Pardillo, but were held, it is stated, at all points. Finally after persisting for 12 hours with tanks in the lead, the rebels were forced to fall back.

Government 'planes have also been bombing rebel troops behind the lines.–Reuter.

145

60,000 REPUBLICAN FORCES?

St. Jean de Luz, July 15.

Lack of strategical leadership is blamed for the halt in the Government offensive north-west of Madrid by an American journalist taken prisoner on that front by the rebels. The views of the journalist whose name is not given, appear to-day in the rebel 'Voz d'Espana'. He is said to have been taken by the rebels near Villanueva del Pardillo.

He states that the Government forces in Madrid are well supplied with men and material, but leadership in the higher command is lacking. The total number of men of all arms used in this offensive is estimated by him at 60,000, including auxillary forces. Of these he is reported to believe that 12,000 are either dead or out of action, in order to achieve an advance of eight miles.

As soon as the advance was checked the Government General Staff was seized with indecision, the result, the American is said to consider, either of the very heavy losses incurred or more probably of the absence of a well-conceived and carefully thought out strategical plan.–Reuter.

REBEL CLAIMS OF AIR SUCCESSES

All attacks by the Government forces in the sectors of Brunete and Villanueva del Pardillo have failed with heavy losses for the Government according to yesterday's communiqué issued in Salamanca and received in London. The communiqué adds:

We brought down four 'Red' 'planes without any loss on our part. All the news broadcast by the 'Red' radio station to encourage their troops, as ten 'planes of ours having been shot down is absolutely false. The only 'Nationalist' 'planes lost in the air fighting are the five mentioned in our communiqué of July 13, while sixty-one 'Red' 'planes were shot down for certain, and probably another twelve. 'Red' aviators whom we have taken prisoner confirm the demoralisation among the communist aviators owing to the heavy losses suffered. The 'Red' command seeks to hide these losses from their own aviators by saying that the 'planes in question came down at other aerodromes from which they have not returned.

According to a Spanish Press Agency message received last night six rebel 'planes were brought down during an aerial battle over Madrid yesterday.

146

A YEAR OF WAR

The Spanish civil war has lasted for twelve months, and
no one can yet say when it will end or who will win. It is
a war of attrition, which the Spaniards wage with innate, fero-
cious stubbornness, a war which consumes them with a more
horrible slowness because the Fascist Powers have from the
start kept it alive for their own purposes. It began with a mutiny
that left the established Government without an army or an
army's equipment. The Government had untrained, half-armed
militia; the rebels had the army, the Moors, and foreign aid.
For, to aid this concerted mutiny at its very birth came Italian
aeroplanes, forerunners of the organised and almost official
aid which from that time onwards Italy gave the rebels. A Government without an army must create one. The Spanish Government set to work to make a modern army out of a people
which dislikes co-operation and resents authority; only now
are the fruits beginning to be seen. A Government which is
without weapons of war must make or buy them, but France
and Britain, saying that the free (and legal) supply of arms
was the first step to competitive intervention and a possible
wider war, denied the Spanish Government its rights. At every
stage since then the cause of the rebels has been carried to
such victories as it has gained by systematic German and Italian
aid. Under this attack, which was not less in some parts of
the field than an invasion, the Spanish Government might well
have gone down long ago. But genuine foreign volunteers
arrived in time to save it and munitions were sent by certain
foreign countries that surreptitiously tried to prevent the Fascist
Powers from establishing a despotism, which would be a satel-
lite of their own breed, in Spain, on the southern frontiers of
France, on the North African coast, in the Western Mediterranean. Let no one accuse the British Government of such guilt.
There are even Tory newspapers and Tory M.P.s who applaud
the cause of Franco.

The Spanish Government is now bringing into the field
its new army, which some reckon at half a million men, and
its factories are beginning to supply it with munitions. But everything depends on the extent of the supplies. There is at present
no sign of any war of movement. The forces whose defeat
or victory might prove to be 'decisive', though even that is
doubtful, are gathered round Madrid. But at Madrid we seem
to be back in the Great War. It is a struggle of trench systems,
wire entanglements, concrete works, and machine-guns every
few yards. It demands a great mechanical apparatus if an attack
is to succeed. Each side may hope that an 'offensive' will lead

to a 'break-through' – who does not think of Nivelle and Haig, of the Somme and Passchendaele? – but each offensive may actually lead, as this last Spanish offensive seems only to have led, to the driving in of a 'salient', to the capture of so many men, so many guns, so many miles, to heavy losses on the attacking side, and to nothing more. But since the Government is growing steadily stronger the near future will be critical. Franco will require more aid from Italy and Germany, who have given him not enough help to make him win but only enough to secure him from defeat. To withdraw their troops, to stop sending Franco munitions, to let him lose would mean for them a triple defeat. It would mean that they had failed to destroy liberty in Spain, since that is what is ultimately at stake and will ultimately emerge; that they had failed to set up a potentially hostile Spain on France's southern frontier; and that they had failed to undermine British and French interests in the Western Mediterranean and therefore everywhere.

The war itself has had the traditional Spanish character. Geography and the national temperament dictate it; it is fought in compartments, it is an affair of 'the Spains' rather than of Spain, of regions and even of cities. There has been no striking military leadership, even on Franco's side although (or perhaps because) he has the professional soldiers. On the Government side none was to be expected unless the miracle which produced Napoleon's marshals was repeated. The rebels have produced no notable plan of war beyond the advance on Madrid. They captured Malaga but derived no profit from it. They took Bilbao by a crushing superiority in material, but the effect, if any, on the fortunes of the war is yet to be seen. The attack on Madrid itself was bungled. They dallied over the relief of Toledo and dallied again at the outskirts of the capital. They involved themselves in a siege which has served the Government well, for the Government had no strength to attack but battered itself against Madrid's defences. Otherwise, campaigns have begun, have appeared in the headlines, and have vanished like rivers that waste away in desert sands: famous names like Saragossa, Cordova, and Oviedo crop up, disappear, and come again. There has been a mention or two of guerrilleros, for whom the Napoleonic and the Carlist wars were famous. But the modern army moves with a constant shield of armoured weapons and with aeroplanes for eyes; the guerrilleros and their ambuscades are reserved for a later stage of the war when the organised forces of one side or the other are in decline. One characteristic of Spanish warfare this civil war retains. Marshal Lannes, when he captured Saragossa in 1809, wrote to Napoleon: 'I have never seen stubbornness equal to the defence of this place. Every house needs a separate assault. In a word, Sire, this a war which horrifies.'

ITALY HOLDS UP DISCUSSION ON 'VOLUNTEERS'
Delaying Tactics on Procedure

GERMANY AND PORTUGAL SUPPORT COUNT GRANDI
Envoys to Consult Their Governments

From our Diplomatic Correspondent

London, Tuesday Night.

The difficulties that were sure to arise in the Committee of Non-Intervention began to-day when the withdrawal of the so-called 'volunteers' from Spain was discussed in accordance with the British plan.

Under that plan the British Government would be authorised to arrange immediately with both sides in Spain for the establishment of international officers in the Spanish ports and for the withdrawal of the 'volunteers'. (The emphasis is on the 'immediately', and it has all along been made clear that speed in carrying out the plan is essential.)

Lord Plymouth proposed to-day that a sub-committee be formed to deal with the withdrawal of the 'volunteers', but Signor Grandi objected and said that the supervision of traffic entering Spain should be dealt with first. The Italian view is that the points in the British plan shall be dealt with in the order they appear in the British White Paper, whereas the British view is that they must be dealt with as rapidly as possible and that there is no reason why one point should not be handled simultaneously with another.

A TRANSPARENT MANOEUVRE

The Italian manoeuvre is perfectly transparent. There is indeed no valid reason why the question of the 'volunteers' should be left until the other questions have been disposed of. Signor Grandi was, of course, supported by Herr Woermann, who is representing Germany in the absence of Herr von Ribbentrop. He also had qualified support from the Portuguese representative, Senhor Monteiro.

It is quite clear that Italy and Germany wish to delay the withdrawal of the 'volunteers' as long as possible. They have secured a delay even now by the tactics they used this morning and afternoon. The Committee has adjourned and will not meet for another two days at least. Its members are to consult their

Governments. It is still too early to say how far Italian and German obstruction would go, but the old difference between the British attitude, which is supported by France and a big majority of the Non-Intervention Committee, including the representatives of all the Powers that are non-partisan, and the German–Italian attitude remains. Germany and Italy are willing to accept the British plan (or, for that matter, any plan) 'in principle' as long as they are spared the necessity of abandoning their intervention on behalf of General Franco in practice.

As it is the practice – indeed, the speedy practice – that matters, the real deadlock underlying the professions of mutual goodwill exists just as it did before the British plan was drafted.

p.6

FIGHTING FOR 48 HOURS
Madrid Battle

REBELS CLAIM BIG ADVANCE
Much Ground Regained?

St. Jean de Luz, July 20.

A series of reports from Salamanca give details of the violent fighting which has been continuing almost without stopping for the last forty-eight hours on the Madrid front in the triangle formed by the towns of Villanueva del Pardillo, Villanueva de la Canada, and Brunete.

The rebels now claim to-day to be to the east of all these three places and to be working along the road leading to Majadahonda to the north and that leading to Boadilla from Brunete to the south. On the base of this triangle the security of large forces of General Miaja's troops, who are some fourteen miles from their base, is threatened by an enveloping movement which, if successful, will change the whole strategical situation west of Madrid.

FIERCE RESISTANCE

Rebel reports from Avila say that a prolonged resistance was made by the International Brigades massed on narrow fronts at Brunete and Pardillo, and offering a terrible target to the artillery, machine-guns, and automatic rifles of the Moors and the rebel regular troops.

For eleven hours they endured a raking fire, and when finally driven from their positions by the Moors after hand-to-hand fighting were then exposed to terrible bombardments

150

by six squadrons of rebel 'planes, which dropped forty tons of bombs on the retreating infantry and on tanks which were endeavouring to cover their retirement.

A petrol-lorry was hit and set fire to eleven other supply wagons as well as to some large petrol reservoirs. The burning petrol spread to some reserve trenches at that moment occupied by a company of the International Brigade. The defenders were driven into the open, where they became an easy target to the advancing rebels only three hundred yards away.

Salamanca says that headquarters at Avila claim to have advanced four miles and to have inflicted at least 8,000 casualties, five thousand of them yesterday alone.–Press Association Foreign Special.

HALF LOST GROUND REGAINED?

Salamanca, July 20.

According to reports from the Madrid front received here the losses of the Government aviation during the last fortnight amount to over 40 machines, including both bombers and fighters. The rebel superiority in the air is given as one of the principal reasons of the setback to the Government offensive at Brunete, where positions won after the advance could not be retained owing to the constant activity of rebel bombers and fighters. The aircraft also simplified the task of the rebel infantry when they began the counter-attack now in progress, the object of which is to restore the former front line of Navalgamella, Villanueva del Pardillo, and Las Rozas.

It is claimed that the rebels are now advancing north of Quijorna and Brunete, and have already won back nearly half the territory penetrated by the Government.–Press Association Foreign Special.

MADRID ADMITS A LOSS

Madrid, July 20.

The Ministry of National Defence to-night issued the following communiqué:– 'Today there has been intense action on the centre front to the west of Madrid. The enemy seriously attacked Hill 660, to the west of Villanueva de la Canada, occupying it after a fierce combat which resulted in many casualties to the enemy.

'On the front from Navalgamella to Perales fierce combats were withstood successfully by our troops, the enemy failing in every effort.'–Press Association Foreign Special.

LULL WEST OF MADRID
Fighting Dies Down

BOTH SIDES TALK OF HEAVY LOSSES

The fighting on the front west of Madrid has died down, and both sides are busy counting the losses of the other side. In Madrid, states Reuter, it is estimated that over 12,000 rebels have been killed or wounded during the past three weeks in the fighting for Brunete.

On the rebel side the 'Voz d'Espana', of San Sebastian, reports that two lieutenants of the Government medical service who were taken prisoner put the number of dead at 16,000 and the wounded at 19,000 in three weeks. The Government medical service had 144 ambulances and 1,800 stretcher-bearers and other personnel on the Brunete sector, the report adds, but these were not sufficient to evacuate the wounded, who suffered terribly from lack of water in the great heat.

CAPTURED MATERIAL

The rebels also speak of much material taken, and an official communiqué from Salamanca states:

As a result of the battle in Brunete arms and material of all kinds are still coming into our linès from the fighting zone. So far we have collected one thousand rifles, 14 machine-guns, and a large quantity of boxes containing guns and ammunition. Sixty-six militiamen came over to our lines to-day on this sector.

Rebel General Headquarters also announce that of the 140 tanks employed by the Government in the Brunete battle fifty-four were destroyed and fifteen captured undamaged and utilisable.

It is held in Madrid that the rebel counter-offensive has reached a dead end. The Government forces are strongly entrenched in new positions and capable of resisting the fiercest attacks. Even if the Government has to relinquish the ground it has recently captured the loyalist troops have inflicted severe losses on the enemy, which the latter cannot afford so easily as the Government.

Rebel sources suggest that the rebels are now preparing for a new thrust against Villanueva de la Canada.

THE POWERS AND SPAIN
Verbal Duelling

VON RIBBENTROP ATTACKS RUSSIA
An Air of Unreality

From our Diplomatic Correspondent

London, Friday.

To-day's meeting of the Sub-committee of the Committee of Non-Intervention ended inconclusively, as was expected. The German and Russian representatives spoke with some vehemence, but there is little genuine ill-feeling amongst the members of the committee, who all have a growing sense of unreality as they follow the proceedings. The verbal duels, like to-day's, tend to increase rather than diminish this sense.

Three main theses now exist:

1. The Russian. – The question of belligerent rights does not concern the Committee. What matters is that the dispatch of men and war material to Spain shall stop and that the so-called 'volunteers' shall be withdrawn. When this has been done, the question of belligerency can be examined, if there is any point in doing so.
2. The German–Italian. – The withdrawal of the 'volunteers' and the simultaneous acceptance of belligerency is acceptable in principle. In reality (as distinct from 'principle') the Germans and Italians demand that a state of belligerency be recognised in any case, and that the 'volunteers' be withdrawn only when General Franco sees fit – that is to say, when he has won the war or is sure he can win it without them.
3. The Anglo-French. – The withdrawal of the 'volunteers' must be carried out as soon as possible, and a state of belligerency can be recognised when the withdrawal is making full progress.

NO PROSPECTS OF COMPROMISE

Between these three theses there has been no real compromise, nor is there any prospect that there will be one. The Sub-committee meets again early next week. It is not believed that it will be able to achieve anything conclusive before it adjourns for August holidays.

Santander and Asturias campaigns – August–October 1937

→ Nationalist attacks

154

Aragón – August–October 1937

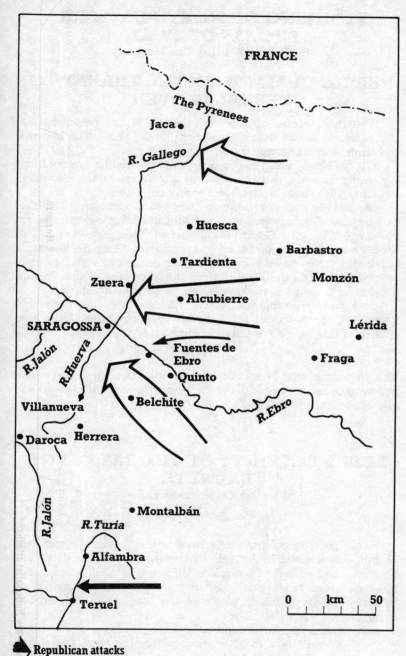

FRANCE

The Pyrenees

Jaca

R. Gallego

Huesca

Barbastro

Tardienta

Monzón

Zuera

Alcubierre

SARAGOSSA

Lérida

R. Jalón

R. Huerva

Fuentes de
Ebro

Fraga

Quinto

Villanueva

Belchite

R. Ebro

Daroca

Herrera

Montalbán

R. Turia

R. Jalón

Alfambra

0   km   50

Teruel

Republican attacks

FIGHTING ON NORTH-EASTERN FRONTS OF SPAIN
Shelling of Madrid This Morning

REBELS CLAIM THAT THE THREAT TO TERUEL IS OVER

The main scene of fighting in Spain is at present in the north-east, around Huesca, Saragossa, and Teruel. The Madrid and Santander fronts are quiet.

On the Huesca and Saragossa fronts the claims are conflicting, but those of the Government, which are more detailed, state that the rebels have been heavily repulsed.

Teruel lies at the extreme south of a long and narrow salient running into Government territory and has for some time been threatened by the Government forces. Now, however, the rebels claim that the threat no longer exists. They declare that in ten days they have taken 350 square miles of territory and have driven the Republicans from the province of the Teruel into the adjoining provinces of Cuenca and Guadalajara.

It is suggested that the rebels will now advance westward towards Cuenca to cut the Madrid–Valencia road there – a vital road that they have failed to cut nearer the capital.

The Republic attack on Teruel was intended to relieve the growing pressure on its forces on the northern front and especially at Santander.

REBEL ACCOUNT OF THE BATTLE OF BRUNETE
Why the Republicans Failed

Salamanca, August 2.

The great Republican offensive in the Brunete sector last month – described in the rebel press as 'Spain's Battle of the Marne' – has ended in complete failure, it is claimed at rebel head-quarters here. Now that it is all over it is possible to sum up and explain this phase of the war, as seen from the rebel side.

Government forces, estimated here at about 30,000 men, pushed forward in a south-westerly direction from Las Rozas on July 6–7. The attack was well planned, for the spearhead of this force of men, tanks, and armoured cars struck the weakest point in the rebel line encountering little resistance, the loyalists advanced under cover of their artillery and within a few days were in possession of Villanueva de la Canada, Quijorna, and Brunete itself.

The rebels holding positions in front of this overwhelming force of men, metal, and machinery were, numerically speaking, negligible. Besides, they had no barbed-wire entanglements, and the Government advance achieved principally down the dusty, dried-up river beds, was fast.

AIMS OF OFFENSIVE

The offensive had three aims – two military and one moral. The first was to reach Navalcarnero and cut the Madrid–Estremadura road, the life-line of the rebel forces in the Casa de Campo, Pozuelo, Aravaca, and other positions west of the capital. But, it is argued here, there was a greater military object in view – to cut off completely all the rebel forces in this area.

This was to be achieved by means of a break-through the lines of General Franco's troops at the Barrio de Usera, on the south-western outskirts of Madrid. The orders of General Miaja to his commander in this sector were, according to prisoners' reports, to strike west along the Estremadura road towards Alcorcon, and to join the troops who had come down through Brunete, thus closing the circle round the rebel positions near Madrid.

ATTACK HELD

But this plan failed. General Varela, directly he heard of the enemy attack launched in the Barrio de Usera sector, is reported to have sent his reserves there. His men responded well, and in spite of a furious barrage of artillery and machine-gun fire, they held their positions, with the result that when the Government forces took Brunete and waited expectantly for the other forces to arrive from the south-east they waited in vain.

The third aim of the offensive was moral. For the past twelve months the Republicans have been almost always on the defensive. Opinion here is that the Valencia authorities felt that something had to be done to show the world that the Madrid side was still one worth supporting.

FIRST PHASE

What may be called the first phase of the battle of Brunete ended after about four days. Six villages had been captured, a breach had been made in the rebel lines, but, owing to the resistance put up by the infantrymen holding trenches west of Villanueva del Pardillo on one side of the salient and as Majadahonda and Boadilla on the other, the hole made by the Republicans could not be widened. Nor, thanks to the desperate resistance of the rebels south of Brunete and to the non-appearance of the Republican column from the Barrio de Usera, could it be deepened.

This defence gave the rebel general time to send reinforcements, including bombers, from the aerodromes of the north.

SECOND PHASE

Then began the second phase of the battle – the fight to prevent the enemy from improving his position. Day after day the Republican infantry threw themselves at the rebel lines. There were also great battles in the air, sometimes as many as 80 machines being engaged at the same time.

On the ground, in that bare, dusty plain of Castille, under a burning sun, which sent the thermometer up to over 105 degrees, the Republicans in spite of enormous losses, came on again and again in waves, but were mown down by the accurate fire of the rebels. For about a week these attacks continued, lessening in force each day.

'WORK OF RECTIFICATION'

With the dying-down of the Republican attempts to break through, the second phase of the battle ended. Then started the third and last phase termed by General Franco 'the work of rectification', which was to sweep the enemy out of the salient.

In this chapter of the battle of Brunete which is now regarded here as drawing to its successful conclusion with the recapture of Brunete and Villafranca, it is the rebel air force which has had the greatest success. The infantry has played little part in this. It has not been asked to do anything more than quietly advance and occupy positions which have been won by the bombers and fighters, and to a lesser extent by the artillery.

During the first week of the Brunete offensive over 40 Government machines were officially reported to have been brought down. During the past fortnight the daily casualty list of loyalist aircraft has continued, and the rebel air ministry claims that no fewer than 100 enemy machines had been destroyed, as against about 15 rebel 'planes.

The total losses of the Republicans are said to have been enormous. Men who have returned from Brunete after its recapture tell how trenches were piled high with corpses. One estimate puts the Government casualties at 30,000 (killed and wounded). The rebel losses are reported to have been comparatively small, and to have occurred in the second phase of the battle, when they were defending their lines against further advances.

It is claimed here that the Republican offensive, though it has interrupted for a time the general plan of campaign, has failed in all three of its objectives with terrible loss of life to the Government side.–Reuter's Special Correspondent with the Rebels.

LULL ON MADRID FRONT

Madrid, August 2.

The calm which has reigned for the past few days on the Madrid front continued to-day, and it is generally believed here that the lull may well last throughout the month. There have been no important modifications of the positions of the two sides, and both Government and rebels are engaged in fortifying their lines.

Military authorities here claim that while the primary objective of freeing Madrid from the threat of attack from close quarters failed, the secondary objective of halting the rebel drive on the northern front succeeded. They claim that large bodies of men and quantities of war material, particularly aeroplanes, had to be withdrawn to stem the Government advance north-west of Madrid.

It is announced to-day that the Valencia Government has appointed a special commission under the Minister of Agriculture to reorganise and hasten evacuation and to improve methods of supply for Madrid. This step is warmly received in to-night's Madrid press.–Reuter.

Monday August 9 1937   *p.12*

VALENCIA'S CHARGES AGAINST GERMANY
'No Leipzig Incident'

Valencia, August 8.

The allegation that the torpedo attack against the German cruiser Leipzig, of which Berlin accused Valencia and which brought about Germany's withdrawal from the Spanish naval control scheme, never actually took place is contained in a Note published here by the Minister of Defence. This Note says:–

The Republican authorities have received the witness of a sailor from the German cruiser Leipzig which shows that this warship was never the object of aggression by a Spanish submarine as the German Government alleged in June. The declaration of the German sailor, whose name is being kept secret for reasons that are easy to understand, proves, moreover, that the commanders of the Leipzig had made preparations to organise a real torpedo attack against the Leipzig themselves in order to be able later to accuse Spain. This comedy was given up on account of the risks that such an attack would entail, and the Leipzig's commanders contended themselves with telling the whole world that an attempt had been made to torpedo the Leipzig.

The first news of the alleged attack on the cruiser Leipzig was given out in an official communiqué in Berlin. The announcement stated that two separate attempts were made to torpedo the cruiser off Oran, three torpedoes being fired on the first occasion and one on the second, but all missed their mark. The communiqué declared that after the first torpedo had been noticed the Leipzig changed her course, and that it was likely that by this manoeuvre either grazed another torpedo or the submarine, as examination of the hull later showed certain dents and scratches.–Reuter.

Wednesday August 18 1937   *p.5*

ADVANCING TO SANTANDER
Rebel Claim

The rebel advance on the Santander front is proceeding 'slowly but surely', according to a Havas correspondent at Reinosa, which was captured from the Government troops late on Sunday. Tanks in groups of three are proceeding without opposition across the hillsides, while artillery and aviation are keeping up a brisk bombardment. At nine o'clock yesterday morning the vanguard was stated to have pushed a few miles farther along the road from Reinosa.

Monday's prisoners are put by the correspondent at over 1,300, and he declares that the precipitacy of the Government troops' flight from Reinosa is exemplified by the fact that they did not destroy the arms foundry, most machinery being intact and the turbines untouched. There were, he says, 100,000 shells in the cellars.

According to a Spanish Press Agency message from Santander, quoted by Reuter, the rebels, while maintaining a violent offensive, 'have failed to reach their objective and have suffered very considerable losses'. The Government claims to have improved its position in one of the sectors, and in the Reinosa sector, where 'a rectification of line' is admitted, it is declared that the new positions have been maintained.

Monday August 23 1937 *p.12*

ISOLATION OF SANTANDER
Immediate Threat

ARMY'S DANGER OF BEING CUT OFF
New Rebel Advance

The rebels last night claimed to be within artillery range of Torrelavega, which lies about 16 miles south-west of Santander. The Havas correspondent with the rebel army states that the town is expected to be taken very soon.

The fall of the town will mean that Santander is isolated and its capture inevitable. For the Government forces the position will be extremely serious, for no retreat westwards will be possible for them as it was after the fall of Bilbao.

General Gamir, commanding the Government army defending Santander, must therefore either concentrate all available troops on the Torrelavega front, thereby weakening his eastern sector, and losing three-quarters of the province of Santander, or he must maintain his present distribution of strength with what seems to be the certain loss of Torrelavega.

'IRON BELT' BROKEN?

The Havas correspondent also states that the 'iron belt' of Santander, constructed in imitation of the famous defences of Bilbao, has broken at the first attack. The break is said to have occurred in the western sector.

The Government, however, denies the rebel claims. An official communiqué issued in Barcelona yesterday stated that the rebels had been repulsed with heavy losses at Barcena and at Ontaneda.

An Italian sergeant taken prisoner stated that four divisions of Italian regulars, as well as Spaniards and Moors, were operating on this front.

FLIGHT BY SEA FROM SANTANDER
10,000 Reported to Have Escaped in All Kinds of Craft

BAYONNE OVERWHELMED BY REFUGEES

Santander, which fell to the rebels when supporters inside the city revolted on Wednesday, was entered by General Franco's troops yesterday.

The city formally surrendered without conditions at nine o'clock in the morning. Troops were drawn up waiting to enter after the city authorities still nominally in control had been given an hour and a half to warn the defenders of their decision. A steady procession of rebel troops entered throughout the day, and last night there were 20,000 in the city.

All day yesterday refugees who had managed to escape by sea from Santander before or during the revolt were arriving on the French coast in all kinds of craft. A report from Santander states that it is estimated that 10,000 Government supporters left the city in fishing-boats and trawlers in the 48 hours before the fall.

Bayonne is overwhelmed by the arrival of refugees. By Wednesday evening some 400 men, women, and children had landed. Early yesterday morning 500 more arrived, and throughout the day more and more came. By last night well over a thousand refugees had reached Bayonne alone.

'FLOATING TOWN' OF REFUGEES

Because of the impossibility of housing this ever-increasing number of refugees in the town it was decided to organise a 'floating town' formed by all the Spanish ships which had arrived. The ships will be moored two miles downstream from Bayonne and placed under the supervision of the Mobile Guard. The measure is only a temporary one while the authorities study the situation.

At La Pallice, farther up the coast, between 500 and 600 militiamen, including many who are wounded, and 2,000 refugees arrived from Santander in 37 trawlers. They too have not been landed. Mobile Guards are patrolling the coast to prevent unauthorised landings.

HOW SANTANDER SURRENDERED
With the Rebels at Santander, August 26

Two men standing on a hilltop this morning formally surrendered Santander to General Franco's army. Thus on the
morning of the thirteenth day since the start of his advance
on Santander from the south General Franco added another
province to the list of territories under his control.

Throughout the night the rebel guns had been trained on
the city from the western and south-western suburbs. While
nine rebel fighter-'planes circled overhead a small car drove
up slowly from a city street to a spot on a hilltop overlooking
the scene of yesterday's fighting. It stopped in front of a group
of rebel generals.

Two men stepped out, one the leader of the Government
shock troops, the other the commander of the Carabiniers. The
first was pale, the second calm. The two men saluted and then
formally handed over the city, with the proviso that women
and children should not be shot. This remark drew grim smiles
from the bystanders.

The rebel generals demanded 100 Republican hostages
as a token that the promose of surrender would be kept. A
few minutes later the two Government officers entered their
car and returned to the city. The leader of the shock troops
sat on the radiator holding out a white cloth attached to a stick.

Tanks and infantry columns waited three miles from the
centre of the city before entering from the south-west, while
the Navarrese column entered by the road farther north.–Press
Association Foreign Special.

Saturday August 28 1937   *p.13*

MUSSOLINI AND FRANCO
Messages Exchanged

THE ITALIANS AT SANTANDER
341 Dead: 1,676 Wounded – Rome Bulletin

While Signor Mussolini and General Franco were exchanging congratulatory telegrams yesterday on the part played by
the Italian Legionaries in the Santander battle, there was published in Rome an official bulletin of the Italian losses. The
casualty list, which covers the period August 14 to 23, is as
follows:–

Officers killed	16
Officers wounded	60
Men killed	325
Men wounded	1,616

THE TELEGRAMS

The following telegram was sent by General Franco to the Duce:–

At the moment in which the valorous Legionaries are entering Santander in close co-operation with the Nationalist troops, both of them in name of Western civilisation in its struggle against Asiatic barbarism, I gratefully testify to your Excellency my pride at having the Italian Legionaries under my command.

The Duce's reply reads:

I am especially happy that the Italian Legionaries have given, during the last ten days' battle, a powerful contribution to the splendid victory of Santander, and that such contribution finds to-day in your telegram a welcome recognition. This intimate fraternity in arms is a guarantee of the final victory which will deliver Spain and the Mediterranean from all menaces against our common civilisation.

Then follows another telegram, from General Teruzzi, who commands the Italian Legionaries in Spain, to the Duce:–

All the Blackshirts have completely and heroically fulfilled their duty. The Duce's orders have been carried out. I desire to assure once more that the Blackshirts wore, as always, the same warlike expression which was shaped for them by your will.–TERUZZI

Signor Mussolini also sent a telegram to the General commanding the Legionaries, for all officers and Legionaries, saying:

My enthusiastic applause. The heroism of the Legionaries is recognised and exalted not only in Italy but in the whole world.

ENTHUSIASM IN ROME

The exchange of telegrams between Signor Mussolini and General Franco has again stirred up in Rome enthusiasm for the capture of Santander and the part played by the Italian

Legionaries. The headings in the papers give the impression that Italy, as much as Spain, has won a national victory.

The 'Giornale d'Italia' claims the victory largely for the Italians. 'General Franco has declared before the world that to-day's victory is in great part an Italian victory; a victory of the Legionaries and the Fascist Leader,' it says. The evening newspapers print columns of exaltation of the Italian Legionaries.–Reuter.

TWELVE ITALIAN GENERALS FIGHTING FOR FRANCO

Rome, August 27.

The Rome newspapers publish to-day the names of twelve Italian generals now serving with General Franco's forces in Spain. The names include General Bastico, of the Italian General Staff, and General Frusci, formerly Commander of the Libyan Division in the Abyssinian war.–Exchange Telegram.

On Monday, August 30, the French Cabinet decided to protest to the Non-Intervention Committee at Mussolini's action in exchanging congratulatory telegrams with General Franco and argued that, by doing so, Italy had been guilty of official intervention in Spain.

Friday September 3 1937   *p.9*

STRONGER FORCE TO COMBAT THE 'PIRATES'
Ministers' Decisions Yesterday

MEDITERRANEAN POWERS TO CONFER
British Cabinet Called for Wednesday

From our Diplomatic Correspondent

London, Thursday Night.

There were two meetings of Ministers, lasting three and half hours altogether, at the Foreign Office to-day. Sir John Simon, the Chancellor of the Exchequer, presided, and Mr. Eden, Lord Halifax, Mr. Duff Cooper, Mr. Hore-Belisha, Mr. Malcolm MacDonald, Mr. Ormsby-Gore, and Mr. Oliver Stanley were present.

The whole situation in the Far East and in the Mediterranean was surveyed, but the special subject of discussion was the 'piracy' going on in the Mediterranean.

The chief result of the meetings was the decision to reinforce the destroyer strength of the fleet in the Western Mediterranean basin. Reinforcements are now under orders to proceed forthwith.

The problem of 'piracy' in the whole of the Mediterranean is regarded as the most urgent of all problems on hand. As an immediate measure, all submarines attacking British shipping are to be hunted down and destroyed without further warning.

By an adequate patrol of destroyers it is believed that the submarine menace can be held in check pending a conference of the Mediterranean Powers, which, at the suggestion of the French Government, will be held in Geneva. Great Britain, France, Yugo-Slavia, Turkey, and Greece will be represented – Italy will, presumably, exclude herself from the conference by her absence from Geneva.

The whole Mediterranean has been made insecure by 'piracy'. A problem has thereby been created that directly affects the vital interests of Great Britain and France. This problem is to be treated, in the first instance at least, as being independent of the Spanish civil war and of 'non-intervention'. There is complete agreement between London and Paris that it must be settled with all speed and, if there is no other way, by drastic action.

A meeting of the Cabinet has been called for next week.

Attacks on merchant shipping were a growing problem throughout 1937. In an attempt to safeguard merchant seamen a joint Anglo-French invitation was extended to Germany, the Soviet Union and all states with a Mediterranean frontier (except Spain) to attend a 'Mediterranean Conference' which would consider how 'piracy' could be ended. The invitation was issued on September 6 and the first meeting took place at Nyon on September 10. Germany and Italy were both absent from the Nyon Conference, having argued that piracy was a question which fell within the preserve of the Non-Intervention Committee and therefore should not be dealt with by a special conference. Italy was later to accept the naval patrol scheme which emerged from the Nyon Conference.

Some indication of the scale of attacks on merchant shipping in the Mediterranean can be gained from a written answer given by R. A. Butler, Under Secretary for Foreign Affairs, on Friday 3 1939. He stated that, since the start of the Spanish Civil War, 99 British ships had been attacked with 26 British subjects killed and a further 26 wounded.

SPANISH GOVERNMENT CLAIM 3,800 PRISONERS IN ARAGON

Rebels Still Deny Capture of Belchite

The following statement has been issued by the headquarters of the Spanish Government eastern army (says a
Reuter message from Barcelona):–

With the capture of Quinto Belchite, the first stage of the
Government offensive on the Aragon front, which, with
Saragossa as its objective, is aimed at relieving the Asturias,
has now been accomplished. The Government have captured
over 350 square miles of enemy territory and 3,800 prisoners.
The enemy losses are estimated at over 5,000, and Government aircraft brought down 20 insurgent warplanes during
the recent advances.

The rebels have not yet acknowledged the fall of Belchite.
In his nightly broadcast from rebel radio stations General
Queipo de Llano on Saturday evening stated that having read
Valencia's detailed accounts of the capture of Belchite he con-
sidered it would be a mistake not to announce its fall frankly.
Accordingly he telephoned General Franco's headquarters and
at 6.30 p.m. was informed that Belchite was still holding out
against the enemy attack up to that hour.

*The Aragon offensive was launched to divert pressure from
the Republican forces in the Basque country.*

NYON POWERS EXTEND THEIR WAR ON 'PIRACY'

Attacks by Aircraft and Warships

NO BOMBING BY 'PLANES OF MERCHANTMEN

Italy Invited to Join the New Pacts

The Nyon Conference ended its talks in Geneva yesterday
by setting up a complete system of defence against illicit warfare by submarines, surface vessels, and aeroplanes in the
Mediterranean.

Under this any aeroplane that attacks a vessel at sea

(a) Without warning; and
(b) Without providing for the safety of the crew

will in future be treated as a pirate.

As it is impossible for any aircraft to fulfil the conditions named, the agreement signed yesterday prohibits air attacks on merchant shipping.

With regard to surface vessels, the proposal to extend the provisions of the Nyon Agreement to attacks by such craft aroused objections from the legal mind of M. Politis (Greece). M. Politis asked what would happen if a Greek destroyer saw an Italian battleship sinking a non-Spanish merchant vessel in Greek territorial waters without regard to the provisions of the London Naval Treaty. What he asked, could a Greek destroyer do in such circumstances?

His scruples were satisfied by the addition of a sentence running as follows:–

In territorial waters the riparian Powers shall decide what action they shall take in the circumstances of the case.

The agreement signed last night consists of a text virtually identical with that signed at Nyon, which provides for measures to end submarine piracy, the only difference being that the words 'aeroplanes and surface vessels' are substituted for the word 'submarine'.

It is accompanied by two annexes to the Nyon Agreement dealing with the routes to be followed and the zones reserved for submarine exercises.

The agreement was signed without reservation by all the nine Nyon Powers, and the text will not be published until to-day to allow of its communication to Italy.

It is understood that the British and French Chargés d'Affaires in Rome were to receive instructions last night to communicate to the Italian Government the text of the new agreement in the same conditions and with the same invitation to participate as was done in the case of the original Nyon Agreement of which this forms an integral part.

NEXT STEPS IN 'NON-INTERVENTION'
Clandestine Help of Little Use: Open Help Difficult

NO ITALIAN REINFORCEMENTS YET

From our Diplomatic Correspondent

London, Wednesday.

There is no truth in the reports that big Italian reinforcements have been sent to Spain, though it does not follow none will ever be sent any more.

Until only a short time ago there was complete confidence in Rome and in Berlin that the fall of Bilbao would precede the fall of Madrid by only a few weeks and that the war would end in a rebel victory before the winter. Piracy in the Mediterranean was, beyond any doubt, intended to accelerate this victory by cutting loyalist Spain off from essential supplies.

Piracy has now been brought to an end, and, so far from being able to attack Madrid, the rebels have not been able to complete the conquest of the Asturias; the miners of Oviedo are stilling holding out. After the conference of naval experts which will open in Paris on Monday Italian patrol ships and aeroplanes will have the privilege of escorting Russian merchantmen with cargoes of war material and petrol as far as the three-mile limit off Valencia, while Italian destroyers will be able to defend Italian merchantmen against Italian submarines.

ITALY'S INTEREST IN REBEL VICTORY

Italy is still as interested in a rebel victory as ever, perhaps more than ever, for the war is presented to the Italian public as an Italian war in which Italian troops are heavily engaged. Germany is also interested in a rebel victory, though less so than Italy, and the German papers do not mention the presence of German troops in Spain.

What is Italy to do now? Spain will certainly be discussed by Herr Hitler and Signor Mussolini when they meet. It is hard to see how Italy and Germany can make General Franco win the war before the winter unless they send reinforcements, for a renewal of piracy would seem to be out of the question. But the attitude of Franco towards 'intervention' has certainly stiffened. It is ceasing to be a matter of special concern to the 'Left' or to the 'Right', and is more and more conceived as a matter touching national security.

The opening of the French frontier would not be sufficient

to counteract a renewed Italian–German interventionist effort. Indeed the total break-down of 'non-intervention' would probably be to the advantage of the Italians and Germans (and of their protégé General Franco) unless it were accompanied by positive counter-measures on the part of the French.

BRITISH ATTITUDE

The British attitude towards intervention has not perhaps stiffened quite as much as the French, but there would certainly be a greater willingness here to support France in any action she might be prepared to take than there was some months ago thanks chiefly to the progress made in British as well as in French rearmament and to the ever-growing solidarity between the two Western Powers. It is fully realised here that the ultimate purpose of such action would be the defence of that security in the Western Mediterranean which is of such vital concern to both Powers alike.

It may be that Italy and Germany will attempt renewed clandestine intervention, though it will be difficult, if not impossible, to intervene within the limits of the clandestine and yet tip the balance in favour of General Franco. The view taken here is that the possibilities of non-intervention have not been exhausted and there would be the greatest reluctance in resorting to another policy. But the limits of what is tolerable under non-intervention have been nearly exceeded even now – there is a point where non-intervention must become meaningless. That point has not been reached, but it may be if Italy and Germany are absolutely determined to make General Franco win this year.

ITALY AND THE PATROL

The participation of Italy in the Mediterranean patrol is welcomed here and in Paris. It is believed that the Anglo-Italian conversations which are to begin in the autumn are more likely to be successful than was apparent some weeks ago. But no real Anglo-Italian understanding is possible as long as there is Italian intervention in Spain. Nor can there be any real Anglo-German understanding as long as there is German intervention in Spain.

It is realised more and more clearly here that the question of Spain and of British security in the Western Mediterranean is vital. The thesis that Italy and Germany are out to scotch so-called 'Bolshevism' in Spain would not bear critical examination. Whether intentionally or not, the Italian and German action in the Western Mediterranean is inimical to British and French vital interests. These interests have hitherto been defended by the policy of 'non-intervention', but if that policy were to collapse they would still remain and would still have to be defended.

GERMANY AGAIN SENDING TROOPS TO SPAIN
Over 100,000 Italians There

STILL MORE MEN GOING TO HELP IN CONQUEST OF COUNTRY

From a Diplomatic Correspondent

London, Friday.

There is ample evidence that German intervention in Spain continues side by side with the Italian, though less openly and on a smaller scale.

Information from Germany which has just reached this country indicates that during September between 100 and 300 men from two German anti-aircraft batteries – the 8th, stationed at Furth, near Nuremberg, and the 25th, stationed at Goppingen, in Wurtemberg – were sent to Spain by way of Italy, together with all the guns and equipment of these two batteries. In the case of the 25th Battery the commander paraded the men, told them that he and they were going to Spain, and asked whether any man was unwilling to go. There was no answer, and he then formally declared the men to be volunteers.

The men were sent in plain clothes, some of them by air but most of them by train, first to Italy and then to the headquarters of the general who is in charge of the German aircraft and anti-aircraft organisation in Spain. Some of the men's relatives have already received letters from them, sent through the Air Ministry in Berlin. By the terms of their service they receive pay and allowances amounting to a little over 24 marks a day, but out of this they pay for their own board and lodging. Previous German 'volunteers' have had the option of returning to Germany after a year's service with a gratuity of about 3,000 marks, and a number of them have already done so.

Meanwhile Italy has in the last few days been pressing on with arrangements for the shipment of further troops and war material. So far these have been landed not only on the Balearic Islands but also in Cadiz, and probably in other rebel ports. In the past three weeks more than 15,000 troops have been disembarked at all harbours, including the Balearic

Islands, in addition to large quantities of munitions and other material, some still on the way, some already landed.

The aims of Italian policy are expressed with considerable frankness in high quarters at Rome. The essential aim, it is said, is the military conquest of Spain, and this seems to be confirmed by the large scale of the present intervention. It is not easy to believe that Italy would invest all this money, men, and material in fighting 'Bolshevism', according to her theory, in Spain, and then leave the country as soon as Franco had won the war. The latest importations bring the total number of Italian troops in Spain up to between 110,000 and 120,000 men.

SUDDEN BREAK IN THE SPANISH DEADLOCK
Concessions by Italy and Germany

PRIORITY FOR 'RECOGNITION' NOW DROPPED
'Volunteers': Fact-Finding Commission

From our Political Correspondent

London, Wednesday.

A sudden Italian change of front has saved the Spanish Non-Intervention Committee from breakdown.

Yesterday the Italians, and with them of course, the Germans, were refusing to agree to any withdrawal of volunteers until belligerent rights had been granted to the two sides in Spain. To-day Count Grandi announced that the Italian Government would agree to withdrawal without this precedent granting of belligerent rights. He proposed, and of course the Germans agreed with them, that belligerent rights should be granted at some point when withdrawal could be said to have reached a substantial stage. That, of course, was the proposal of the British plan, and indeed Count Grandi was insistent that Italy by these proposals was adopting the British plan in its entirety.

THE INQUIRY

If that had been all that Count Grandi proposed, then much of the satisfaction that is being professed at the Italian change of front would be justified. But Count Grandi also proposed that a commission should go out to Spain and discover the exact number of foreign nationals serving on either side. The result of this investigation would be to make it possible to decide 'in what manner and in what proportion the withdrawals shall take place'. While this Commission makes its inquiries the Italian Government (and with it the German) will agree to the 'preliminary and immediate withdrawal' of an equal number of volunteers from either side.

THREE POINTS

The decision as to when a sufficient withdrawal has taken place to merit the granting of belligerent rights is to be made either by the Non-Intervention Committee or by some other body appointed for the purpose. The Italian plan then is as follows:–

(1) Token withdrawal;
(2) Main withdrawal; and
(3) Belligerent rights granted at some point during the main withdrawal.

And that is, of course, substantially the British plan.

The one and crucial departure from the British plan is the proposal for a commission to establish the relative strength of the volunteers on either side. The British plan only contemplated a commission to 'make arrangements for, and supervise, the withdrawal of foreign nationals'. How long will it take for this commission to carry out an enumeration of the foreign combatants on either side? An authority who has perhaps become too sophisticated through attending the Non-Intervention Committee answered the question by saying, 'Three months or the duration of the war.' Whether it is a cynical delaying plan of that kind or not it would obviously be a long job counting foreign heads on the two sides. It means, for instance, on the rebel side visits to three fronts.

On the worst view the Italian project gains time for Mussolini's arms in Spain and relieves him from the obloquy of bringing about the failure of non-intervention. And if the worst view is taken it is entirely his own fault, for it requires some explaining why last night Italy should have been against any withdrawals until belligerent rights were granted and to-night should have accepted withdrawal first with belligerent rights granted when substantial withdrawal has taken place.

The Italian proposals seem to have won the acceptance of the whole Committee save the Russians. Mr. Maisky has reserved his observations on them. He will no doubt give them at the resumed meeting of the Committee on Friday. Perhaps the British and French Governments are less enamoured of the Italian proposals than they are pretending to be to-night, but they probably feel that Signor Mussolini, having made some concessions, even though they are apparent rather than real, may as time goes on be driven into yielding substantial points.

TOKEN WITHDRAWALS

There appears to have been pretty general agreement in the Committee outside the Russians that the 'token' withdrawal should be equal since it would be a prelude to complete withdrawal, but the question has been postponed for fuller discussion at Friday's meeting. Then, too, will be discussed the size of the token withdrawal.

It is understood that the two sides in Spain will be approached immediately after Friday's meeting, if that goes well, in order to discover whether they will accept the Commission of Inquiry into 'volunteer' strengths. Meantime, on the Committee's suggestion, investigation is to begin at once on the technical questions involved in withdrawal, like the shipping required and where (a question apt to be overlooked) many of the volunteers are to be taken. This certainly suggests expedition. But there is still that commission on 'volunteer' strengths to be remembered.

Friday October 22 1937   *p.11*

GIJON SURRENDERS AFTER RISING INSIDE TOWN
The Northern Front Wiped Out

LONG SIEGE OF OVIEDO COLLAPSES: THOUSANDS OF TROOPS CUT OFF

Gijon, the last Government stronghold in the north of Spain, has fallen as Santander fell – to the 'fifth army' of rebel sympathisers within the town. After two hours' fighting they got control, and at once the town surrendered.

With its fall General Franco has achieved his long-threatened 'liquidation' of the northern front and a new phase in the Spanish civil war is begun.

The rebel communiqué received early this morning announcing the surrender of Gijon stated:

The Asturian front has been completely overcome by our

174

troops, and the enemy, defeated and abandoned by their leaders, are surrendering their arms to the 'Nationalist' columns.

The civil population in a tremendous manifestation has turned out into the streets carrying the 'Nationalist' flag. With the entry of the 'Nationalist' army, peace, order, and justice have been restored.

The northern front is no more.

OVIEDO RELIEVED

The collapse of the Austurians' resistance brought immediate relief to Oviedo, in which a garrison of rebel troops has been besieged for 15 months. Whole battalions are stated to have surrendered to the rebels around Oviedo, and one report estimates that 60,000 troops have either surrendered, been taken prisoner, or been surrounded.

IMPORTANCE OF FALL OF GIJON

The fall of Gijon, in that it means the wiping out of the northern front, is of the greatest importance. Since the beginning of the war this front has occupied forces that the rebels needed elsewhere. The advance on Madrid had to wait until, by the taking of San Sebastian and Irun, the loyalist North had been cut off from communication with France. Then, when the attacks against Madrid failed and the advance in the south was held, it was to the north that General Franco turned, hoping that he could quickly end the war there and so release his troops for the other fronts. But it has proved a long business.

Now some 80,000 to 100,000 men from the north are available to attack either at Madrid, in the south, or, more likely, in Aragon. Further, the rebel warships that since April have been fully occupied in trying to maintain the naval blockade in the north will be available for appearance off the Catalan coast.

The rebels, therefore, are in a state of great optimism. Broadcasting last night from the rebel wireless station Radio Nacional, the announcer said, 'The liberation of Gijon is the penultimate stage of the civil war. The last stage will not be long. Therefore have courage and patience.'

FOREIGN ARMIES IN SPAIN
Nearly 100,000 for Franco Against 15,000 for Government

From a Diplomatic Correspondent

London, Friday.

The task of the Commission which will have to discover the number of foreign volunteers fighting in Spain need not be a long one. It can be simplified by the use of the information which is already in the Non-Intervention Committee's possession.

The latest and most careful inquiries have shown that on the side of Valencia not more than 15,000 volunteers are fighting. A surprising fact which has emerged from these inquiries is that the number of Russian volunteers does not exceed 1,000. The other volunteers of the Valencia Government, apart from Germans and Italians, are mostly French, Yugo-Slavs, Poles, Americans and Swiss.

Equally careful inquiries about the foreign volunteers fighting under Franco have shown that he has at least 80,000 Italian soldiers at his disposal. In addition, the number of Italians in Spain who have various kinds of non-combatant connection with the civil war is between 20,000 and 30,000.

In addition to the Italians, there are on Franco's side between 12,000 and 15,000 Germans, who, apart from complete air formations and air defence units, are mainly serving as specialists. The Germans, even when not serving in large units, work with extreme discipline, and their organising activity has been of great use to Franco.

In addition to the Italians and Germans, Franco has between 2,000 and 3,000 other volunteers of various nationalities.

Friday November 5 1937 p.11

WITHDRAWAL OF FOREIGNERS FROM SPAIN
Immediate Approach to Both Sides

LORD PLYMOUTH AUTHORISED TO ACT

The two parties in Spain are to be approached immediately with a view to securing their assent to the terms of a resolution embodying the British plan for the withdrawal of foreign combatants from Spain. Lord Plymouth, the chairman, was authorised at a full meeting of the Non-Intervention Committee last night to communicate to the British Government the terms of the communication to be made to Spain, and the British Government will be asked to transmit this statement immediately.

The resolution embodying the British plan for the withdrawal of foreigners was accepted by all the Powers represented with the exception of Russia, which again abstained from voting on the clause relating to the granting of belligerent rights. The Committee unanimously accepted a resolution authorising the chairman to approach the two parties in Spain to obtain their agreement to the resolution as a whole. In making this approach Lord Plymouth will make clear the attitude of the various Governments and will point out that Russia has abstained from voting on the belligerent rights clause.

The Committee further decided unanimously that pending receipt of the replies from Spain the Chairman's Sub-committee shall continue examination of the concrete questions concerned with execution of the various parts of the British plan. The Sub-committee will also take into consideration the practical methods required to meet Russia's abstention from voting.

After the resolutions before the Committee had been dealt with the chairman said he regarded their acceptance as authorisation to him to approach the two parties in Spain forthwith. He asked that the exact words of the communication to be made to Valencia and Salamanca should be left to him, and to this the Committee agreed. Lord Plymouth said he was familiar with the positions which had been adopted by the various representatives on the Committee, and he would put the whole matter to the two parties in Spain in as clear and precise manner as he could. He would ask the two sides in Spain to treat the matter as urgent and to reply as quickly as possible.

THE MILITARY POSITION

From our Diplomatic Correspondent

London, Thursday.

The proceedings at to-day's meeting of the full Non-Intervention Committee followed the expected course. Great Britain will now submit the British plan for ending intervention to both parties in the Spanish civil war.

The principal purpose of this plan is to secure the speedy withdrawal of all the foreign 'volunteers' in Spain. The loyalists are in favour of complete withdrawal, seeing that it would be very much to their advantage. It is possible that the rebels will, with the sanction of the Italian and German Governments, agree to the actual withdrawal of some volunteers. But it is regarded as most unlikely here that there will be a withdrawal of 'volunteers' big enough to alter the relative strengths of the two armies. In other words, the bulk of the 'volunteers' on the rebel side – and therefore on the loyalist side – will remain at least as long as there is no change in the military situation.

There is no change in sight. As far as can be judged from here, there is no massive concentration of rebel troops and war material for an offensive on any sector of the Spanish front. It would therefore seem that no big offensive can be expected in the near future.

Even if there is an offensive it does not follow that it will decide the war. The odds are generally regarded as being heavily in favour of the rebels, but it may well be that the loyalists can hold up any rebel advance for a long time to come. As things are now the outlook is that the war will drag on indefinitely, with ever-growing hardship for both sides (though for the loyalists far more than for the rebels) and with no real change either in the military situation or in the policy of the interested Powers (whether interventionist or non-interventionist). The question of 'volunteers' is therefore likely to remain much as it is now, even if a certain number is withdrawn from both sides.

Monday November 8 1937   *p.12*

THE DEFENCE OF MADRID
First Anniversary

REBELS REPULSED IN ARAGON

Barcelona, November 7.

Republican Spain to-day celebrated the anniversary of the start of Madrid's defence against the rebels.

Senor Prieto, the Minister for National Defence, issued a statement eulogising General Miaja and the defenders which is to be read to every member of the loyalist armed forces. The celebrations include great meetings, theatre and cinema shows, and physical culture displays. In Madrid there was a special celebration in which the International Brigade took part.

Desperate fighting took place on the Aragon front to-day when the rebels launched offensives against the Government positions.

After an artillery barrage the rebels advanced with massed infantry, but were driven back. A second attempt followed with fresh troops, but these, too, were repulsed with heavy losses. At nightfall the Government still held the line. The rebels, it is stated, were using every kind of modern arms.–Reuter.

Tuesday November 9 1937   *p.11*

WITHDRAWAL OF INFANTRY
Italy's Policy

HER 'VOLUNTEERS' DOWN TO 60,000
Ratio Still Ten to One

From our Diplomatic Correspondent

London, Monday.

Withdrawal of Italian infantry from Spain (as distinguished from aeroplanes, guns, tanks, and so forth) is now going on. No certain figures are available, but it is believed that the Italian 'volunteers' serving with the rebel army now number no more than 50,000 or 60,000 and the German 'volunteers' 10,000 at the most.

The number of 'volunteers' on the Loyalist side has also been dwindling. The strength of the International Brigade is unknown – it is probably not more than a few thousand, for the column has had very heavy losses during the last few months. Many Russian 'volunteers' have been withdrawn: only about 800 remain in the service of the Loyalists. Most of them are pilots and staff officers.

The proportion of 'volunteers', however, remains much as it was – that is to say, about ten to one in favour of the rebels.

LOYALIST DEFENCE

The Loyalist Army is hardly able to conduct a big offensive, chiefly because it has not enough aeroplanes, tanks, and ammunition to replace the heavy losses which an offensive against a trench system and fortified position would inflict. But the Loyalists should be well able to put up a powerful defence.

They continue to receive arms from abroad, but these arms, most of which now arrive at Barcelona, are not of the highest quality. Their Army has greatly improved in discipline and organisation. The spirit of their Air Force and of the troops defending Madrid is particularly high.

The spirit of the civilian population does not seem to have changed much. There are many signs of war-weariness, but not conspicuously more than there were a year ago. The Catalans are making a much bigger contribution to the common cause than they were six months ago, and the discipline along the Aragon front, which is held chiefly by Catalans, is excellent.

There is a shortage of food almost everywhere in Government territory now, but the Spaniard can live on an astonishingly small ration, and there is no sign of starvation. The population of Madrid continues to face the war with the same kind of fatalism as ever, and there is no sign that shortage, bombardments, and air raids have produced any demoralisation.

OFFENSIVE BEFORE LONG

The initiative is certainly in the hands of the rebels and it is expected that they will begin offensive operations before long. It would seem that unfavourable weather conditions have delayed the concentration of their forces. It will probably be insufficient for them to win isolated victories.

If the war is not to drag on indefinitely, they will have to effect a 'break through' and follow it with an advance on a broad front. Not only will they need large forces to man their lengthening front and lines of communication but also to hold the territory they have occupied, for there will be arms left with secret Loyalist supporters in every village. The rebels are immensely superior in the air and in artillery.

Wednesday November 17 1937   *p.14*

'VOLUNTEERS' PLAN
Russia's Concession

ITS RESERVATION WITHDRAWN

Russia sprang a surprise at yesterday's meeting of the Chairman's Sub-committee of the Non-Intervention Committee by dropping her reservations on the belligerent rights section of the British plan for withdrawing foreigners from Spain.

Mr. Maisky, the Soviet Ambassador, addressing the Committee, which had met at the Foreign Office to consider reports by technical sub-committees regarding the strengthening of control and dealing with the withdrawal of foreigners, said:

The Soviet Government, in order to facilitate still further the practical work of the Non-Intervention Committee for the withdrawal of foreign combatants from Spain, accepts the resolution of November 4 in toto without any reservations whatsoever leaving, along with the other Governments, its interpretation of the term 'substantial withdrawal' until the time when this question will come up for consideration in the Committee.

I hope, Mr. Chairman, that my statement will assist you in guiding the work of the Committee towards a speedy realisation of the withdrawal of foreign combatants from Spain.

It was on this subject that there was so much discussion at meetings on October 20 and November 4. Italy contending that unanimity was essential and that Russia's attitude on belligerent rights made this impossible, but eventually the Soviet Government accepted all the other points of the resolution on the British plan, but announced its abstention on the problem of belligerent rights. By this means it was possible to adopt the resolution and send the plan to both sides in Spain, the question of Russia's abstention being held over.

Monday November 22 1937   *p.14*

COMMISSION ON 'VOLUNTEERS'
Franco Accepts

SOME RESERVATIONS & DETAILS SOUGHT

General Franco has accepted in principle the proposal to send a commission of inquiry to both sides in the Spanish war to arrange for the eventual withdrawal of 'volunteers'. A Note to this effect, states Reuter, was handed to the British Government's representative at San Sebastian on Saturday by Senor Sangroniz, chief of the Salamanca diplomatic Cabinet.

The Note, which is lengthy, while accepting in principle, makes certain reservations and asks for further elucidation on certain points.

The commissions to be dispatched to both sides in Spain are provided for under the British draft plan of July 14, which was finally approved by the Non-Intervention Committee on November 4. The duties of the commissions will be:–

(1) To estimate the total number of non-Spanish nationals on both sides to be withdrawn and to report to the Non-Intervention Committee:
(2) To arrange with the appropriate authorities in Spain for the withdrawal; and

181

(3) To carry out, in the manner determined by the Non-Intervention Committee, the withdrawal from both sides in accordance with the proportion of non-Spanish nationals on each side.

The Spanish Government last week promised that its reply on the receiving of a commission will be given at an early date.

Saturday November 27 1937   *p.17*

AN INTERVIEW WITH DR. NEGRIN
The Coming Offensive

From our Barcelona Correspondent

In an interview with your correspondent Dr. Negrin, the Spanish Prime Minister, declared that General Franco's great offensive, announced some time ago, was expected to start shortly. Neither he nor the great military expert and Chief of Staff, General Rojo, place any faith in the reports of the retirement of Italian troops.

General Rojo did not state at what point on the front this attack was expected. From his remarks it appeared possible that it would be launched in several places simultaneously.

Dr. Negrin said that the most important internal problem, that of the relations between Catalonia and the rest of loyal Spain, was settled before the Government moved to Barcelona during the interviews arranged by Senor Companys, President of Catalonia. The autonomy of the region is to be fully respected. The Government, on coming to Barcelona, made an excellent impression on Catalan public opinion by various proclamations which stated and reaffirmed this agreement. To this has been added the improvement in the food supply in the last few days.

Jestingly, the Prime Minister stated that his next residence would be in Saragossa, 'But not immediately,' he added. 'The war will be over within two more years.' These words were a second and very definite denial of the rumours of an armistice.

'I WILL IMPOSE MY WILL'
No Mediation – General Franco

Paris, November 26.

'I will impose my will by victory and will not enter into discussion,' declared General Franco in an interview with the special correspondent of the Havas Agency at Burgos. Asked whether this meant a denial of rumours that he was willing to exchange views with European Powers regarding mediation General Franco said, 'Exactly.'

'We open our arms to all Spaniards and offer them the opportunity of helping to form the Spain of to-morrow which will be a land of justice, mercy, and fraternity. The war is already won on the battlefields as in the economic, commercial, industrial, and even social spheres. I will only agree to end it militarily.' The correspondent asked, 'What if the Spanish Government, through the intermediary of a European Power, shortly offered an armistice?' General Franco replied, 'I would refuse even to enter into contact. My troops will advance. The choice for the enemy is fight or unconditional surrender, nothing else.'–Reuter.

Tuesday November 30 1937   *p.11*

REBEL THREAT OF BLOCKADE
Representations By Britain

NO RIGHT ADMITTED

The Commander-in-Chief of the Mediterranean Fleet has been instructed to raise with Admiral Moreno, the chief of the rebel naval forces at Palma, Majorca, the announcement made by rebel wireless stations on Sunday that General Franco intends to take vigorous naval action to blockade Spanish Government ports. The action threatened was that ships in Spanish Government waters would be liable to attack.

The British Government does not admit the right of General Franco to impose a blockade, since no belligerent rights have been granted. Further, even, if belligerent rights were to be granted, there would be no right of attack, although there would then be right of capture.

The British Government has issued by broadcast from Gibraltar and Malta a warning to British shipping that the rebels have announced that they intend to establish this 'blockade' of the Spanish Government coast – that is, from Almeria to the French frontier – and a reminder that while British shipping will as far as possible receive the protection of the British Fleet at sea this protection cannot be given in territorial waters.

The determination of the British Government to protect British shipping on the high seas is evident here. The sea lanes were the arteries of the Empire. Britain regarded the freedom of the seas and her capacity to protect her merchant fleet as being of paramount importance both to her prosperity in time of peace and to her survival in time of war.

Teruel offensive – December 1937–February 1938

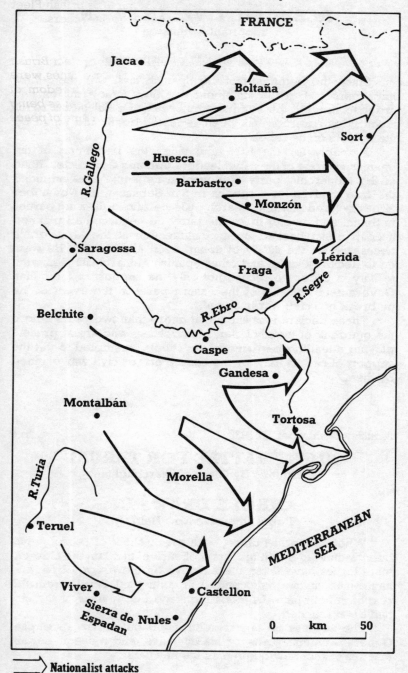

Nationalist attacks

185

REBEL MOTIVES IN SPAIN
Important Admission

From a Diplomatic Correspondent

Since the beginning of the Spanish civil war the rebels have persisted in the statement that they took arms only in order to prevent the imminent outbreak of a Bolshevist revolution. This assertion has been repeated again and again by the leaders of the rebels.

Probably for the first time since the beginning of the Spanish war one of the rebel leaders, Antonio Goicoectea, head of the Monarchist party 'Renovacion Espanola', has admitted the true motives. In a speech in San Sebastian on November 22 he declared that since March, 1934, certain Right-wing parties in Spain, and among those the party he headed, had planned a coup d'état backed by an insurrection of the army or, 'if necessary for the safety of Spain, even a civil war'. He went on to declare that he and other Spanish Monarchists then went to Italy in order 'to secure not only the support of the Italian Government but also of the Fascist party in the event of the outbreak of a civil war in Spain'.

These declarations show that, more than two years before the outbreak of the civil war, Monarchists, who are at present playing a leading part among the rebels, attempted to get the support of Fascist Italy for the coup d'état or civil war planned by them.

NIGHT BATTLE FOR TERUEL
Fighting by Glare of Searchlights

CIRCLE DRAWS IN
Rebel Offensive Now Held Up

While General Franco, with much show of secrecy, has been waiting to begin his 'great offensive' in Spain the Government forces have taken the initiative on the Aragon front and have, it is claimed, succeeded in cutting off Teruel from the rest of rebel Spain. Late last night the first houses of the city had been reached.

The success is important in itself, but it has also upset General Franco's plans for his offensive, and it seems certain that this cannot now begin until the new year.

Yesterday was the fifth day of fighting for Teruel, and a communiqué received from Barcelona early this morning stated that the day's results were 'frankly satisfactory'. The communiqué, according to the Spanish Press Agency, added:

At 6 p.m. the order for a general attack was given and a Republican force reached the first houses of the city. Another column simultaneously attacked Teruel from the east.

At 9 30 p.m. the attack was still continuing, carried out under the rays of Republican searchlights which lit up the city.

All the rebel counter-attacks were repulsed with enormous losses, and rebel aviation was unable to give much support.

The circle round Teruel, far from being broken, is drawn closer. The number of prisoners is enormous but not exactly known.

Republican aviation brilliantly co-operated in the fighting. Two Government planes were brought down by rebel anti-aircraft guns.

OFFER TO CITIZENS

Yesterday morning before the attack began the Government delivered a message to the inhabitants and troops of Teruel stating that civilians would be allowed to leave the city before nine o'clock in the morning and the lives of soldiers who laid down their arms before that time would be spared.

Rebel headquarters at Salamanca admit that attacks have been made in the Teruel sector but declare that they have been unsuccessful. A rebel communiqué states that the dead among the Government forces numbered over 2,000.

It is certain, however, that the Government's attack in the Teruel sector came as a great surprise to the rebels, and people arriving at Gibraltar from Seville affirm that preparations for a rebel offensive are now at a standstill. It is generally believed that a new plan is being devised as a result of the vigorous Government attacks.

The Republican attack on Teruel was intended to disrupt Franco's plans for a rebel offensive against Guadalajara. It not only served that purpose but had the added advantage of shortening the Republic's lines of communication between New Castile and Aragon.

REBELS HOLD OUT AT TERUEL
Fighting in Blinding Snowstorms

The rebels are holding out at Teruel, but they are hard pressed.

A message from St. Jean de Luz last night emphasised the good organisation of the offensive, the best ever achieved by the Government forces. The surprise was complete: the attack was launched in the darkness with the support of groups of tanks that completely encircled the rebel advance posts.

The surrounding hills were first occupied and then the villages of Concud and Villastar. From Concud the road to Saragossa was cut, and the advance continued from Villastar and from Rubiales.

The narrow passage between the town and the rebel rearguard along the banks of the Guadalaviar still remains open, although the fighting line had last night been pushed forward into the outskirts of the town.

The defence is made easier to a certain extent because Teruel stands on a hill. The blinding snow and rain storms are impeding the work of the artillery, and the defenders are using automatic arms. As a result there is bitter fighting and great bloodshed. The attacking Government troops are estimated at some 30,000, with a great quantity of material, states Reuter.

APPEAL TO SURRENDER

A Spanish Press Agency message from Madrid states that Republican aircraft yesterday scattered over Teruel pamphlets stating, 'Our troops dominate your city completely,' and inviting the defender to surrender. The Government, it was stated,

guarantees you your liberty, your independence, and your lives. Do not listen to the promises of great reinforcements which are being made to you. They will not arrive ... Lay down your arms, all of you – soldiers, chiefs, officers, – and thus render a great service to Spain, to our Spain free from invaders, without Germans, without Italians.

If you do not do so you will be crushed and conquered – for Spain and for the Republic. Do not shed in your resistance useless blood.

BARCELONA BOMBED

Barcelona was heavily bombed late on Sunday night and again yesterday morning. There were many victims, though the number is not known, in Sunday's raid, during which two hospitals were hit. Yesterday eight people were killed and thirty wounded.

Port Bou, on the Franco-Spanish frontier, was bombed twice early yesterday. Twenty bombs were dropped in the first raid and ten of a heavier type in the second. No damage was done to the railway.

Monday January 3 1938

BATTLE FOR TERUEL AMIDST BLINDING SNOW
Fate of the City Still Undecided

DESPERATE FIGHTING FOR KEY HILL
49 Killed in Barcelona Air Raid

The rebels now seem to have abandoned the claim that their relief forces are in Teruel. But outside the city the position is still obscure; nothing is known with certainty except that the fighting goes on.

In blinding snow, in intense cold, with enormous losses, the fighting goes on.

Last night the battle was being fought desperately for the Muela de Teruel (in English, the 'Tooth of Teruel'), the great plateau that lies south-west of the city and dominates it. Reports of the way in which the fighting is going contradict each other. Barcelona says that the Government troops are holding their ground in this part of the front; rebel sources claim that the loyalists have been pushed back to the main road leading east from the city.

EFFORTS 'TO REACH' THE CITY

The Government communiqué on yesterday's operations, received early this morning, reported that fighting had continued without a break along the whole front, and added: 'The results were frankly favourable to the Government forces.'

Up to an early hour this morning there had been no official rebel communiqué. But there was a phrase in a Havas correspondent's message from Saragossa, the rebel headquarters, that revealed that the rebels were not in Teruel, at least on Saturday. He declared that the heavy falls of snow were 'seriously impeding rebel efforts to reach the city'. On Saturday Salamanca had claimed that the rebel relief had made contact with the besieged garrison as early as Friday afternoon 'amid scenes of the greatest enthusiasm'.

Last night, however, it was again reported, by way of Lisbon, that the city had been entered at three points.

The official Barcelona communiqué on Saturday's fighting, received yesterday, was less vague than statements from the Government side have been of late, while the latest Salamanca communiqué was in the most general terms. The Government communiqué read:

On the Aragon front the enemy this morning (Saturday) continued their offensive from two directions, using many aeroplanes and a strong force of artillery.

In the plain we were obliged to abandon Concud, but our infantry reformed on the old positions held by the enemy outside near-by villages. All attempts by the enemy on this line failed.

South of the Muela de Teruel the enemy made an attack in the direction of Hill 1076. We abandoned this position early in the afternoon, but retook it to-night after a vigorous counter-attack.

We then warded off all enemy attacks and repulsed all attempts at infiltration into Teruel.

The Salamanca communiqué merely said:

In spite of the storm raging on the Teruel front the pursuit of the enemy continued to-day (Saturday). The Reds suffered enormous losses.

100 CASUALTIES IN BARCELONA

Forty-nine persons were killed and 50 wounded in a rebel air raid on Barcelona on Saturday night, according to official figures issued yesterday. Three three-engined 'planes coming from the direction of Majorca carried out the raid, dropping bombs on the centre of the city. No military objectives were hit.

STRENGTH OF GOVERNMENT FORCES IN SPAIN
Franco's Small Chance of Military Victory

POSSIBILITY OF WINNING BY PEACEFUL METHODS

From our Diplomatic Correspondent
London, Tuesday.

The progress of the fighting around Teruel confirms the impression that was made here by the capture of the town by the Government forces. That the preparations for the loyalist offensive could have been kept secret showed a great improvement in discipline and organisation: that the main objective could have been reached showed that the Army had far greater striking power than had been generally assumed, and that the objective can in the main be held by loyalist forces with very little foreign aid against the rebels, who not only have German and Italian aid but great superiority in armaments and also reinforcements from the former Asturian front – all this shows that the Government's Army is formidable.

It is, of course, possible that Teruel will be retaken by the rebels, but even now the attempt has meant days of desperate fighting with heavy losses. The Teruel area is a minute fraction of the whole war zone, and if a minor gain like that can only be made at such a heavy cost, an advance on all fronts, or even on one broad front, would seem quite unattainable by General Franco.

FRANCO'S SURPRISING DELAYS

The view has now become almost general here that if the loyalists can go on feeding their population General Franco cannot win the war. Some observers, who are friendly to him, think he would be well advised to abandon offensive operations altogether. Their reasons are briefly as follows:–

General Franco has missed his last chance of inflicting decisive defeat on the loyalists in battle through his delay in advancing on the Aragon front with reinforcements that could have been rushed up from the Asturias in the late autumn. The organisation of the loyalist army was not as good then as it is now, and the Government had far less authority, was threatened by internal political divisions, and was pervaded with pessimism.

Indeed, to some observers the failure of General Franco

191

to advance on Barcelona in the late autumn is as incomprehensible as his failure to enter Madrid over a year ago when, for a few days, nothing stood in his way.

THE WEAPON OF HUNGER

His principal weapon now is hunger. If he just holds his fronts and reverts to peace-time conditions behind the lines, cutting down military expenditure, encouraging normal trade, restoring some slight measure of political freedom, and carrying out social reforms – then, so some observers argue, he will in the end prevail. The loyalists cannot revert to normal conditions because they cannot, as long as Franco holds the main agricultural areas, feed their population adequately, even if they can go on with the war for some considerable time, perhaps for years.

By offensive operations, so it is argued, General Franco can gain nothing and will suffer far heavier losses in men and material than the loyalists. He will increase his own difficulties without greatly increasing theirs. But, so it is thought, a peaceful, normal, and well-fed Spain is bound in the end to triumph over a revolutionary, abnormal, undernourished Spain.

But it would seem that General Franco himself still hopes for decisive military victory. It will, no doubt, be difficult for him, in view of his constant assurances of an early and final triumph, to give up hope of winning on the battlefields. But it must be said that this hope does not seem to be shared nearly as widely as it was by those of his sympathisers who have any objective judgment.

Saturday January 8 1938   *p.17*

1,500 SURRENDER AT TERUEL
Rebel Commander's Decision

ITALIANS APPEAR

Barcelona, January 7.

Colonel Rey Dancourt, who was the rebel military commander at Teruel, has surrendered with 1,500 men, it is claimed here. The Colonel is reported to have said that a small group of rebels remained in the Convent of Santa Clara, with whom he had been out of touch. His surrender would seem to mean that only a handful of rebels are now putting up resistance in the city.

Outside the city the battle still continues with unabated

fury. The rebels are daily massing new troops in order to recapture the city. These troops are being withdrawn from other fronts.

The Republican Command declares that the rebels outside Teruel to-day employed the famous Italian 'Black Arrows' for the first time on this front.

FIERCEST DAY

Throughout yesterday, which saw the fiercest fighting since the rebel counter-offensive began, the rebels made repeated attacks from the village of Concud, north-west of Teruel. Preceded by intense artillery and aviation bombardments these attacks were supported by tanks and armoured-cars. The Republican infantry, it is claimed here, not only maintained their positions but forced the attackers to retire with heavy losses.

In the Muela de Teruel sector the Republicans took the offensive and occupied several positions, which they held under fire, on the Villastar–Teruel road.

The rebel Army is considered here a spent and weary force. During the last eight days it has suffered several setbacks and enormous casualties. It is felt that the rebel determination to recover Teruel is dictated by the knowledge that its presence in the hands of the Government must completely upset plans for any offensive on other fronts.

Monday January 10 1938   *p.12*

GROWTH OF REPUBLICAN WAR MACHINE
Ex-Premier Interviewed on Teruel

From a Barcelona Correspondent

With the taking of Teruel the year 1938 begins auspiciously for the Spanish Republic and the war enters a new phase. The victory at Teruel was made possible not only by the development of the new Republican army but also by the reorganisation behind the lines. Indeed, it may almost be said that the most important military factor is the building, now almost completed, of the new Government machine, which will profoundly influence the course of the war in the new year.

In these circumstances an interview given to the writer by Senor Portela Valladares, who was Prime Minister during the 1936 elections, is of particular interest in that his views are those of an experienced observer who, since he has taken no part in any of the war Governments, has been able to form an independent judgment.

STRENGTH OF NEW ARMY

Asked to what he attributed the fall of Teruel, Senor Portela said:

My opinion is that the Republican army is stronger than the rebel army. I said this three months ago, and now the capture of Teruel has proved it to the world. The northern front collapsed because it was technically impossible to defend, because it lacked unity of command, and because it was geographically inaccessible. In spite of his 80,000 Italians and 10,000 Germans, in spite of all the supplies provided by these two great nations, Franco is now being defeated because he has aroused the spirit of independence in the Spanish people.

Ten thousand officers are graduating from the Republican academies each year. War production has been organised. The Republican command, which contains 6,000 officers belonging to the former Spanish army, has growing intelligence and technical services. But nothing is more tremendous than the spirit of resistance which has withstood all defeats. The war of the Republic is only now beginning.

The Negrin Government has restored order in Republican Spain to such a degree that the percentage of crimes is lower than ever before. It has instituted full and normal constitutional law and respect for this law.

KIND OF PEACE SOUGHT

Expression of opinion in the press is even allowed a scope that I consider excessive in time of war. The leaders of Spanish public opinion surely ought all to realise the necessity of giving Spain a Westphalian peace as far as religion is concerned, a political peace based on the existing Constitution, and a social peace which consolidates the genuine advances made up to the present time.

On the rebel side a national syndicalism has been built up which, according to its official programme, is much more damaging to property and a greater menace to capitalism. And cruelty and barbarism have reached limits hitherto unknown.

On February 17, 1936, in view of the victory of the People's Front, the Right wing leaders came to me and begged me to become Dictator, and that very day General Franco offered me the Dictatorship for myself personally. Again, on

194

the 19th. Franco and the others insisted on this. I refused: and agreed to resign, so as to hand over the government to the People's Front. The Right wing leaders had remained in Parliament until the civil war: they collaborated in the working of that Parliament, and thus acknowledged the validity of its power.

Tuesday January 11 1938   *p.9*

FRANCO'S NON-SUCCESS IN SPITE OF MORE FOREIGN HELP
Fascist States Send 'Planes & Specialists

LOYALISTS RELYING ON THEIR OWN EFFORTS
German Propaganda at Bilbao

From our Diplomatic Correspondent

London, Monday.

More importance than ever is attached to the battle of Teruel now that the loyalist victory stands. The civil war has not been regarded here as a struggle between two parties in Spain as much as an attempt on the part of Germany and Italy to secure a foothold in the Western Mediterranean. The battle of Teruel is interpreted as a distinct check to that effort. Indeed, some observers, who are by no means 'pro-loyalists', are inclined to attribute historical importance to the battle and refer to it as 'a kind of Verdun'.

The battle has certainly influenced opinion here in favour of the loyalists. Their military efficiency has been demonstrated, and all the available evidence would seem to show that it is growing. Nor are they under the influence of political 'extremism' any longer, so that there can be no question of any decisive Communist or Russian influence in loyalist Spain, while the influence of Germany and Italy on the rebel side is as great as ever.

MORE INTERVENTION

There is no sign of an end to the war, and it is possible that German and Italian intervention will now increase. It is not believed here that Germany and Italy mean to relax their effort in Spain. It is true that Italian infantry have been withdrawn in considerable numbers, but supplies of war material, as well as pilots, artillerymen, engineers, and other specialists, continue to reach the rebels. German military aeroplanes arrive after non-stop flights. They leave Germany immediately after dark, pass over the Swiss Jura, and, at great heights, over Southern France, crossing the Pyrenees at various points. Whenever attempts are made to get into wireless communication with them they immediately put out their lights.

THE GERMANS AT BILBAO

The Germans are making a special effort to strengthen their political and economic position in Bilbao. They are investing capital in Bilbao industries partly with a view to counteracting British commercial influence. They have started a vigorous pro-German propagandist campaign, using the German Consulate at Bilbao as a base. Nazi pamphlets in Spanish are being circulated all over loyalist territory, courses in the German language that have a pronounced political tendency are being encouraged in Bilbao, and Nazi propagandist films (such as 'The Triumph of the Will') are being shown in the picture-theatres.

The Italian effort is similar, though perhaps less successful, for the Italians are on the whole more unpopular than the Germans, chiefly, it would seem, because they are more numerous and because they have been much more forward than the Germans in claiming to be the 'saviours' of Spain – a claim that has given some offence, especially as there is a feeling amongst the rebels that Spain has not been 'saved' as yet.

There is a good deal of pessimism among both the Germans and the Italians. Both are dissatisfied with the course of the war. That the year 1937 should have come to an end without bringing victory any nearer is a source of keen disappointment to them.

REBEL DISUNITY

Unlike the loyalists, who have created a powerful unity in their own ranks, political disunity continues amongst the rebels. The conflict between Franco and the Falange (the large Nationalist propaganda body with Fascist ideas) has disappeared from the surface, but it goes on nevertheless. German and Italian observers attribute the defective prosecution of the war by the rebels to their internal dissensions. There is considerable uneasiness on this account amongst the German and Italian officers; nor do they anticipate any improvement in the near future.

Prices are rising steeply in rebel Spain, and the resulting popular discontent helps to increase the following of the Falange.

CONTRIBUTION TO SECURITY

From the purely British point of view the battle of Teruel and the growing military strength of the loyalists are, of course, welcomed, for they at least postpone, and perhaps even avert, the necessity of taking action which, it is considered, would have become necessary if Germany and Italy established themselves in Spain in a way that might threaten to become permanent.

German and Italian foothold in Spain would mean a weakening of the British strategic position in the Mediterranean at a time when naval forces now in the Mediterranean may be needed elsewhere (in the Fast East, for example).

Generally speaking, the battle of Teruel is regarded here as a contribution to the security of Western Europe even by observers who would, if British vital interests were not affected, feel a natural sympathy for the rebel cause.

Tuesday January 18 1938   *p.12*

FIGHTING AGAIN FOR TERUEL
New Rebel Push

LOYALISTS GIVE GROUND

Saragossa, January 17.

As a result of a new push to-day on the Teruel front the rebels claim to have captured two important positions never previously held by them.

The first position taken was a hill near Celadas, three miles due north of Teruel. The rebels then pressed on to the south-south-east, taken El Muleton, another hill a mile farther on. Rebel aircraft claim to have brought down twelve Republican machines to-day.–Press Association Foreign Special.

GOVERNMENT ADMISSION

Barcelona, January 17.

The Ministry of Defence issued a communiqué to-day stating that the enemy, after a period of inactivity caused by the great losses suffered in the course of the first attempt to retake Teruel, resumed an offensive movement towards that city this morning. A strong attack was made towards the heights of Celadas, supported by intense artillery fire and a large mass of aircraft. The defence lines were slightly altered.

Loyalist squadrons engaged in a battle with a large number of rebel 'planes. Five enemy 'planes were shot down and two pursuit 'planes were lost by the defender.–Spanish Press Agency.

Tuesday February 1 1938   *p.12*

REBEL SPAIN
Franco's New Form of Government

BUT NOT FINAL

Hendaye, January 31.

General Franco's new Constitution for rebel Spain, announced in a decree to-day, does not commit 'The New Spain' either to a monarchy or to a Republic, according to telegrams from Salamanca.

Article 16 lays down that 'the Presidency of the Ministry (i.e. the Prime Ministership) is coincident with the Chief of State'. This is held by General Franco himself. The same article states that the Ministers in Council with the Chief of State constitute the Government of the nation.

In the preamble to the decree it is explained that the new arrangement is 'without prejudice to any ultimate form of Government'. The preamble also says that the organisation of the new Spanish State will be 'subject to the constant influence of the national movement'.

Under the Constitution General Franco will have dictatorial powers. It stated that the president, as Chief of State, has supreme power to determine the general lines of procedure. He will issue decrees after consulting the Cabinet, and they will have the force of law. Among the list of functions of the Minister of Foreign Affairs special mention is made of 'relations with the Holy See'.

Article seven, which sets up the new Ministry of National Defence reserved to General Franco supreme command of the armed forces.–Press Association Foreign Special.

FRANCO CALLS UP BOYS OF 18
2 Years Before Time

San Sebastian, January 31.

General Franco has called to the colours men born in the first quarter of 1919. These men are not normally due for military service until 1940. The total number involved is not known.

All men in rebel Spain between the ages of 18 and 21 are now serving with the colours.–Reuter.

Wednesday February 23 1938   *p.6*

RETURN TO TERUEL'S RUINS
Republicans Fight Their Way Out Through Rebel Lines

NEW STAND BEING TAKEN TO SOUTH

The rebels who abandoned Teruel at the end of December regained it completely yesterday. At eight o'clock in the morning, after eight days of bitter fighting, General Franco's forces were back in the ruins of the town.

The Republican Ministry of National Defence in Barcelona yesterday afternoon officially admitted the evacuation of the city by its defenders, states Reuter. The announcement was based on a telegram received by the Ministry from the General Officer Commanding the Army of the Levant (North-east Spain) which read:

As Teruel was completely surrounded by the rebels, the G.O.C. 40th Division, carrying out orders received, collected his forces, and forming an attack column broke through and left the city with all his troops and war materials.

Neither men, arms, munitions, nor food were left behind in Teruel.

Having broken through, the column joined the Republican forces outside Teruel and with them launched a strong counter-attack against the enemy. They are reported to have re-formed their line along the road to Valencia a short distance south of Teruel. This they intend to hold at all costs.

The plateau the Government holds is an important position and is a natural starting-place for a rebel push to the coast towards Valencia.

Reports of the last stages of the advance on Teruel and its final re-occupation received from rebel sources told of tremendous artillery and aerial bombardments, cavalry charges, street fighting, and the capture of quantities of supplies and prisoners.

Street fighting lasted for two hours after the occupation of Teruel yesterday morning, it was reported. One report claimed that 2,600 prisoners had been taken, as well as a large quantity of war material, including machine-guns, rifles, mortars and munitions.

CLAIM OF 5,300 PRISONERS

St. Jean de Luz, February 22.

The rebel press bureau at St. Jean de Luz late to-night sent Reuter a special report to say that following a partial occupation of Teruel at 9 a.m. to-day two Galicean divisions under General Aranda marched into the town at one o'clock this afternoon.

'All conditions proposed by the deputation of the defenders were refused at midday,' the report adds, 'and 4,600 men laid down their arms unconditionally, though it is believed that many militia men are still hiding in the cellars, caves, and underground passages which honeycomb the city.

'More than 900 machine-guns and 7,000,000 rounds of ammunition have already been found, but it will be days before all the booty captured can be checked.

'The important fact would seem to be not so much the recapture of Teruel itself as the rout and demoralisation of the whole Republican Army on the Southern Aragon front.'

A later message says that the number of prisoners at 4 p.m. had risen to 5,300.–Press Association Foreign Special.

Monday February 28 1938   *p.6*

CONFIDENCE IN VICTORY
Dr. Negrin Broadcasts

Barcelona, February 27.

Dr. Negrin Premier of Spain, declared in a broadcast speech last night that production of armaments was to be increased and 'ultimate victory was assured'.

'The loss of Teruel', he declared, 'was an episode of the war brought about by the enormous quantity of arms and men sent to the assistance of Franco by Italy and Germany. We need the aid of no one. With the men, material, and ideals at our disposal we are certain of ultimate victory, which has been so long postponed. The delay in victory is due solely to the intervention of foreign Powers and the injustice of the Non-Intervention Committee which hinders our purchase of armaments.

'We believe that German and Italian superiority in armaments will not last long and that the Spanish Government with its resources will supply the Republican Army with all the aeroplanes and war material which are required, superior to the Fascists. The Spanish people have shown in history what they are capable of when their country and liberties are in danger and at stake. The country of so much suffering and of so great morale will win in the long run.

'An international adventurer has proclaimed to the world that he will conquer our country, but he will never succeed in his ambitions.'–Reuter.

Wednesday March 2 1938

RUSSIA AGREES TO PLAN FOR WITHDRAWAL FROM SPAIN
First Hint of Details of the Scheme

From our London Correspondent

Fleet Street, Tuesday.

The Russian Ambassador called to-day on Lord Plymouth to say that his Government accepted in principle the British formula on the proportion of foreign 'volunteers' to be withdrawn from Spain, agreeing to the initial figure of 20,000 men mentioned in the formula on which the proportionate withdrawals would be based as a 'substantial withdrawal', Italy and Germany agreed last week to the formula, but without committing themselves to any initial number as the basis of withdrawal. This initial number is important, for without agreement there it will be possible and even easy for Italy to continue her delaying tactics, which have held up the deciding operations in the Spanish Non-Intervention Committee for over a year. The formula has never been officially published, but it is known that 20,000 volunteers is the number mentioned as the basis for withdrawal in this way.

It is proposed that when the Commission (which under the plan the Non-Intervention Committee would send out) has reached its conclusion as to the numbers of volunteers on each side, it should then decree which has the smaller number. From that side 20,000 should be sent back, while the other side, with the larger number, should send back the same proportion of its total as the 20,000 is of the total volunteers in the lesser force. For instance, if the Government side has 40,000 volunteers it sends back 20,000 – that is, 50 per cent – and on that basis if the rebel side had 100,000 it would send back 50,000. The formula also lays down how the withdrawals should be made in order to include all units of the forces.

It can easily be understood that good faith is essential to the carrying out of the scheme, and that until the initial number is accepted hopes cannot be built upon it. The suspicion that Italy may begin again with her old tactics and put forward a basis of 5,000 as 'substantial withdrawal', however, can easily be allayed by the Italian Ambassador's making his declaration on the point as the other representatives have done.

No date has yet been fixed for the next meeting of the Non-Intervention Committee.

BELCHITE FALLS
Rebel Success in Aragon

Belchite has fallen to the rebels. It was taken from them in a successful Government offensive in the autumn, but the rebels claim that in their present offensive nearly all the ground then lost has been regained.

According to a Salamanca communiqué the rebel advance, which covers a front some 50 miles long, has been 'carried to a great depth'. Troops on the left front are reported to have followed the capture of Belchite with the taking of several villages. Gains are also claimed for rebel forces in the centre and on the right front.

The communiqué states that 'terrific' casualties have been inflicted on the Republicans and that over 3,500 prisoners and 'enormous' quantities of war material have been taken.

It is reported that Belchite was defended mainly by soldiers of the International Brigade, the majority of whom were Canadians. About 100 foreign prisoners have been taken. The centre of three columns used for the offensive was at first delayed through having to encircle a hill held by the Republicans, but caught up with the other columns on Thursday, partly through a spectacular cavalry charge which General Franco personally watched.

Extending the front of their offensive, rebel troops yesterday started a push down from the Ebro River valley from the village of Fuentes de Ebro.

The Republican communiqué states: 'We took a large number of prisoners, many of whom were Italians belonging to Italian divisions taking part in the offensive. Aerial activity was very great. Two battles took place. The enemy lost three two-engined 'planes, and we also brought down two Messer Schmidt fighters and two Fiats.'

In addition to retaking territory lost to the Republic in the previous autumn, the Nationalists' success at Belchite gave them a springboard from which to launch an offensive against Catalonia.

Wednesday March 16 1938   *p.11*

FASCIST POWERS REDOUBLE THEIR EFFORTS IN SPAIN
Arms Sent in Vast Quantities

FRANCO DRIVING TOWARDS THE MEDITERRANEAN COAST
Imminent Danger to Catalonia

The Spanish rebels are only fifteen miles from the Catalan border and still advancing. In a straight line they are some forty miles from the Mediterranean coast, threatening to cut Government territory in two between Valencia and Barcelona.

With Italian and German assistance the rebels are immensely superior in the air and in their artillery, and their rate of advance seems to be controlled only by the rate at which they can keep a barrage of shells ahead of them. Government resistance is slight, though the Minister of Defence promises that the rebel offensive 'will be checked within 48 hours'.

A French cruiser, a destroyer, and a torpedo-boat are on their way to Barcelona to protect French nationals, it is learned in Paris.

MORE GERMANS?

The Spanish Embassy in London announced last night that the Spanish Foreign Office has received information that 'thirty thousand Storm Troops with their officers, specially trained in infantry and artillery technique by Reichswehr experts, left Germany for Spain on Monday in German ships'.

In Berlin last night the allegation was described as nonsense.

There were rumours yesterday, strongly denied from Barcelona, that the Catalan Government was seeking peace with the rebels, and last night it was reported in Paris that the Spanish Government was seeking the assistance of other Powers in arranging an armistice.

A Reuter message from Toulouse received at two o'clock this morning stated that Senor Azana, the Spanish President, and Senor Prieto, Minister of Defence, were due to arrive at Toulouse by air 'at any moment'.

A British steamer was bombed by rebel 'planes in Tarragona Harbour yesterday. Two members of the crew were killed and four were injured. The non-intervention observer on board was also wounded.

p.11

WHY THE REBELS ARE WINNING
Formidable Intervention by the Fascist Powers

From our Diplomatic Correspondent

London, Tuesday.

The gravest possible view is taken here of the Spanish situation. The impending defeat of loyalist Spain has been announced so often that there is some reluctance in regarding it as imminent now. But it must certainly be considered possible.

Hitherto either side in the civil war could hold up the offensive of the other because there has all along been insufficient weight of metal to overcome the rifle and the machine-gun in a terrain so difficult as the Spanish. It was impossible to produce anything at all like the barrages of the Great War. But this has now been achieved by the rebels.

Their superiority in light and heavy guns and in bombing and fighter 'planes is now so enormous that they can produce the equivalent of a creeping barrage of shells and bombs on fairly wide sectors. A hail of metal descends on the advanced positions of the Loyalists, and having smashed the defences and annihilated the defenders passes on to the second line. Against this fire the Loyalist infantry are helpless.

ITALY'S NEW INTERVENTION

A new form of 'intervention' has made this possible. Italian aeroplanes arrive for each rebel thrust, take part in the operations, and then return to Italy. General Franco and his staff have only to state what they need and the needs are supplied.

New German aeroplanes are also present in considerable numbers. They are far superior to the Junker and Heinkel 'planes that took part in the earlier operations. The Russian 'planes serving with the loyalist forces are now wholly outclassed.

Counter-attack in the air and reprisals are almost impossible, for even if loyalist 'planes elude the rebel fighter 'planes they are kept so high by the rebel anti-aircraft artillery (which is mostly Germany) that they are quite unable to hit their targets. The loyalists, on the other hand, are at the mercy of rebel air raids.

The rebels are chiefly advancing along the valley of the Ebro, which offers them the most favourable terrain. But the natural obstacles that still lie between them and the coast are great, and it is possible that the offensive will be held up in two or three days by the ravines and mountain ranges.

SUPREME CRISIS?

The implications of this crisis – which may be the supreme crisis – in the Spanish civil war are very grave in any case.

The question of the 'volunteers' has now become meaningless. Italian and German intervention is now more formidable than it has been at any time and would remain almost unaffected by the withdrawal of 'volunteers'.

The Anglo-Italian conversations are now being resumed. So far the results have been scanty. Italy demands that the British Government recognise Abyssinia directly and not through the League of Nations. She professes to regard the presence of a large army in Libya as a result of tension in the Mediterranean, and makes the withdrawal of unspecified numbers of Italian troops from Libya contingent on a Mediterranean agreement, although she is still reinforcing her Libyan army and is constructing barracks and fortified positions which leave no doubt that she means to maintain a large and permanent Libyan army.

ITALIAN ATTITUDE

As for the Spanish problems, it is, according to the Italian thesis, being adequately dealt with by the Committee of Non-Intervention.

The precise relations between Italy and Germany are still obscure, but the point is rapidly being reached when both the British and the French Governments will be compelled to adapt their own policies to a European situation which has been transformed by the conquest of Austria, by the crisis in the Spanish 'v' [sic] war, and by German-Italian relations which seem to have been made closer by the conquest of Austria.

That conquest cannot be agreeable to Italy, but it is irremediable and removes the main conflict between German and Italian vital interests.

IMPORTANCE OF SPAIN

Without a Spanish settlement there can be no Anglo-Italian settlement that is not a sham. Final judgement on the conversations in Rome must be suspended, for they are still in their beginnings. But the crisis in the Spanish civil war would seem to be robbing them of whatever meaning they may have had.

Time is now on the side of Italy and Germany. By gaining time Italy and Germany may hope to win the civil war. Their victory, coming as it would close on the prodigious German victory in Central Europe, would be of the greatest importance in promoting the plans for a German hegemony east of the Rhine and an Italian hegemony in the Mediterranean. The balance of power, strongly tipped against the western Powers by the German conquest of Austria, and the German-Hungarian Entente, which is certainly impending whether the Hungarians fancy it or not, will be made even more unfavourable by the direct menace to French and British vital interests in the Mediterranean and Eastern Atlantic.

Decisions that may determine the future of Europe and the status of this country and France as Great Powers have become a matter of immediate urgency: it will be noted that Mr. Chamberlain in his statement, to the House of Commons yesterday, said that we must consider the new situation 'quickly'. It is coming to be realised that the transition from a passive to an active foreign policy cannot be delayed much longer.

Friday March 18 1938   *p.11*

EIGHT HUNDRED KILLED AND A THOUSAND WOUNDED
Homeless Flee Into the Country

Barcelona, March 17.

Barcelona to-night is a city distracted. From late last night to late to-night it has been bombed by rebel 'planes.

According to a conservative estimate the death-roll is 800, and the number of injured is placed at over a thousand.

The first air raid began at ten o'clock last night and lasted intermittently until two o'clock this morning. Then there was a respite for a few hours until 7.45 this morning. This was the worst raid of the day: the early figures showed 126 dead and 100 wounded.

Another raid came at half-past ten, another at two o'clock. To-night it looked as though the programme was being repeated, for after ten o'clock the rebel 'planes appeared again.

All the 'planes came from the direction of Palma, Majorca. Flying at a height of about 25,000ft. over the centre of the city, they bombed indiscriminately.

Whole blocks of modern apartment buildings have been demolished. In the ruins still lie scores of mangled bodies – men, women, and children.

The buildings were set on fire by incendiary bombs, and to-night the city lies beneath clouds of smoke.

The streets are thick with broken glass. Not a house or a shop in the centre of the city has its windows intact.

The streets surrounding one block of apartments hit by bombs were littered with shattered glass that crunched under one's boots like hard snow.

All vehicles, including British and American, have been commandeered for rescue work.

Trying to escape the ghastly scene homeless families carrying little bundles, all that is left of their possessions, are trailing out into the countryside.–Reuter, Exchange, Spanish Press Agency.

24,000 ITALIANS IN ARAGON

A Press Association correspondent who has been with the Spanish rebels last night sent an uncensored message from Hendaye, on the Franco-Spanish frontier, giving details of the foreign troops taking part in General Franco's present offensive on the Aragon front.

He found that the centre column which took Alcaniz contained two complete divisions of Italian 'volunteers', numbering about 12,000 men each. In addition there is a mixed division of the Foreign Legion – Blue and Black Arrows – in which 90 per cent of the men and probably a slightly lower percentage of the officers are Spanish. This column is supported by the first Navarre Brigade under General Garcia Vilino.

The northern column under General Yague, is composed of Spanish regiments-of-the-line and Moroccan regiments. The latter consist partly but by no means exclusively of Moors. The southern column, under General Aranda, is entirely Spanish and is composed mainly of Galicians. The rebels probably have a total of about 180,000 men of all nationalities in the field.

There are no Germans fighting apart from those engaged

in artillery and air activities. The Germans deal with technical problems, engineering, transport, and communications.

Private inquiries at Pasajes, on the north coast of Spain, indicate that it is untrue that any foreign troops have landed there recently.

A different version, in that it omits to mention the Italians, was given yesterday by the rebels themselves from Burgos.

There it was officially stated that the forces operating on the Aragon front were made up of divisions of Spanish troops from Navarre, Galicia, and Castille. The troops known as the Moorish Army Corps were not all Moors and included the 5th Division Navarre and sections of Requetes and Phalanx and National Militia. The divisions of the Legion known as 'Blue and Black Arrows' were stated to be 90 per cent Spaniards.

Speaking in the Italian Chamber of Deputies General Valle, the Under Secretary for Air, said it was no exaggeration to say that most of the victories on the north front in Spain had been due to Italian aviation. Recently the commander-in-chief of the Nationalist Air Forces in Spain had published an order of the day stating that 75 per cent of the victory at Teruel had been won by the Italians.–Reuter and Exchange.

BRITAIN AND FRANCE PROTEST TO FRANCO
Horror at Barcelona Bombings

USE OF GERMAN AND ITALIAN 'PLANES
Paris Sends Evidence to London

The British and French Governments have jointly sent a strong protest to General Franco against the recent bombings of Barcelona. The French Government has also sent a separate appeal to the rebels asking to stop such bombardments, and is approaching the Vatican for its support in an Anglo-French move to get the bombing of civilians in Spain stopped altogether.

The rebels defend the raids as being directed at military objectives. Barcelona had a respite over the week-end, but a number of coastal villages were bombed.

LETTERS TO THE EDITOR

REBEL BOMBING OF CIVILIANS
Senor del Vayo's Appeal

To the Editor of the 'Manchester Guardian'

I am sure that the whole of Great Britain will have shuddered with horror on reading the news of the most recent bombardments of Barcelona.

But I can assure you, after having visited the entire city in which two thousand people have been killed and an equal number wounded, that the most terrible predictions of the coming aerial warfare have been converted here into the most abominable reality.

The Spanish people turn towards Great Britain and ask you to raise your voice against the extermination of the civilian population of Barcelona and against a policy which prevents the Spanish Government from acquiring the means necessary to defend itself from this murder of more than a thousand women and children in a single day.

ALVAREZ DEL VAYO,
(former Spanish Foreign Minister).

Tuesday March 22 1938   *p.11*

THE BOMBING OF BARCELONA
American Horror

MR. CORDELL HULL'S APPEAL

From our own Correspondent

New York, March 21.

The Secretary of State. Mr. Cordell Hull, undoubtedly spoke, as he said, for the whole American people when to-day he vigorously protested against the bombing of Barcelona by Franco's aeroplanes. The 'sense of horror' which he said he shared with other Americans had been demonstrated in hundreds of ways by all sorts of people in the past few days.

No formal action will be taken in the sense of a Note to Franco in view of the fact that the United States Government's opinion is already on record in this matter, but Mr. Hull's vigorous language left no doubt that this country considers the bombing of non-combatants inhuman and unjustified.

FRANCO EXPLAINS
'Strictly Military Objectives'

General Franco's regret for the 'victims caused amongst the civilian population', and his censure of the Republican authorities for 'violating all the laws of humanity and warfare', are contained in the following message from Salamanca issued by Spanish Press Services Limited:–

The air raids carried out by the 'Nationalist' air force on military objectives in Barcelona have been reported with notorious mendacity by the 'Red' press and part of the foreign press, too. The 'Nationalist' air force has sought only to destroy strictly military objectives.

'Red' barbarity has converted the district situated in the centre of towns into huge stores of explosives and war material. 'Red' propaganda states that some of the 'Nationalist' bombs fell in the Cataluna Square, on the underground station of the Metro, and the main northern railway station.

It omitted to say, however, that these two points had been converted into huge munition dumps, a fact which is proved by the several explosions which took place after the falling of the bombs. These explosions caused the collapse of several buildings such as the Barcelona Theatre and others in the Cataluna Square.

We regret the victims caused amongst the civilian population, but responsibility for these rests with the 'Red' authorities who, violating all the laws of humanity and warfare, have placed huge powder dumps in the middle of large cities.

(The Hague air war rules, which though not binding on any nation, form the standard for air warfare, declare that if military objectives cannot be bombarded 'without the indiscriminate bombardment of the civil population, the aircraft must abstain from bombardment.')

THIRD REBEL OFFENSIVE BEGUN IN ARAGON
Italians Boast of Their Share

SPANISH NOTE TO BRITAIN ON THE LATEST FOREIGN HELP

A third offensive in Aragon was begun by General Franco yesterday and the rebels succeeded in crossing the Ebro.

They recently captured the territory along the south bank of the Ebro from Saragossa to Caspe. On Tuesday they began a new thrust in the region of Huesca, and the latest action is apparently aimed at trapping the Government forces in the Huesca–Saragossa–Pina triangle.

A Press Association correspondent reports from Saragossa that the rebels attacking the Quinto sector crossed the Ebro by means of pontoons. The attackers are now striking north-east into Government territory. The Government forces put up a powerful resistance, machine-gunning the pontoons. Their defence was eventually broken by artillery and 'planes, and the rebel infantry began to pour across the river.

The advance continued with astonishing rapidity, and from the south bank it was possible to see the rebel banner waving from hill after hill as the troops moved forward. The Government troops retired eastwards, their artillery almost silent and their aviation out of action.

For the first time in the war the rebels yesterday used a smoke-screen to cover their advance.

Around Huesca the rebels claim to have advanced six miles in two directions. North of the city the Republicans admit the loss of Lierta and they also admit a 'slight retreat' near Almudevar. In this sector the rebel claims are vague.

SPANISH NOTE

The Spanish Embassy in London yesterday sent a Note to the Foreign Office giving information of the Italian and German share in the rebel offensive on the Aragon front.

The Spanish Ambassador also called on Sir Alexander Cadogan, Permanent Under Secretary of State for Foreign Affairs, and stressed the importance which the Spanish Government attributed to the dispatch by Germany and Italy of large quantities of war material, aeroplanes, and men for this offensive. He declared:

With this material Italy and Germany have once again

attempted – and once again unsuccessfully – to be in a position to confront the British Government with the accomplished fact of a rebel victory for such time as the Spanish question shall come to the fore in the British negotiations with Italy.

The attempt has been a manifest failure in spite of the retreat of the Republican Army, with the consequent loss of ground. The military situation has, in essentials, remained unchanged.

'GOOD AUGURY'

The 'essential' role of the Italian legionaries in Spain is emphasised in a resolution passed by the National Directorate of the Fascist party yesterday, the 19th anniversary of the foundation of the Fasci. The resolution reads:—

The directorate of the party stresses with pride before the Blackshirts and Italian people the valour of the legionaries who are once again an essential factor in the victory in Spain. The participation of the '23rd March' Division in the battle that is engaged is a good augury and illuminates to-day's historical date.

The extremist Rome newspaper 'Tevere' in an article on French reaction to the war in Spain says:

Is France determined to intervene? As responsible voices are silent we shall reply ourselves with brutal clarity. If France intervenes there will most certainly be trouble. If France decides to play Moscow's game she will find who holds the best cards.

If France wants to take the opportunity to use force, let her prepare to meet force. If France moves a finger beyond the Spanish frontier the movement will be general. With the greatest calm we warn France of the mortal danger which intervention would bring on her head.

FRANCO TO HITLER

General Franco, reports Reuter's Berlin correspondent, has sent the following telegram to Herr Hitler:–

From the victorious front of the war against Communism I send your Excellency the greetings of Spain and my own in this solemn hour in which Germany has rendered a service to the West by sparing Europe danger and bloodshed.

This is presumably a reference to Herr Hitler's declaration

212

that he entered Austria to save it from becoming another Spain. In his reply Herr Hitler expressed the hope that final victory of 'Nationalist' Spain would soon be won.

Monday March 28 1938

REBELS REACH AND ENTER CATALONIA
Cutting Loyal Spain in Two

FRANCO ONLY THIRTY MILES FROM THE COAST
Advance of 'Fantastic Rapidity'

The Spanish rebels last night entered Catalonia and are not twenty miles from Lerida, after Barcelona the largest town of Catalonia.

Farther to the south they have reached the borders of Castellon, a province of Valencia, and are there little over thirty miles from the Mediterranean coast.

These latter forces, which consist to a great extent of Italians, are aiming at reaching Tortosa – or the ruins of this many-time bombed town. If they succeed Republican Spain will have been cut in two and the position of the Spanish Government will be desperate.

FIRST CATALAN VILLAGE FALLS

The threat to Lerida is equally serious and more immediate. The rebels yesterday advanced along the main road from Saragossa (making detours where the bridges had been blown up), and reached the River Cinca.

Here the Government forces had been expected to make a determined stand, but by the evening the rebels had crossed the river and taken their first Catalan village, Masalcorreig. They then turned north again towards the main road to Lerida, and the latest news last night was that they were investing Fraga.

A correspondent with the rebels on the Aragon front describes the advance has [sic] having been carried out with 'fantastic rapidity'.

The Republicans are putting up what resistance they can, but the mass of arms against them is so overwhelming that men alone cannot stand out against it.

The long rebel communiqué issued from Salamanca yesterday was a recital of numerous villages occupied, of hundreds

of men made prisoners, and of great quantities of arms taken
– including a million rounds of ammunition. The latest Barcelona
communiqué is short, but its admission of the loss of a few
villages means the loss of most of those the rebels claim.

MONOPOLY IN INTERVENTION

The Italian headquarters staff at Salamanca has issued a
communiqué showing the large part played by the Italians in
the present fighting. In Rome yesterday a semi-official communiqué was issued that contained a 'warning' to France that any
help by her for the Spanish Government might lead to a European war.

Friday April 1 1938

STRONG STAND AT LERIDA
Men but Little Material

MOORS HELD AT BAY
Republicans Attack Near Madrid

Lerida was still holding out last night against General
Franco's Moors. For a day and a half they have been pounding
at the city – a city made famous during the Moorish occupation,
– but they have not entered.

A message from Saragossa admits, further, that there is
no immediate prospect of their entering.

The battle has been fierce and uninterrupted, and is going
on not only at the city but in the countryside around. Last night
it was still in full swing, with Government artillery fire heavy
in the north and east of the city.

For over two thousand years Lerida has been a centre
of military importance. It is a natural fortress, and if the Government had artillery, aviation, and supplies equal to those of the
rebels it might hold out as long as it has often done in sieges
of the last two centuries.

But the condition of the Government forces is shown by
the thousand or two who have fled over the Pyrenees into
France. 'The militia men', says a message from Luchon, in the
Haute Garonne, 'are well equipped in everything but arms.
Many have only sporting rifles and daggers.'

Nevertheless the morale of the troops in Lerida is high.
Leaflets have been distributed among them exhorting them
to resistance and promising them plentiful war material shortly.

ITALIANS PRESS ON

While the Moorish columns are fighting for Lerida the predominantly Italian columns are overcoming resistance farther south and have drawn a little nearer to the sea. It was claimed yesterday that the provinces of Castellon and Tarragona had been entered.

It is suggested from Saragossa that the rebels will first try to reach the coast at Tortosa and then advance on Barcelona, hoping that the city may be forced to surrender by a rising of the 'Fifth Army' – rebel sympathisers within the city.

Somewhere along the front Burgos claims that an entire battalion of the International Brigade has been captured by Franco's troops. All are said to be British including the commander.

Apparently with the idea of drawing rebel troops away from Catalonia, the Government forces yesterday began an offensive on the Guadalajara front, north-east of Madrid. It was here that the Italian forces were routed last year. Whether it is a full-scale offensive is not yet clear, but the Republicans have had considerable success.

Reuter's Barcelona correspondent reports that the capital is outwardly unperturbed by the latest news from the front. Life is going on normally.

The President of Catalonia, Senor Companys, has broadcast a call for general mobilisation for the front and for fortification work. Plans are being made for a determined resistance.

Senor Azcarate, Spanish Ambassador to Britain, in an interview in Paris with Reuter yesterday, said that morale in Barcelona was wonderful. The Ambassador is leaving for London to-day after a visit to Barcelona, where he saw the Prime Minister, Dr. Negrin.

NON-INTERVENTION

The Non-Intervention Sub-committee met yesterday for the first time since the beginning of February. Its meeting showed that there is still disagreement over the basic figure of 'volunteers' to be withdrawn – the Soviet Union considers the 10,000 to which the other Powers agree to be too few.

It also disclosed that the observation scheme is in danger of coming to an end completely, since the big Powers have not paid any contributions since October.

SPAIN AN 'EPISODE'
Republican Appeal to the English People

Barcelona, April 3.

The Spanish People's Front, representative of all parties in Government Spain, has issued a message to the English people which says:–

'Italy and Germany are attempting to defeat us in a decisive manner and have launched an unmasked attack in the hope of crushing us. They are not only attacking us with troops disguised as volunteers but also with tremendous quantities of war material, which increases a hundredfold the damage and injury to our independence.

'Spain is merely an episode in what is being prepared and a foretaste of what threatens the world in the future. But Spain can cease to be an episode and can be made to represent a definite barrier which will put a stop to this criminal aggression.'–Spanish Press Agency.

LOYAL SPAIN CUT IN TWO?
De Llano's Claim

DRIVE TO THE SEA ENDING
The Italians Hurry

General Queipo de Llano, the rebel general, broadcasting from Seville late last night, claimed that Tortosa had been taken. If the claim is correct – it is not made from any other source – General Franco's drive to the Mediterranean has been accomplished and Government Spain is cut in two.

Tortosa lies a few miles from the sea, but the main coast road runs through it, and the minor coast road will be untenable if Tortosa has fallen.

The last certain news was that General Franco's Italians were within seven miles of the sea. Having taken Gandesa, they were advancing along the road to Tortosa, already brought to ruins by German and Italian 'planes.

Early yesterday they had had their first sight of the Mediterranean, fifteen miles away.

When the sea is reached, and the time when it is cannot be far off, the rebels will be able to advance on Barcelona along the coast as well as along the road from Lerida.

The rebels are now in control of Lerida, but are still meeting resistance on the outskirts. They claim to have made 8,000 prisoners.

The battle-cruiser Hood has arrived at Barcelona, and her commander will discuss with British authorities there questions affecting the safety of British subjects.

Tortosa fell to the Nationalists on April 18.

Wednesday April 6 1938   *p.9*

SPAIN APPEALS TO CONSCIENCES OF BRITAIN AND FRANCE
'Appalling Injustice' Done to Her

ASKING ONLY FOR RIGHT TO BUY ARMS
'Still Time' to Stem Invasion

The Spanish Government, faced with the most critical situation of the civil war, yesterday appealed to the conscience of Britain and France to allow it to buy arms.

Notes were delivered to the British and French Offices that set out the injustice of the policy of non-intervention in practice – injustice which the Notes call 'appalling and dangerous', and 'profound and unbearable'. Now, 'while there is still time,' the Spanish Government asks to be given back its right 'to obtain the war material necessary for it to drive back the foreign invasion'.

The Spanish Government concedes that a policy of non-intervention would have had merit if it had meant that Spaniards alone could have solved their problems but as it has worked it has had entirely the opposite effect. 'Its open violation in favour of the rebels, publicly and unashamedly acknowledged by the Governments of Germany and Italy, is so notorious that no man of public affairs with any sense of his responsibilities longer dares to deny it.'

A new Spanish Cabinet was formed last night. The main change is the displacement of Senor Prieto, who was Minister for War. Dr. Negrin, who remains Premier, takes over the War Ministry as well. Senor del Vayo returns as Foreign Minister.

One of the most remarkable features of the new Government is the presence of a Syndicalist – at the Ministry of Education. Otherwise the political complexion of the Cabinet is not greatly changed.

217

General Franco's drive to the Mediterranean is developing into a race between Italians and Spaniards and a message from Saragossa suggests that the Spaniards may win.

The race, however, is not going too quickly, for along the route of the main advance the Republicans have withdrawn only a mile since Sunday.

General Queipo de Llano, in an after-dinner broadcast on Monday night, had claimed that Tortosa was already taken, but the latest dispatches indicate that the town will hold out for some little time yet.

Thursday April 7 1938   *p.6*

SPAIN'S GREAT EFFORT TO DEFEND HERSELF
Workers Rally to Government

CABINET'S MANIFESTO AGAINST 'MOST MONSTROUS PLOT'

Loyal Spain, dwindling in size, is making a great effort to stem the rebels. Army, Government, anti-Fascist parties, and the trade unions are co-operating more effectively under the present danger than they have done before.

The Spanish Cabinet, reorganised on a rather wider basis, has issued the following manifesto:—

The Government of the Republic addresses itself to all Spaniards on the fighting front, in the Republican rear, and on rebel territory fighting against the armies of invasion, and declares its absolute will to continue the struggle for the independence of Spain until the country is delivered from those who have attacked and invaded it in the most monstrous international plot ever known.

After praising the Government armies on all fronts, the manifesto adds: 'The Government resolved to reward services to the Fatherland and to strike without delay and with the full severity of Republican law against traitors.'

To some extent the rebel advance into Catalonia has been checked: in the most critical sector, around Tortosa, where three rebel columns are trying to reach the coast, Government resistance is strong, and the rebels refrain from making many claims.

North of Lerida, however, they have captured a town that

218

gives them control of much of Barcelona's electric power supply.

A big recruiting drive is going on in Republican Spain, and during the past eight days 16,034 volunteers have been enlisted. The highest totals are for Barcelona (2,718), Jaen (2,583), and Madrid (2,212). With the slogan, 'For every volunteer to the front one woman for industry,' the National Committee of Anti-Fascist Women is mobilising 150,000 of its members in the recruiting campaign.

The U.G.T., the Socialist trade union, numbering some 2,000,000 members, has agreed to urge its associates belonging to classes not yet called to arms by the Government to join the Army.

The different sections of the several syndicates have been asking their members to co-operate in the war by increased production in all factories connected with war industries.

The United Socialist Youth, which includes the Communist Youth, is now conducting an intense campaign aiming at recruiting 100,000 volunteers.

BRITISH APPEALS FOR MODERATION

The British Minister at Barcelona, Mr. H. Leche, has been instructed to inform the Spanish Government that the British Government sincerely trusted that, in the event of a further retreat on the Catalan front, the Spanish Government would take all possible steps to ensure that no looting of property or acts of revenge on political prisoners and hostages in Barcelona or elsewhere on the part of irresponsible elements would be tolerated.

At the same time, the British Agent at Burgos, Sir Robert Hodgeson, was instructed to inform the rebel authorities that the British Government sincerely trusted that they would ensure that adherents should refrain from taking the law into their own hands and that strict discipline would be maintained until General Franco's administration had been established in districts occupied.

Each side has been informed of the representations made to the other.

200 'PLANES OVER BARCELONA
Government Shows Its Strength

THE REBELS HELD

Squadrons of Spanish Government warplanes flew in formation over Barcelona on Saturday, dropping leaflets. The Spanish Press Agency puts their numbers at 200 three-engined bombers and pursuit 'planes. After the demonstration most of the 'planes left for the front.

The leaflets contained a second appeal by Dr. Negrin, the Prime Minister, for resistance to the end against the rebels. In one made less than a fortnight ago he had said:

> We will be tenacious until we equalise superiority in the air. Hundreds and hundreds of young pilots are waiting with deep impatience for the 'planes which will permit them to confront the Germans and Italians.

The appeal dropped from the sky yesterday ran as follows, states Reuter:–

> I ask, first, the regular officers of the old Army and the genuine representatives of the democratic traditions of the old Spanish infantry, as well as officers risen from the Militia, to fight for their liberties. I ask war commissars to make extra efforts, setting an example to the Army. I ask soldiers not to abandon their posts until the death. I count upon your obedience for the triumph of national independence and the frustration of the ambitions of two European Powers.
>
> I, the same as you, have a profound conviction that we will win the war. There is only one path to victory: resist: resist until the death. There is one object only: victory.

GOVERNMENT ATTACKS

For the most part the Spanish Government forces are holding the rebels in their advance in Catalonia. In the Morella sector, at the extreme south of the front, the Republicans have been counter-attacking, but the rebels dispute that they had any success.

A Spanish Press Agency message from Barcelona claims that the initiative in the fighting around Lerida and in the lower Ebro sector has passed to the Republicans. The Moors on the Lerida front have confined themselves to defending their positions, and the Italian troops attempting to reach the sea at or near Tortosa have had to retreat in several places.

ITALIAN AID IN SPAIN
Premier's Admission

FRANCO'S RECENT REINFORCEMENTS
No 'Material' Change

The Premier admitted for the first time in the House of Commons yesterday that there had been recent Italian reinforcements to General Franco.

He had been asked by Miss Rathbone (Ind.–English Universities) whether he would forward evidence she had sent him to the Italian Government, and his reply contained the phrase:

> I have no reason to think that the position in Spain has been materially altered by the recent imports of Italian reinforcements to General Franco.

This point was seized upon by Mr. Alexander, and the Premier added: 'I do not deny that there may have been reinforcements to both sides,' repeating his belief that the situation had not been materially changed.

It was announced in answer to another question that Britain has refused the recent appeal by the Government in Spain for the right to buy arms. The British reply stated that the Government did not see its way to modify its declared policy of non-intervention in Spain.

THREE SPAINS

By reaching the sea at Vinaroz yesterday the rebel army has achieved the main object of its present offensive, and loyal Spain is once again divided by hostile territory. General Arganda's Galician troops, beating the Italian legionaries in race to the sea, have cut the last road connecting Catalonia with the rest of Republican territory, and from now on the Spanish Government in Barcelona can visit Valencia and Madrid only by air or sea. It would be foolish to under-estimate the gravity of the blow. The Republican army is cut in half and must again defend two fronts while the rebels enjoy the advantage of interior lines. The war industries of Catalonia are

221

separated from the food-producing areas of Valencia, and the problem of supply and distribution will become more acute. But it would be no less foolish to think that the war will soon be over. Too late, perhaps, to save Spain, but not so late as to be useless, the Catalans are roused to the highest pitch of determination. They have nothing to hope from General Franco, who detests their claims to autonomy as much as their support of the Spanish Government. There is not likely to be any political wavering there. It seems likely that General Franco will attempt first to crush Catalonia, because it is the smaller part and also, in a sense, the more dangerous. It has the men and the industries: also it lies next to France and is therefore the last hope of direct intervention, a point which may influence Franco's German and Italian allies. But to crush Catalonia is a formidable task which must in any case take several months and may be possible at all only with the aid of Franco's three great allies – Germany, Italy, and non-intervention.

Wednesday April 20 1938   *p.13*

SPAIN AGAIN APPEALING TO THE LEAGUE
'Growing Foreign Intervention'

FRANCO BOASTS THAT HE HAS WON THE WAR
'Last Days of the Reconquest'

For the third time Spain is to appeal to the League of Nations. Senor del Vayo, the Foreign Minister, yesterday asked that the League Council should consider the Spanish question when it meets on May 9. The basis of the appeal will be that of the previous appeals of May and September last year – the help that Germany and Italy are giving to General Franco and its threat to the peace of Europe.

Senor del Vayo points out that since the League last met and recognised the danger of foreign intervention in Spain Germany and Italy have been intervening more and more. He is going to lay before the Council 'concrete information' of this.

'This growing intervention in Spain', adds the Spanish Foreign Minister, increases 'the gravity of the danger to general peace already emphasised by the Council a year ago.'

'WE HAVE WON'

General Franco yesterday announced over the wireless, 'We have won the war.' This was repeating a declaration that he made at the beginning of the year, but yesterday he added, 'Our Navy, Army, and Air Force are now fighting in the last days of the reconquest of Spain.'

He also announced that after the war (the rebels winning) Spain was going to be a great Power again, with a big Navy and a big Army, and attractions for tourists.

The Chairman's Sub-committee of the Non-Intervention Committee will meet on Monday to consider its financial position. When it last met, on March 31, Mr. Hemming, the secretary, announced that the committee's funds were 'mainly conjectural', and it was then decided to send to the Governments an appeal to pay their arrears at once. There is no indication of the response that has been made.

TORTOSA ABOUT TO FALL?

Tortosa seems to be in danger of falling soon. The greater part of the town lies to the north of the wide Ebro and would be difficult to take by direct assault, but it is claimed that the Italian columns have managed to cross the Ebro above the town. If this is so the Republicans are in danger of being caught in their rear.

Last night the rebels claimed to have widened their corridor to the sea, both to the north and to the south. They now say they are in possession of thirty miles of the coast.

Wednesday May 4 1938   *p.13*

FRANCO'S HOPES DEFERRED
Government Strength

SPIRIT OF ITS ARMY RESTORED
Air Power Strengthened

From our Diplomatic Correspondent

London, Tuesday.

There would seem to be a certain stagnation in the Spanish civil war, but it is clear that the resistance of the Spanish Government is going to be much more formidable than was recently expected.

The heavy defeat which seemed the beginning of a general

223

collapse of the Government forces in Spain was the result of an immense superiority on the part of the rebels in heavy guns, bombing 'planes, and heavy tanks, as well as the use (for the first time in the civil war) of a smokescreen on a very wide front. The Government forces were overwhelmed by sheer weight of metal and their aeroplanes were outnumbered by about ten to one. The troops could not see where they were, and they broke in the first main onset. Nothing (so it appeared) stood between General Franco and Barcelona. But all signs of demoralisation have now vanished and the spirit of the Government Army appears to have been fully restored.

The rebels are still superior in the air, but the Government has received considerable numbers of bombing 'planes, and the disparity is not quite as great as it was. Meanwhile Barcelona is being fortified, as Madrid was fortified at the end of the year 1936. The Government hopes to make it as impregnable as Madrid to direct assault, and even if Barcelona should fall the possibility of continued resistance in the vast region comprised by the triangle Madrid–Valencia–Cartagena remains.

Wednesday May 11 1938   *p.6*

AMERICANS & ARMS FOR SPAIN
Changing Situation

From our own Correspondent

Paris, May 10.

The news from Washington that Senator Nye's amendment to the Neutrality Act to enable arms to be sold to Spain is unlikely to be passed has caused disappointment and anxiety in Spanish Government quarters here, as well as among all those who considered that the removal of the arms embargo would enormously improve the position of the Spanish Government.

It is held that the great majority of American opinion is as revolted as ever by the 'non-intervention' policy and would heartily welcome the renewal of American arms shipments to the Government side, but it is strongly suspected here that the British Government, fearing that this would 'perpetuate the Spanish war' and would also oblige Great Britain and France to choose between following the United States (and at least not hindering them) and continuing 'non-intervention', has advised Washington against any change in the Neutrality Act.

PROPOSED ALTERATION TO NEUTRALITY ACT

The question at Washington is whether to repeal that section of the Neutrality Act which stops the supply of American arms in the event of 'civil conflict'. Senator Nye, the well-known isolationist, has introduced a resolution for the repeal of this clause. The matter is now before the President and his Ministers.

Rumours of an impending change in the Neutrality Act had been rife in Washington since May 5. On May 13, any likelihood that the Act would be repealed was ended when the Foreign Relations Committee voted by 17 to 1 to shelve Senator Nye's resolution that would have permitted the export of arms to Spain. It is probable that the protests generated in the United States by reports of the Nationalist bombing campaign provided the spur for Nye's proposal. (See report of Tuesday March 22 1938.)

Thursday May 12 1938 p.6

SPANISH FOREIGN MINISTER'S DEMAND
'An End to Sham Non-Intervention'

DANGER OF FASCIST POWERS' LUST FOR EXPANSION

In his speech at the public meeting of the League Council at Geneva yesterday Senor del Vayo made a vigorous attack on the policy of non-intervention and asked the League to restore Spain's right to buy war material. He said:

Let us put an end to this sham non-intervention, whose sinister spectre taints the international atmosphere, and let us restore the question to its natural jurisdiction the League of Nations.
    What is the situation today? Unfortunately it is worse than it was yesterday. I do not intend to take up the time of the Council in placing before it irrefutable proof of facts which to-day no man of goodwill and upright judgement will attempt to deny. The intensification of foreign intervention in recent months and its immediate and direct effect on the latest offensive on the Aragon front are only too well known.

'ONLY PRACTICAL POLICY'

Lord Halifax said his Government remained convinced that non-intervention was not only the best but the only practical policy, and intended to persevere with it.

'They deeply deplore the tragic loss of life which is inseparable from modern war', he went on, 'and their sympathy with the Spanish people is the more profound as the struggle which is raging in Spain has all the added bitterness of fratricidal strife.

'From the outbreak of the tragic struggle his Majesty's Government, and indeed, the British people, have felt the necessity of doing whatever lay in their power to relieve the sufferings which have fallen upon the Spanish people.

'This necessity is no less imperious to-day, and we would urge that no effort should be spared to mitigate the disasters of this unhappy war to the wounded and the non-combatants.

'His Majesty's Government appreciate the longing with which all patriotic sons of Spain must await the day when their country will no longer thus be desolated, and they would fain hope that some settlement based on reason and goodwill might soon be found to spare further agony to that unhappy country and to enable them to play their full part in the community of nations with the vigour and courage which they have always shown.

'The League of Nations may be held to have peculiar qualifications for acting as an organ of conciliation. If any time there was anything which this institution could contribute towards bringing together the two contending parties in Spain no one would be better pleased than his Majesty's Government.

'Moreover, I think all of us have the interests of the League and of Spain at heart and hope that a time will come when the League may be able to play a part in reconstruction of Spain once this unhappy strife is a thing of the past.'

Friday May 13 1938   *p.14*

FRANCO STARTS AGAIN
Valencia the Aim

RAIDS ON CITIES AND VILLAGES

The Spanish war is under way again. For a fortnight heavy rains have kept the rebels for the most part inactive, but with the weather set fair once more another offensive in the direction of Valencia has begun, and rebel 'planes have taken to the air, bombing Valencia and Barcelona.

The messages from Burgos about the resumption of the offensive are in general terms. It is stated that yesterday General Franco's troops were closing the pocket that is taking shape between Teruel and the sea. It contains possibly 10,000 Government troops.

Republican battalions, it is suggested, expected a push from another direction. They may try to make their escape southwards over pathless mountains, but loss of roads, it is stated, makes it impossible for them to remove heavy material.

Burgos claims that, in spite of heavy Republican resistance, there has been an advance of five miles over a thirty-mile front in little over 24 hours.

There were two raids on Valencia during the night. Twenty-two people were killed and 80 were wounded. A heavy load of bombs was dropped on Barcelona in two raids yesterday afternoon and some 35 people were killed. Villages along the coast near Valencia has been attacked, and one razed to the ground.

Ebro offensive – July–November 1938

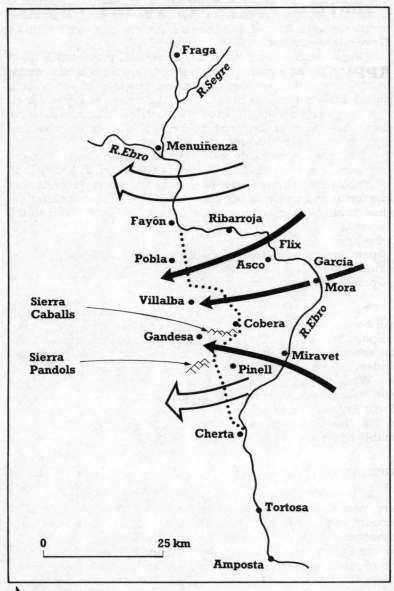

Republican attacks

•••• Limit of Republican advances at the end of October 1938

BRITISH PLAN ON 'VOLUNTEERS' ACCEPTED
Russia Likely to Agree

APPEAL TO BARCELONA AND BURGOS TO-DAY
Four Powers Pay Instalment of Cost

From a Diplomatic Correspondent

London, Tuesday.

The full Non-Intervention Committee, meeting for the first time for eight months, to-day passed unanimously the scheme which is officially called

the British compromise for the withdrawal of volunteers from Spain, for the granting in certain circumstances of belligerent rights to the two parties, and for the observation of the Spanish frontiers by land and by sea.

To-morrow, at the request of the committee, the formula will be dispatched by the British Government to the two sides in Spain. When it has been received in Barcelona and in Burgos the scheme will be published as a White Paper, probably on Friday.

While a reply is awaited from the two sides in Spain the Non-Intervention Committee will pursue its preliminary work. Great Britain, France, Italy, and Germany to-day each handed to the Non-Intervention Committee a cheque for £12,500 to enable this work to go on.

RUSSIAN OBJECTIONS

In to-day's plenary meeting Lord Halifax, Foreign Secretary, who took Lord Plymouth's place as chairman, gave a full account of the British plan and paid a high tribute to Lord Plymouth's work. No objections were raised to the plan except by the Soviet representative, Mr. Kagan, who suggested that the regulations for the establishment of an international control at sea and land ought to be revised. He desired to make these regulations uniform so that they should either both work in stages or both start completely at the same time. The compromise arrived at in the meeting gives reasons to assume that the Soviet Government will not approve of the decision reached by the meeting.

It was pointed out to-day that the passing of the British formula meant real progress. Much naturally depends on the attitude of Barcelona and Burgos. Early consideration of the British formula by Barcelona and Burgos would certainly further increase the importance of to-day's decision.

POSITION OF ITALIANS

It is expected that Franco's reply on the bombing of British ships and the Italian attitude towards Spain will be discussed at to-morrow's meeting of the Cabinet. The Government may then be in possession of the report which Lord Perth, the British Ambassador in Rome, has given of his recent talks with Count Ciano. It is believed that this report will give an account of the conversations which were undertaken, possibly with a view to creating the conditions for an early completion of the Anglo-Italian Agreement.

Though the Italian attitude towards such a suggestion has not been made known, certain quarters seem not to have given up hope that Signor Mussolini will ultimately agree to an ostentatious withdrawal that might be used to justify the completion of the Anglo-Italian Agreement. It is obvious that a withdrawal of 10,000 or 15,000 Italian troops from Spain, however much publicity were given to it, would not considerably alter the situation. The military position would hardly be affected by the withdrawal of 10,000 or 15,000 not so valuable Italian infantry if such a withdrawal did not include the specialists and special troops. Certainly the essential problem of intervention would remain.

Intervention is at present more than ever a matter of specialists and special troops stationed in Spain. The recent bombing of British ships has shown that the special troops, particularly those in Majorca, have been working independently of the rebel military command. There is, moreover, reason to assume that in some instances the bombing of British ships was carried out by seaplanes, which started from their base at Genoa and returned there again after the attacks.

This aspect of intervention emphasises the vital importance of including special troops and specialists in the withdrawal, not only with a view to the situation in Spain but also to the general spheres of interest which are affected by it.

GERMANY AND ITALIAN PACT

Germany's attitude towards the question of an early ratification of the Anglo-Italian Agreement is of great significance for the international political situation. There is reason to suppose the heads of the National Socialist State hope that the ratification of the agreement will take place before the Spanish

question is settled and, in particular, before the substantial withdrawal of 'volunteers' has been effected. Berlin is firmly convinced that such an event would create the fundamental wedge
between Great Britain and France which they desire. It is difficult to foresee whether this attitude of Berlin corresponds to
the attitude of Rome or whether it represents the policy of
the Third Realm only.

No light is thrown upon this question by certain occur-
rences which at first sight seem to have a bearing upon it
– for example, the fact that since the Anglo-Italian Agreement
was concluded Italian activity in Palestine has decreased while
German activity has been increasing.

Monday July 11 1938   *p.12*

A CALL FROM SPAIN THAT MUSSOLINI HEARD
'Could Not be Left Unanswered'

Rome, July 9.

Praise for the exploits of Italian forces in Spain is contained
in an article by Signor Mussolini appearing to-day as preface
to the third five-year series of Acts of the Fascist Grand Council.

'We just had time', he writes, 'to salute this victory (that
is, Abyssinia) when from over the Mediterranean came an
appeal that could not be left unanswered. Since the Bolsheviks
made the Spanish war 'their war' the battalions that had just
returned from the conquest of empire were reorganised. The
new deeds have passed into history under the names of Malaga,
Guadalajara, Santander, Bilbao, Tortosa.

'The publication of the Grand Council Acts is taking place
while, nothwithstanding Franco-Russian aid, Franco's army is
winning. The event is of an enormous historic importance. It
is the first time (but will it be also the last?) when Blackshirts
have faced on an international ground the Bolshevik forces;
it is the first encounter between the two revolutions, between
this of last century and ours.

'We do not know whether such encounter may develop
to-morrow on a European scale or involving the whole world.
What we know is that Fascism does not fear a fight which ought
to decide the future of the Continent.'

In a reference to Italian foreign policy, Signor Mussolini
says that, 'in spite of being inclined to wider forms of collaboration, it is based decidedly on the Rome–Berlin axis and on
the Rome–Berlin–Tokio triangle.' Later he adds: 'Those

foreigners who once cheated us now hate us, and this hatred, which is intensely reciprocated, we are very proud of.'–Reuter.

2,000 'VOLUNTEERS' A DAY TO LEAVE SPAIN
What the British Plan Proposes

PROHIBITION OF TRANSPORT OF WAR MATERIAL
No Passports for Propagandists

The British plan, approved by the Non-Intervention Committee, for securing the evacuation of foreign combatants from Spain, which was published as a White Paper in London last night, provides for–

The handing over by the two armies in Spain of at least 2,000 foreigners every day;

The disembarkation in London, as a prelude to repatriation, of volunteers from Britain, Eire, and, if from the Republican side, from Belgium, Denmark, and other North European countries;

The disembarkation of other foreign combatants in Hamburg (German), Lisbon (Portuguese), Marseilles (French), and Genoa (Italian).

A prohibition against people going to Spain who might engage in propaganda for either side; and

The prohibition of ships flying the flags of the signatory Powers from carrying war material from any port to Spanish ports (British ships are already prohibited from doing this).

The plan generally is designed to secure the withdrawal of foreign volunteers, to bring about the recognition in certain circumstances that the two parties in Spain have a status which would justify them in exercising belligerent rights, and to put into operation the observation of land and sea frontiers in order to prevent the arrival of prohibited materials.

The task of withdrawing volunteers will be entrusted to two commissions attached respectively to the headquarters of the two sides. For the Spanish possessions and dependencies there will be 'branch establishments' working under the commissions. Eventually the two commissions will sit as a joint commission to determine the proportion in which the withdrawals will be made.

232

In the event of one side's having more volunteers than the other, the numbers handed over will vary proportionately, but the total of the two batches must reach 2,000 every day.

The first of the daily quota will be transferred to the evacuation areas on the 46th day after the final adoption of the plan by the International Committee (it was only provisionally adopted on July 5). The first embarkation on transports will take place on the 51st day after the final adoption of the plan. On the 101st day the commissions will begin the task of verifying that no foreign volunteers remain unevacuated. It is estimated that the complete process will be finished by the 164th day.

Political exiles fighting in Spain are to go back to the country in which they were 'habitually resident'.

p.16

SPANISH CHARGES IN NOTE TO BRITAIN
Italians to stay Under Spanish Names

On the day that the British volunteers withdrawal plan was published the Spanish Government issued documents communicated to Britain alleging a plan to keep Italian troops in Franco's Foreign Legion under assumed Spanish names and giving details of the alleged landing of Italian soldiers and arms in Spain in the past three months.

A Note was handed to the Foreign Office by the Spanish Ambassador in London accompanying, 'for the information of the United Kingdom Government and eventual communication to the Non-Intervention Committee, certain reports relating to recent Italian intervention in Spain.'

These reports,' it was added, 'proceed from sources which my Government considered reliable, and although, given the impossibility of submitting them to detailed verification, the Spanish Government cannot answer for the exactitude of each and every concrete point in question, it does not hesitate to declare that taken in conjunction they correspond to the real facts.'

The first document stated:

'The Italians have informed Franco of the necessity to yield to English pressure in the matter of the withdrawal of the Italians without this measure extending to the war material employed at present by the Italian division.

'Arising from this communication there have been several conversations between the chief of the Italian forces and the Italian Ambassador on the one side, and Franco, Francisco

Morano, and Jordana on the other. The result of these conversations is as follows:–

'In the event of Italy's being forced to yield to British pressure, some 10,000 men, most of them incapacitated and sick, would be transferred to Italy.

'The remainder of the Italian troops would be incorporated into the Spanish Foreign Legion, as volunteers, together with their officers. They would wear the uniforms of the Tercio, both officers and ranks.

'The Italians have made it a condition that these new "banderas" (battalions) of the Spanish Tercio would be commanded exclusively by commanding officers and officers of the Italian Army, to which Franco agreed.

'The members of the Aviacion Legionaria would employ the same procedure, wearing uniforms of the Spanish Air Force, and passing as Spaniards under assumed names.

'The advisers of the Italian General Staff attached to the General Headquarters of the Generalissimo will remain in their posts, but will pass henceforward as attachés of the Italian Embassy and continue their services in civilian dress.'

The second document gives details of alleged landing of arms and men since April from Italy. Over 7,000 men are alleged to have reached Spain and it is alleged that important reinforcements are being prepared for embarkation in Italy.

Friday July 15 1938   *p.22*

LETTERS TO THE EDITOR

'NON-INTERVENTION' IN SPAIN
Unsatisfactory Features of the New Scheme

To the Editor of the Manchester Guardian

Sir,–The scheme of the Non-Intervention Committee which has now been submitted for the approval of both sides in Spain is a complicated document requiring much study. But before accepting the view that it represents a big step towards real 'non-intervention' at last it is as well to remember certain drawbacks, some inherent in the scheme itself and some arising from the circumstances in which it is being initiated.

The worst drawbacks to the scheme are these: First, it makes no provision for the withdrawal of foreign munitions or engines of war, though the supply of these – to both sides but by far the more abundantly to the insurgents – is at least as important a factor in the war as the foreign 'volunteers'. Secondly, it provides no machinery for checking the arrival of fresh material or combatants on the warships of the participating countries. Only merchant ships are to carry 'observers', though, notoriously, much of the help that has reached the insurgents, and virtually none of that which has reached the Republicans, has been brought in warships. Thirdly, it provides no means of observing or checking the arrival of foreign aircraft by air, though the German 'planes and those whose exploits are openly boasted of in the Italian press are known to come that way, while similar aid that, say, Russia or Mexico chose to send to the Spanish Republic could only come by ship and so would be 'observed'. These defects in the scheme – all favourable to Franco – are fatal to its chances of securing real non-intervention.

Nevertheless, within the compass it attempts the scheme will have a limited value if it does result in the withdrawal of foreign combatants. But the chances of that have been largely destroyed by its own parents, the British and French Governments. Obviously the scheme cannot succeed unless the Spanish Government and the Burgos authorities genuinely facilitate the counting and withdrawal of 'volunteers'. But why should General Franco facilitate a withdrawal by which he stands to lose far more than the Republicans (who have abundant manpower) now that he has been granted beforehand the two advantages which were to have been his reward – namely, the closing of the French frontier, intended to result from the reinstatement of 'observers', and the right to intercept neutral shipping, which should have accompanied the recognition of belligerency? Without waiting for observers, on June 11 the French Government re-established rigid control of its frontier. On June 14 Mr. Chamberlain announced that he saw no way of stopping the bombing of British ships, and so gave Franco more than he could gain by a blockade which he has not naval power to enforce and which would not in any case legalise the sinking of ships and machine-gunning of crews.

As to the closing of the frontier, the two Governments have shown their bad consciences by trying to shift the responsibility on to each other's shoulders. It was reported from Paris and universally believed that the French action was due to strong British pressure until, after a fortnight of evasive replies to Parliamentary questions, Mr. Chamberlain astonishingly declared that his Government 'had never suggested that in present circumstances the French Government should take unilateral action in closing its frontier' and that it was its own 'independent action'. If this is so, the motive was presumably the desire of the French to follow in British footsteps by concluding an agreement with Italy.

Signor Mussolini is known to be infuriated by the continued resistance of the Spanish Republic. So to placate him the French have closed the one door by which the great disparity in the supply of arms to either side could be reduced, while our Government has done its utmost to discourage British ships from bringing food to the stricken population. It is just as though two men watching a fight were to help to tie up the arms and legs of one of the combatants, pouncing on him to tighten the bonds whenever they tended to loosen, and while he was being beaten to death continued to protest their complete neutrality. Yet the British people, especially the wearers of old school ties who follow Mr. Chamberlain pride themselves on their sportsmanship and sense of fair play!

What have we gained by all this, we and the French? If by our help Franco wins our strategic position in war-time will be immeasurably worsened, as Captain Liddell Hart shows in an article in the June 'Fortnightly'. Signor Mussolini shows his contempt for us by deed and word. He has refused to co-operate in protest to Germany over the Austrian loan and in the Evian conference. He encouraged his aviators to bomb our ships and kill our seamen, and when the Spanish Republic threatened to retaliate, while Mr. Chamberlain contented himself with verbal protests, he sneered at him through his mouthpiece Signor Gayda by saying that if Italian ships or ports were touched he would reply 'not with Notes of protest but with guns'. Finally, there was his furious outburst at Aprilia against 'the great demoplutocracies', with their 'ridiculous abject, nasty faces', from whom the Italian people would ask no help but 'would remember at any time in peace or war'. That is Mussolini's answer to those who cringe to him, and perhaps it is the answer they deserve.

Yours, & c.,
ELEANOR F. RATHBONE, House of Commons, July 13.

Eleanor Rathbone was an Independent MP in the House of Commons representing the English Universities.

TWO YEARS OF WAR
Spain Unconquered

'STRUGGLE TO THE LAST MAN'
Republican Resolve

Two years ago to-day the Spanish civil war began. Senor del Vayo, the Republican Foreign Minister, in a statement yesterday said: 'The totalitarian States had no idea of what it meant to capture Spain.' He went on to declare that Spain would 'struggle until the last man', saying:

Republican Spain is entering the third year of the war with something more than confidence in victory, with the decision to struggle until the end, until the last man, for the last piece of Spanish soil.

The Government's resistance is being felt in rebel territory. They counted the days to victory in March, whereas Senor Negrin said the war would be a long one.

General Franco, however, in an interview with Reuter's Burgos correspondent yesterday predicted that the third year of the war would bring a Nationalist victory.

The third year of the war opens gravely for the Government, for the rebels are steadily advancing on Sagunto, the one large town that bars the way to Valencia. The resistance is bitter, and the rebel gains like most of those of the past year, have been made only at great cost of lives.

Franco's Cabinet yesterday marked the last day of what in the rebel calendar is known as the 'Second Triumphant Year' by conferring titles on General Göring and Count Ciano, the Italian Foreign Minister. General Göring is given the title of Grand Knight and the Collar of the Imperial Grand Order of the Red Arrow. Count Ciano is made a Knight of the Order of Isabella the Catholic.

The year that has now ended has seen the wiping out of the Northern front, the first offensive of the new Government army that led to the capture and then the loss of Teruel, the great rebel sweep across the plains of Aragon, the reaching of the Mediterranean, and the cutting of Government Spain in two.

It has seen the worst air raids of the war when in ten days in March 815 people were killed and 2,200 were injured in Barcelona. At the opening of the year there began the piracy on the high seas that was ended by the Nyon agreement, and towards the end of the year there came the repeated attacks on shipping in Republican ports.

FRANCO'S ADDRESS TO SPAIN
Republican Ministers Described as 'Servants of Russia'

PRAISE OF HIS FOREIGN TROOPS

Burgos, July 18.

General Franco to-day addressed the Spanish nation on the occasion of the second anniversary of the beginning of the Spanish civil war.

He said that celebrating the commemoration of the national rising was to glorify something not only of interest for Spain but a phase in the world's history crowning the process of Bolshevik revolution. Spain, the champion of the faith and of civilisation, had her culture seriously threatened by the Red Communist principles. The Russian Comintern persisted in its efforts to overthrow by violence the social and traditional order of the nations, said General Franco. All nations were threatened by the Seventh International Congress, particularly the British Empire, Africa, and India.

Popular Front Governments were formed in coalition with the left parties to facilitate revolutions. With the help of outworn Liberalism those who failed in Spain in 1934 succeeded in 1936 in occupying political power and offering to Russia the Bolshevisation of Spain.

FRANCO'S 'CRUSADE'

'Our fight is therefore a crusade in which Europe's fate is at stake,' said General Franco. 'That is why since the beginning Russia has taken her place unconditionally on the side of the Spanish Republic by sending tanks and a thousand warplanes, and by mobilising the undesirables of all Europe to fight for the Red Army. Our triumph is immense, in spite of the difficulties of the enterprise. No difficulties have prevented the rescue of over three million Spaniards from Red barbarism during the second triumphal year.

'I beg your affectionate remembrance of our brothers who are suffering from the effects of lawlessness in the Red zone, and your prayers for the martyrs of our cause. I pay tribute to those who have fallen far from their own countries – the natives, the volunteers, the legionaries who left their home to enrol in the forces of the crusade and to demonstrate in Spain the fullness of their countries' identification with the cause of firmness and friendship professed by them towards Spain.

'The Reds assassinated over 70,000 in Madrid, 20,000 in Valencia, 54,000 in Barcelona. Such crimes are the work of the

Comintern and its agents Rosenberg, Marti, Negrin, Del Vayo – all servants of Soviet Russia.

'Spaniards have a duty to remember that Christian charity is boundless for the deluded and the repentant but they must observe the dictates of prudence and not allow the infiltration of the recalcitrant enemies of Spain. Those proceeding from a politically infested area must undergo quarantine to avoid the contamination of the community.

FOREIGN INVASION

'I denounce the new Red campaigns of those posing as defenders of Spanish independence against foreign invasion. The foreign invasion came through the Catalan frontier, whence entered the undesirables who sacked and destroyed Spanish towns and villages, looted banks, destroyed homes, and stole our patrimony of art.

'The Reds who pursued these treacherous tactics in the Nationalist rear, in attempting to destroy our unity, will continue these tactics after the war, when our vigilance and our care for the purity of our creed must increase. The Nationalist movement has ousted the old political intrigues and is guiding the nation to greatness and prosperity.

'Spain was great when she had a State Executive with a missionary character. Her ideals decayed when a serious leader was replaced by assemblies of irresponsible men, adopting foreign thought and manners. The nation needs unity to face modern problems, particularly in Spain after the severest trial of her history.

'Separatism and class war must be abolished and justice and education must be imposed. The new leaders must be characterised by austerity, morality, and industry.

'Spaniards must adopt the military and religious virtues of discipline and austerity,' concluded General Franco. 'All elements of discord must be removed.'–Press Association Foreign Special.

FRANCO'S RAPID SUCCESS IN S.W. SPAIN

Big Slice of Territory Occupied

CLAIM TO HAVE TAKEN MANY TOWNS AND PRISONERS

The rebels in their surprise pincer movement in Estremadura, the south-west corner of Spain near the Portuguese frontier, claim to have captured a big slice of territory and many prisoners and munitions.

A Franco official report, quoted by Reuter, claims that the area captured amounts to nearly 1,050 square miles, with a population of over 400,000 people. This area includes the rich Serena Valley and fertile River Guadiana plains.

Batteries, armoured cars, machine-guns, and large quantities of ammunition are included in the haul.

It is said that cavalry, who have taken a major part in the operations, continue to advance, capturing 'dispersed and wandering' Republican units still at large. The Republican losses are put at 1,000 dead. Several thousand have been taken prisoner.

The rebels claim that near one town they surprised an entire Republican unit that was going in lorries to reinforce their comrades resisting in the town. At Castuera, an ammunition dump containing 10,000 artillery shells and many millions of rifle cartridges was captured, and also several thousand head of cattle.

An advance to a depth of several miles on the Valencia front is also claimed by the rebels. Here the Republicans are estimated from Saragossa to have 100,000 men equipped with a greatly increased number of tanks and armoured cars, more shells and an active air force.

The Government, however, in its official report says that on the Valencia front 'Spanish soldiers completely repulsed the attacks which the invaders launched against their positions'.

OFFENSIVE

Across the Ebro

Barcelona, July 25.

The Republicans to-night claimed that they had been successful in a new offensive just south of Tortosa, near the Mediterranean coast, about half-way between Barcelona and Valencia. A communiqué states that forces crossed the River

Ebro at dawn between Amposta and Mequinenza and put insurgent troops to flight at several points, taking 500 prisoners and much war material. The advance continued throughout the day.–Reuter.

Salamanca, July 25.

General Franco's headquarters here to-night admitted that Republican troops had crossed the River Ebro between Tortosa and Amposta, but declared that they had suffered heavy losses.

Bridges which the Republicans had built across the river during the night were destroyed by insurgent aircraft, and concentrations of troops preparing to cross were heavily punished, adds the Salamanca communiqué.–Reuter.

The crossing of the River Ebro was the beginning of the Republic's last major offensive and, with its failure, Catalonia was exposed to the Nationalist forces.

Wednesday July 27 1938   *p.11*

REPUBLICANS RECROSS THE RIVER THAT HELD THE REBELS
Advances Along Ninety-Mile Front

CLAIM THAT 3,000 PRISONERS HAVE BEEN TAKEN

The offensive that the Republicans have unexpectedly begun along the banks of the River Ebro is going well for them. When the rebels reached the Mediterranean in April the Government forces fell back to the left bank, and there managed to make a stand. At no point along the Ebro below its junction with the Segre were the rebels able to cross.

Now the Republican forces are attacking along a 90-mile front from the mouth of the Ebro, and a Barcelona telegram last night claimed that the river had been crossed at eleven points. Bridges were thrown across the river, surprising the rebels everywhere, it is reported, and the Republicans now claim to be about a mile from Gandesa, a town of considerable strategic importance.

PRISONERS TAKEN IN THEIR SLEEP

Altogether 3,000 prisoners are stated to have been captured, 500 of them while they were asleep. Republican batteries which

241

crossed to the right bank of the Ebro bombarded Franco's positions before the town of Gandesa. Troops to try to stem the advance are being hurried from the town of Lerida and from the Balaguer sector.

Last night's Barcelona communiqué stated: 'Brilliant operations of the Spanish soldiers continued to-day. They are still advancing victoriously. The enemy was dislodged and pursued from the majority of his positions. In those cases where he feared resistance he was surrounded and overcome.'

General Franco's headquarters admit that the Republicans have crossed the Ebro, but claim that losses amounting to 'several thousand' have been inflicted on them. A communiqué declares that bridges which the Republicans had built across the river at night were destroyed by aircraft and that concentrations of troops preparing to cross were heavily punished. The Republicans, it is said, were aided by 'Red villagers'.

The communiqué received early this morning from Salamanca admits that the Republican attacks are continuing, but it is claimed that the offensive is being carried out only by 'small detachments'. One regiment is alleged to have been wiped out and other Republican forces have been surrounded.

In the Pyrenees sector the Republicans are attacking Sort, the electricity power centre north of Balaguer. Neither side, however, has much to say of the fighting in this sector.

The sudden rebel offensive in South-west Spain seems to have achieved its purpose, and yesterday there was no further news of it. On the main battle front, south of Castellon and south-east of Teruel, on which the future of Valencia will depend, there is a break in the bitter fighting that had lasted a fortnight. For the present both Republicans and rebels are more occupied with the diversions that each side is creating, but that on the Ebro may become a diversion of some importance.

Thursday July 28 1938   *p.12*

BARCELONA'S OBJECTIONS TO THE VOLUNTEERS PLAN
'Unjust' Air and Sea Control

BELIEF THAT SCHEME WILL END IN 'PROFOUND DISORDER'

A translation of the Spanish Government's official reply to the plan for the withdrawal of foreigners was issued by the Foreign Office in London last night.

The Spanish Government commends the 'meticulous care' with which the arrangements for withdrawal have been drawn up, and says that it accepts, for its own part, these arrangements, and adds the assurance that when the case arises it will loyally collaborate in their application. Nevertheless, it feels obliged to make a number of observations. It calls attention to the absolute necessity of the counting commissions not limiting themselves to the collection of reports from the respective authorities, but of proceeding on their own account to whatever investigations may be necessary to ensure that information corresponds to reality. For its own part it declares itself ready to concede to the Commission in its own territory ample facilities for the officials to inform themselves of the exactitude of information given by Republican authorities.

Friday July 29 1938   *p.6*

BATTLE OF THE EBRO
Town Threatened

REBELS FIGHT BACK FROM THE AIR

Barcelona, July 28.

The Republicans are closing in on Gandesa, the important town west of the Ebro, where Franco is making a determined effort to stem their advance. The town is hemmed in on three sides, and the only road still open is that due west of the town that goes to Alcaniz.

This is the fourth day of the unexpected Republican offensive west and south of the Ebro from Catalonia. Their troops are showing great persistence in the face of constant air attacks on their makeshift bridges over the river, which were raided more than thirty times yesterday. The bridges are rebuilt as soon as they are destroyed, and the passage of troops and supplies has continued almost without interruption.

GARRISON SURPRISED

The Republicans advanced more than twelve and a half miles beyond the Ebro yesterday before meeting with resistance a few miles north of Gandesa. The garrison of Corbera (three miles north-east of Gandesa) was taken so completely by surprise that the town fell with hardly a shot being fired. Villalba was also taken without resistance.

A whole supply train, on the way to Castellon loaded with

243

provisions and clothing, was captured at Asco, and another train was blocked in a tunnel.–Reuter.

Madrid, July 28.

One result of the Republican offensive has been the withdrawal of warplanes from the Teruel–Sagunto road sector to the Ebro front. The attack on Valencia has died down while General Franco's aircraft fly to meet the threat on his flank.–Reuter.

THE REBEL VERSION

Saragossa, July 28.

The control of the situation along the Ebro is now, it is claimed here, passing entirely into the hands of the Nationalists. The systematic destruction of their bridges, it is maintained, means the isolation of the Republicans from their supplies of food, ammunition, and reinforcements, and the impossibility of withdrawing their wounded.

With the continued pressure by the Nationalists to-day the present situation of the Republicans is thus considered here to be fraught with dangerous consequences. For success the Republicans should have seized Gandesa immediately and struck deep into the heart of enemy territory and before the Nationalists had time to react. Now, however, what was to have been the overture to a big-scale offensive has become, it is held here, merely an audacious and spectacular exploit, which the Nationalists suggest will be probably suicidal.

It is considered here that the Republicans having shown that they are unable to follow through after taking the initiative, and their failure is attributed partly to the fact that the manoeuvre was not protected by aviation and partly to the Nationalists' speed in mobilising their reserves.

200 REBEL 'PLANES

The Nationalist aviation is reported pouring torrents of bombs on the enemy vanguards and mercilessly pounding their communications. At certain moments as many as two hundred Franco planes were to be seen together.

It is believed that a great part of the Catalonian Army was brought down for this offensive and in its early stages the Nationalists were fighting in a minority of eight or ten to one. The Republican claim to have taken 4,000 prisoners is therefore described as ludicrous.–Press Association Foreign Special.

FRANCO STRIKES HARD TO PUSH BACK REPUBLICANS

Fierce Bombardment on Ebro Front

REBELS' DAILY TASK OF DESTROYING BRIDGES FROM THE AIR

General Franco's forces are trying desperately to drive the Republicans from the foothold they have gained on the right bank of the Ebro in the region of Gandesa. At dawn yesterday a tremendous bombardment of Republican positions began, and the pressure increased as the day wore on. Reuter's correspondent at Saragossa reported last night: 'The extent of the progress achieved by the insurgents is not yet specified.'

General Franco is throwing his heaviest forces against Republican concentrations on his right wing, and it is claimed that progress was maintained steadily throughout the morning, although the advance was bitterly contested. Artillery and infantry were powerfully supported by aircraft, which, after carrying out their early morning duty of destroying the bridges rebuilt by the Republicans during the night, opened a withering bombardment of the enemy positions.

The Republicans were on Saturday consolidating positions captured north and south of Gandesa. These positions enabled them to dominate the road running west from Gandesa to Alcaniz. The Nationalists resisted strongly on the heights around the city.

A Reuter telegram from Barcelona said that enemy aircraft were still playing a great part in the fighting, but were not succeeding in holding up the Republicans, who have now crossed the Ebro in considerable numbers. It is reported that the Nationalists have concentrated the bulk of their troops on the Ebro front to withstand the Republican offensive.

Saturday's Republican communiqué claimed that the advance had continued in the sector south of Gandesa, where they had occupied ten hills. 'The enemy, who continued to bring up reinforcements from other fronts', it said, 'offered great resistance, which was overcome by the spirit of our soldiers.' 'Notable progress' was made in the district of Fayon, north of Gandesa, where two hundred prisoners and war material were taken.

IMPORTANCE OF EBRO BATTLE
Local Republican Offensives as Best Means of Defence

WEARING OUT THE REBEL FORCES

Barcelona, August 5.

After three months of reorganisation and efficient training the Republicans by their well-planned but unexpected advance to Gandesa, have diverted the Nationalists from their advance on Valencia. They have relieved the weary defenders on the Levant front, whose stubborn and gradual withdrawal during three months had inflicted the maximum losses on the exhausted forces of General Franco and absorbed their reserves.

And this has been done by an offensive carried through with a minimum of losses in its first stages because it was through territory only weakly held: the insurgents thought the Ebro a sufficient obstacle to any Republican counter-attack.

By advancing on Gandesa and conquering the Ebro loop the Republicans have gained a wide 'bridgehead' across the Ebro. Their left flank is protected by wild mountains and their right by the Ebro in the neighbourhood of Fayon. The Republicans have gained limited objectives and wisely consolidated to await the counter-attacks which they hope will be very costly to the insurgents.

The Republicans' main difficulty is to maintain communications across the Ebro, and by varying the level of the River Ebro through their control of the dams at Tremp the insurgents have added a new complication to the task. Republican transport has to make its way to and fro across the river by ferries, trestle and pontoon bridges – some constructed with boats collected from the coast, – which are bombed all day long by massed aircraft. Anti-aircraft fire, however, keeps the 'planes high, and damage is immediately repaired by engineers, who work in the great heat under showers of bomb and anti-aircraft shell fragments.

Northward from Fayon to the French frontier, while the Nationalists concentrated on Valencia, the Republicans have been fortifying since April. They are modern defences, expertly planned, and extend for miles behind the front. Foreign observers have been immensely impressed and consider now that Catalonia should be almost impregnable.

They also consider that the operations indicate high quantities of moral and organisation, counteracted only by Franco's overwhelming superiority in aircraft and technical resources. Under present circumstances observers feel that it is impossible to foretell the war's duration and result. Meanwhile the Republicans, fired by the genuinely nationalistic propaganda of Senor Negrin, the Premier, evidently aim at wearing out the Nationalist morale by resistance and occasional local offensives, which are considered the best method of defence.

In the Estremadura operations (South-west Spain) the insurgents have thrust by a wide and weakly held plain at the main gateway to Spain's central plateau, but it is considered unlikely to develop into a major operation, since General Franco's reserves are believed to be concentrated on Valencia.—Press Association Foreign Special.

Tuesday August 9 1938 p.9

ITALY'S HELP FOR FRANCO
'Volunteer' Air Force Busy

FACTS FROM ROME

An official communiqué from Saragossa was issued in Rome yesterday which disclosed the extent of the assistance in the air that Italy has given General Franco in trying to push back the Spanish Government forces along the Ebro. The period covered by the communiqué is from July 25 to August 5, and thus does not cover the fighting on Saturday or Sunday when the rebel counter-offensive reached its height. The communiqué runs:

The losses on the enemy by the volunteer Air Force have been very heavy.

The contribution of the Italian volunteers was as follows:— 158 bombing actions took place with the use of 541 aircraft and the dropping of 455,000 kilograms (about 450 tons) of explosives.

Intense action was carried out by pursuit craft, both in accompanying bomber squadrons and in reconnaissance flights. Thirteen flights were made accompanying bombers, with a total participation of 327 aircraft, and thirteen reconnaissance flights, with a total use of 352 machines.

In all, the legionaries carried out 1,672 flights, with a total flying time of 2,825 hours.

WOUNDED ITALIANS

A Reuter message from Naples states that flowers were thrown and the Fascist salute given by members of the public when the hospital ship Aquileia arrived from Spain with

247

wounded Italian officers and men on board. The wounded consisted of 45 officers, 63 subalterns, and 525 soldiers. There were 103 stretcher cases.

Barcelona, though admitting a reverse on the Ebro front at the hands of what it terms 'the forces of invasion', yesterday declared that the offensive as a whole is only 'indirectly affected'. Around Gandesa, the centre of their resistance, the Republicans have withstood all attacks from the air or on land.

p.12

THE REPUBLICAN REVERSE ON THE EBRO FRONT
Barcelona Disputes Its Extent

FRANCE DENIES THAT ARMS ARE GOING TO SPAIN

The Spanish Government yesterday declared that the reverse its troops have suffered on the Ebro will not greatly affect the offensive as a whole. The right wing of the Republican Army has been pushed back, but the rebel claim that the whole of the right bank of the Ebro north of Fayon has been retaken is disputed in Barcelona.

There appears to have been no large-scale fighting yesterday and of the operations on the Ebro front the rebel communiqué received early this morning merely said: 'Punishment of the enemy still continues.'

The latest communiqué issued by the Ministry of Defence in Barcelona states:

All the insurgent attacks on the Republican lines in the Ebro sector made by picked troops withdrawn from the Levant and Lerida–Balaguer fronts were broken by Government resistance. The insurgents suffered very heavy losses.

Fighting was particularly fierce in the Gandesa sector. No sacrifice appeared too great for the insurgents in their attempt to break the Republican defence system especially along the curve of the Ebro, a nerve-centre for the insurgent command.

North of this bend the insurgents, with the use of large German and Italian bombers and more than a hundred tanks, succeeded in taking Alto de Los Auts. This position is east of the Sierra de Mequinenza and north of Fayon, with but only indirect importance for Republican operations in the curve of the Ebro sector.

The rebel claims refer only to that part of the front north of Fayon and of the successes there, the Salamanca communiqué of yesterday stated:—

The Red 42nd Division which was holding the position in this sector, has been wiped out, all the men have been killed, taken prisoners, or drowned. Our salvage corps has collected all the arms abandoned by the Reds in the trenches as well as the wounded abandoned by them in an unattended condition.

Over 1,000 prisoners were taken. It is impossible to estimate the number of dead. To those picked up in the trenches and on the roads must be added the hundreds abandoned in the gorges and ravines and the large number drowned in the waters of the Ebro River.

Our air arm continued its intense activity in the Ebro sector, bombing the enemy concentrations and destroying the bridges laid by them across the Ebro River.

One hundred bombs were dropped on the suburbs of Alicante in a raid yesterday by six insurgent 'planes, states an Exchange Madrid message. No casualties are reported, and the boats in the port were not hit. The raiders were driven off by anti-aircraft batteries. Senor Callejon, the British Consular Agent at Alicante who was injured in an air raid on Saturday, is now out of danger and continues to improve.

MATERIAL FOR SPAIN: FRENCH DENIAL

The French Ministry for Foreign Affairs yesterday issued an emphatic denial of reports appearing in foreign newspapers that France was permitting the delivery of war material to Spain and the passage of volunteers across her frontier.

The official statement cites certain detailed allegations that truckloads of anti-aircraft and machine-guns, with ammunition, had recently passed through Paris from Switzerland on their way to Barcelona, that other machine-guns of French manufacture had been dispatched by sea from France to Barcelona, and that the French Vice-Premier had reached an agreement with the Spanish Ambassador in Paris regarding the passage of 8,000 volunteers into Spain. The Foreign Office, states Reuter, gives the most emphatic and categorical denial to all these allegations, which it declares are false in every particular.

STRENGTHENING POLITICAL FRONT
Spanish Prime Minister Seizes His Opportunity

Barcelona, August 17.

The reorganisation of the Republican Cabinet has left it stronger. So secure does Dr. Negrin feel that he has left Spain for Switzerland to attend an international congress of physiology. The Cabinet now, as before, represents the main trade union and Popular Front parties as well as the Catalan and Basque Nationalists.

Taking advantage of the favourable military situation, which is considered the best for months, with the insurgent advance to Sagunta and Valencia checked by the successful drives across the Ebro and Segre Rivers, and with distant Estremadura the only doubtful front, the Negrin Government turned to Catalonia for a final strengthening of the political front. It began by decreeing the militarisation of war industries and the port and court authorities.

Elements discontented with Negrin and his policy of 'war to a finish' tried to provoke a crisis by raising pretended issues of Catalan and Basque autonomy as against the anti-autonomous Nationalist decrees, but the Popular Front support of Negrin, both in the front-line trenches and in the rearguard, spoilt these plans. The strength of the Negrin Government was shown by refusing to change the autonomy decrees and by replacing Catalan and Basque representatives in the Cabinet by two other men of the same races.

In announcing the changes the Spanish Government issued a communiqué, in which it stated:

The Government of the Republic takes this opportunity of affirming once more its unalterable respect for the personality and right of the autonomous regions, and its pleasure in the fact that the continued representation of the Catalans and the Basques in the heart of the Government preserves its character as a Government of national union pledged to maintain the independence and the existence of Spain, while at the same time defending local freedom.

Following the reshuffle, the Spanish Socialist party, the Basque Socialists, the General Workers' Union, the Spanish Communists, the Unified Catalan Socialist Youth, the Unified Catalan Socialist party, and the Catalan section of the General Trade Union, all announced their support of the Cabinet.–Press Association Foreign Special.

BASQUE SUPPORT

Barcelona, August 17.

The Central Committee of the Basque Socialist party has made the following declaration:—

Until the end of the war we shall in no way hinder the freedom of movement which is necessary to the Republican Government. The war must be won, so that the liberty of our country, stolen by foreigners, may be restored and that our brothers living in slavery in Euzkadi (the Basque country) may be freed. That the war may be won we give loyalty and complete support to the Government of the Republic.

—Spanish Press Agency.

Not only was political support forthcoming for the reorganisation of Negrin's Cabinet, but the changes also received the backing of the Republic's military leadership. A telegram to that effect was sent to Negrin signed by General Miaja, Commander-in-Chief, Senor Hernandez, Commissar, and the General Staff of the Army of the Centre.

Monday August 22 1938   *p.9*

FRANCO REJECTS THE PLAN FOR WITHDRAWING FOREIGNERS
Belligerent Rights Demanded in Advance

EQUAL NUMBERS MUST GO FROM EACH SIDE
Committee's Scheme Torn to Pieces

General Franco's reply to the Non-Intervention Committee's plans for withdrawing foreign combatants from Spain was issued in London last night.

Franco accepts the scheme 'in principle' but makes demands which, if accepted, would alter it completely.

TWO CHIEF POINTS

His two main points are —

That belligerent rights should be granted unconditionally in advance of the withdrawal.

251

That equal numbers should be withdrawn from both sides.

The committee's scheme that the greater number should be withdrawn by the side that has the greater number of foreigners is described as presenting difficulties which would 'emasculate and sterilise' the scheme.

NO TRUCE

Difficulties of counting the foreigners are stressed and it is said that there can be no suspension of hostilities even for a single moment while the counting goes on.

Franco objects to the proposed commission that was to count the foreigners and fears that its agents would be harmful to the Franco cause. The same suspicion is shown in the allegation that 'many ships' with non-intervention officers have carried munitions.

Franco refers to an earlier scheme now dead, under which 3,000 men were to be withdrawn as a start, and goes on:

In its desire to offer to the world an obvious proof of its effective collaboration in the laudable efforts of the Non-Intervention Committee, the National Government of Spain is disposed as from now to increase to 10,000 the number of foreigners to be withdrawn immediately.

BELLIGERENT RIGHTS

Under the Non-Intervention Committee's plan belligerent rights would be granted when the withdrawal scheme had made some progress and the parties were less dependent on foreign support. Now belligerent rights are demanded in advance.

The proposals limiting the goods that under belligerent rights could be declared contraband are also rejected and complete freedom is demanded.

It is made clear that control at the airports would not be accepted, and the committee's plans for control at the ports are strongly criticised.

GERMAN AND ITALIAN SUPPORT FOR FRANCO

Messages from Berlin and Rome show that Franco's reply has the support of the German and Italian Governments. In Berlin it is said that the answer is regarded as very conciliatory and as meeting the Non-Intervention Committee more than half-way.

In Rome it is made clear that the insistence on the granting of belligerent rights before a withdrawal has the support of the Italian Government. The German and Italian Governments, however, agreed to the original plan which Franco now tears to pieces.

The Non-Intervention Committee's scheme was accepted by the Spanish Government – which the rebels in their Note describe as 'the Red Faction' – some time ago with suggestions for improving the scheme of control.

Wednesday August 24 1938   *p.5*

PRETENCE OF 'NON-INTERVENTION' TO CONTINUE

From our Diplomatic Correspondent

London, Tuesday.

The slight shock administered by General Franco's Note has begun to wear off: it was a shock, although, being not altogether unexpected, it was slight. 'Non-intervention', so it is believed here, must go on. As General Franco agrees to the withdrawal of the 'volunteers' in principle, though he rejects it in actual fact, there may be some further correspondence with him as to what he means in preciser terms than those used in his Note.

And so – as a result of 'second thoughts' – General Franco's rejection, which is secretly felt to be insulting to the German and Italian, no less than British, French, and Russian proposal for the withdrawal of the 'volunteers', will serve as a means of perpetuating the pretence that 'non-intervention' is a positive policy. It is now clear that General Franco's reply will not make the slightest difference and that 'non-intervention' will go on as though nothing had ever happened.

It has been suggested here that one of the consequences of General Franco's reply is that France will open her Pyrenean frontier. There is no reason, at least none perceptible from this side of the Channel, for any change in French policy. The general outcome of recent diplomatic exchanges between London on the one hand and Burgos and Rome on the other is that Germany and Italy – and of these two Germany has by far the greater influence at Burgos – mean to maintain 'intervention' at no less than its present level, and may increase it if the situation demands, until the Spanish Government has been finally defeated, while France and Great Britain mean to keep the machinery of 'non-intervention' working now as before.

FRANCO DECLARES HE HAS WON
Will Not Be Robbed of the Fruits of Victory

Burgos, August 28.

'Nationalist Spain has won and will not allow anyone or anything to rob her of the fruits of victory,' declared General Franco, commenting on the Non-Intervention Committee's plan for the withdrawal of foreigners in an interview with the Press Association correspondent here to-day. General Franco said that misunderstandings which had arisen were due to the ignoring of realities and the absence of an interested country from the body drawing up the plan. He added:

'Many members of the committee probably do not know that over 50 per cent of the foreigners in the "Red" ranks are not comprised in the plan. The committee's preoccupation for peace in Europe had caused the consideration of only the European volunteers, whereas according to facts recently published in the American press over 12,000 persons have been recruited in the New World for the "Red" army, and that, furthermore, among the prisoners and dead which have fallen into Nationalist hands recently approximately 50 per cent only were Europeans.

'The equitable withdrawal of foreigners would not alter the prospects of a Nationalist victory, whereas for the "Reds" it would mean the withdrawal of commanders of the expert Chekas, whose terrorism imposes discipline on the militia.

'Barcelona accepted the plan only because it had not thought of observing its decisions. Foreigners have been provided with false passports of Spanish nationality and hidden away among the Spanish fighters. The solution of the withdrawal problem is difficult, but not unattainable. The most just and the cheapest plan is ours for the withdrawal of equal numbers from both sides.

'Un-Spanish are those who knowing that their cause is lost continue sacrificing the lives of militiamen in sterile efforts to prolong the struggle and destroy the country. What would the English think if their bank funds were depleted, art treasures exported, churches destroyed and profaned, children exiled, homes desecrated, and law courts supplanted by "Chekas"? Those guilty of such things in Spain show that the future of the country does not concern them.'

NO MEDIATION

Speaking of mediation, General Franco said: 'The Spanish war is not an artificial conflict but the crowning and historic fight of country versus anti-country, unity versus secession, and the spirit versus materialism.

'The only possible solution is the absolute victory of pure and eternal principles over bastard anti-Spanish ideology. Supporters of mediation favour a divided, subjugated, im-poverished, and materialistic Spain. Peace to-day would mean another war to-morrow. Nationalist Spain has won, and will not allow anyone or anything to rob her of the fruits of victory.'– Press Association Foreign Special.

Monday September 5 1938   *p.13*

FRANCO ATTACKS ON THE EBRO AGAIN
Town Retaken Near Grandesa [sic]

BITTER STRUGGLE

General Franco has resumed his counter-offensive on the Ebro front in yet one more attempt to dislodge the Republicans from the right bank of the river. Yesterday he claimed to have retaken Corbera, a town which fell to Spanish Government troops on July 26. It lies five miles from Gandesa on the main road to Falset.

A Reuter message from Burgos says that many hundreds of prisoners were taken when the insurgents occupied the town. The battlefield is stated to have been strewn with Republican dead. The insurgents also seized two anti-tank guns and many light machine guns.

Their advance has continued throughout the morning and Corbera was surrounded on two sides by noon. A number of Republican trenches were captured during the advance, which was assisted by great artillery and air activity.

REVERSES ADMITTED BY BARCELONA

Barcelona, September 4.

To-night's Ministry of National Defence communiqué issued here admits that General Franco's troops launched violent attacks on Republican positions in the Gandesa sector of the Ebro front to-day and succeeded in capturing three hills. The communiqué adds that the Republican counter-offensive on the Estremadura front continued successfully.–Reuter.

DEL VAYO'S BITTER ATTACK ON WESTERN DEMOCRACIES
'Temporising With the Aggressors'

LEAGUE 'AN OFFICE FOR RECORDING THE DEFEATS'

From our own Correspondent

Geneva, September 19.

Senor Alvarez del Vayo, the Spanish Foreign Minister, was the principal speaker at a meeting of the League Assembly this morning. He said that the tactics of temporising with the aggressor and ignoring aggression had brought them inevitably to the hours of alarm and distress through which Europe was passing. No one had done more to precipitate events in the direction of war than those whose mission it was to save peace.

The Chinese people had been abandoned to their fate. He rendered homage to their heroism with that feeling of solidarity experienced by one who had known the anguish of war but also shared the pride of preferring death to the disappearance of his country as a nation.

They had seen a free and independent State which a year ago enjoyed the prerogative of a member of the League disappear, as it were, overnight from among them. One might look in vain in the Secretary General's report for a few words of condolence or farewell in its honour. Aggressors now knew that a State member of the League of Nations could disappear with impunity, and that in the annals of the greatest institution of peace its disappearance would not even be recorded in the list of international agreements. The Spanish Delegation would like at least to be allowed to direct to the spot once occupied by the Austrian Delegation a glance of indignant protest.

POLICY OF 'REALISM'

It was to be expected that the magnificent effects of the introduction of the so-called realist policy in international affairs, with its contempt for peace and law, should result in the present fresh attempt at aggression against Czecho-Slovakia. It was not on the aggressors but on their accomplices that the greatest responsibility fell. The aggressors, after all, followed the law of their destiny. It was the nations who had proclaimed their respect for the sovereignty of States, but who had always in the name of peace neglected their duty and had turned the League of Nations into a great registration office for recording the defeats suffered in the accomplishment of this mission, who were responsible for the present situation.

Senor del Vayo said that he was entitled to speak in this manner, for no other country had made so great an effort as Spain had made to prevent the conflict raging on its territory from degenerating into a general conflagration. They had resisted all provocations, even those made by the countries that called themselves their friends and yet played the game of the totalitarian States. In the general atmosphere of irresponsibility the Spanish people had given proof of a high sense of international responsibility. Who would dare to claim that in order to save themselves they had hoped to involve other nations in a general war?

The safety of Spain was entrusted to the Republican Army. When two years ago he foretold before the Assembly their resistance and their final victory he was fully conscious of a certain scepticism. He hoped that when he renewed that prophecy to-day those who sincerely believed that the only solution was to capitulate to the totalitarian States would have changed their opinion in the light of events in Spain. Such a change would be of particular value at this moment when international opinion was yielding in so tragic a manner. The greatest contribution that Republican Spain was making at Geneva to-day was its example in confronting aggression without being overcome by the aggressors. If, however the aggressor were given the impression that one State could be swallowed up while others remained unmoved by the event without any League action, then, indeed, nations were in danger and peace was imperilled.

IF SPAIN HAD FALLEN

If in March, 1938, those who were ready to welcome with relief the collapse of the Spanish Republic had been in the right France would have had another frontier to defend, and the aggression against Czecho-Slovakia would by now have taken place. Spain had served the cause of peace; but let no one cherish the illusion that her sacrifices should be indefinitely exploited or become the object of negotiation. Spain was not an aggressor or territory to be thrown to the aggressors temporarily to appease their appetite.

The policy of systematic concessions had brought about the decline of collective security and had forced nations to negotiate their own security at the expense of that of others. Their position grew daily more difficult before the aggressor States, who had been converted by the tactics of capitulation and flattery on the part of others into the lords of war and peace. They still held only a very illusory sway, and would at once cease to exercise their tyranny if the real forces of peace – who were still in the majority – were ready to follow a strong lead and to re-establish a common front at Geneva. Since one must pay the price of the aggressors for provisional freedom from war and since it was far more patriotic and pleasant to make others pay for this freedom, the skill required in this new international policy outside the Covenant consisted in endeavouring to convince the States' victims of aggression that they should allow themselves to be invaded quietly, or at least that they should give up that part of their territory which was demanded of them without too great a protest.

Spain had resisted aggression without receiving the slightest assistance from the League of Nations. The Non-Intervention Committee was welcomed by the 'pacifists' of passivity and the partisans of abstention with an undisguised joy and enthusiasm. This had not weakened his Government's resolve to fight with ever-greater determination for a vigilant, strong, and self-assured League of Nations. He had recalled all this to say that with the assistance of the League Republican Spain's resistance would long ago have had definite results, with the consequent savings of many hundreds of Spanish lives.

'ONLY WAY' TO A STRONGER LEAGUE

Senor del Vayo continued:–

In the course of this debate the hope has been held out by those who would like to reassure us that at some more or less distant date the security of nations will be restored, and we are asked meanwhile to let the League live as and how it can. The Spanish Delegation consider that in view of present prospects it cannot be expected that the strengthening of the League of Nations will be brought about by a miracle.

The only way for the League of Nations to consolidate itself is to put an end to the methods which have been responsible for its weakness. Does anyone contest that any future Assembly, where an even greater number of members will be victims of aggression and will even, perhaps, have disappeared as independent States, can be in a better position than the present one for accomplishing this mission?

Before they take action within the framework of the League of Nations are the great Western democracies going to wait until half the European nations represented here have become paralysed for the task of peace by disillusion, by panic, or because they have ceased to exist as independent States?

With regard to the sanctions article of the Covenant, Senor del Vayo said it was true that the vacillations of the great Western democracies had discredited the system of collective security, but that an instrument which, wielded with greater tenacity and energy, could yet bring together in defence of peace all those who were not disposed to let Europe and the world sink into the chaos of international terrorism ought not to be destroyed.

Mr. Selter (Estonia) and Mr. Munters (Latvia) declared on behalf of their respective Governments that they considered article 16 to be no longer obligatory.

The crisis occasioned by German demands upon Czecho-slovakia, and the response to those demands in London and Paris, had destroyed any last hope that the British and French Governments were prepared to stand up to the aggressor nations in the foreseeable future.

Thursday September 22 1938   *p.11*

INTERVENTION IN SPAIN
The Next Stage

BIG ITALIAN FORCES WAITING TO GO

From our Diplomatic Correspondent

London, Wednesday.

The first consequences of the capitulation of the Western Powers are evident even now. It is not known here what Mussolini's full price for his support of Hitler has been, but part of it is certainly German support for Italian intervention in Spain.

The Italian Government has made all the necessary preparations for an intervention which is intended to be decisive. There are large concentrations in several parts of Italy of troops that are to embark for Spain in a few days.

This renewed intervention by Italy has not been demanded by General Franco. It seems that he has not even been asked. Both Hitler and Mussolini are now indifferent to what Government Spain will have as long as that Government is a docile instrument in their own hands.

REPUBLICANS' BOLD MOVE
No Foreign Troops

Geneva, September 21.

Dr. Negrin, the Spanish Prime Minister, announced here to-day that the Spanish Republican Government had decided to order the immediate withdrawal of all non-Spanish combatants fighting on the Government side.

This withdrawal would apply to all foreigners, without distinction of nationality, including those who had assumed Spanish nationality since the outbreak of the Spanish civil war.

Dr. Negrin asked for the immediate appointment by the League of Nations of an international commission to see that this withdrawal was carried out.–Reuter.

Monday October 10 1938   *p.11*

THE ITALIANS IN SPAIN
'Veterans' to Go

BUT THE AIRMEN WILL REMAIN
Maximum Concession

It was officially announced in Burgos on Saturday night that Italians who have had more than 18 months' service with General Franco's forces in Spain are to be repatriated at once. The announcement quoted by Reuter runs:–

Generalissimo Franco is preparing for the immediate repatriation of Italian Legionaries who have done more than eighteen months' active service in Nationalist Spain.

By ordering this substantial withdrawal of volunteers Nationalist Spain is contributing effectively to the confirmation of good international relations as well as fulfilling the wish expressed by the Non-Intervention Committee.

This, it appears from comment in the official Italian 'Diplomatic Information' last night, is the maximum concession that Italy is willing to make unilaterally to obtain the ratification of the Anglo-Italian Agreement. Its extent is not yet clear, but in Rome it is estimated that some 10,000 Italians will be repatriated.

INFANTRY ONLY

It is noted in political quarters in Rome, states Reuter, that the men affected are all infantrymen and that aviators and specialists will remain.

For some time reports have been current in Rome that General Franco no longer requires the assistance of the Italian infantry, as he has by now sufficient man-power of his own. On the other hand, he is averse from losing the assistance of the Legionary Air Force which, according to Italian press reports, is still playing an important part in the insurgent attacks in the Ebro sector.

Italians are anxious to know whether the concession will be accepted by the British Government as adequate for the recognition of Abyssinia and the ratification of the Anglo-Italian Agreement. It is understood in Rome, however, that no public decision is likely to be taken in London, or to be made known in London before Parliament meets on November 1.

The comment in the 'Diplomatic Information' runs:–

Apart from developments in Anglo-Italian relations the repatriation is substantial, and in responsible Roman quarters it is thought that it might furnish Great Britain with the occasion for making effective those agreements of April 16 which have remained since then for too many months lying in the archives of the Foreign Office. If this happens, so much the better.

In responsible Roman quarters it is held that, having carried out this not merely symbolic but effective repatriation of volunteers, Italy will not go any further unilaterally.

Thursday October 13 1938   *pp.9 and 10*

LEAVING SPAIN
The British Battalion

A FINE RECORD
Stern Fighting and Many Hardships

By Tom Wintringham

The international brigades are leaving Spain and the men of the British Battalion are expected to reach London this month. They will be welcomed home by many; many others who have regretted their 'interference' in a foreign war, or distrust the politics for which they fought, may feel a reluctant pride that English, Scots, Welsh, and Irish have left behind them so great a name in Spain. Their reputation is that of a battalion impossible to shift until in danger of encirclement. Against frontal or flank attack, tanks or 'planes, it seemed able to hold its ground 'until the Spanish summer freezes'. This reputation was won in spite of many difficulties.

In briefest outline these difficulties included recruitment in secret, lack of trained officers, the wide gap between British military practice and that of most Continental countries, and the even wider gap between British standards and habits and those of the Continent in matters of food and cooking.

UNACCUSTOMED FOOD

The men in the line got better food than was elsewhere available in Government Spain. Even so, they had usually to fight on bread, beans, olive oil, and goat or mule. Mild forms of dysentery were endemic; recovery of the wounded, often surprisingly rapid, was sometimes hampered by a lack of suitable food and an English aversion to olive oil. It was not good to see a lad from Yorkshire, with five bullets through him, trying to tackle Spanish sausages. These, as we met them, were either romantic and dangerous with bitter red herbs or classically enduring, able to resist, unchanged knives, teeth, and the ferments of digestion.

I doubt if even the lack of trained officers was a more serious handicap than that connected with food and cigarettes, but it was serious enough. Not one of those who commanded the battalion in action had been an officer 'in a real army'. Wilfred Macartney, author and critic and our first commandant, who was accidentally wounded before we went into the line, had been an officer in the war and was therefore able to give much to our training. He was followed by myself, journalist, Jock Cunningham, coalminer, and Fred Copeman, steelworker. I do not know what had been the employment of Peter Daly, the battalion's next commander, in peaceful Ireland. Nothing neat and tidy, I am certain, remembering a tear in his breeches wider even than his smile. Harry Fry had recently left the Scots Guards, his term of service ended. Sam Wilde has been a sailor.

There were one or two other commanders of the battalion for short periods; casualties were particularly heavy among officers. Of those named above, Daly and Fry are dead, and the other five share over a dozen wounds.

NAVAL EXPERIENCE

We had to make do without the military experience at the disposal of most other nationalities in the brigade. Cunningham and Fry had been infantry corporals. I had endured plenty of O.T.C. as well as two years in the ranks in France. Daly was trained by the Irish Republican Army, as was Kit Conway, who led our Irish contingent with the first company. Copeman and Wilde had the Navy's training behind them.

'Thank God we've got a Navy,' used to be our wry comment in France twenty years ago on our efforts to make an amateur army work. Under Copeman and Wilde the British Battalion did not necessarily use the same phrase (discipline is discipline) but may well have felt the same emotion. The fleet, it seems, lives up to its tradition. It turns out men who can make 'a Navy-shape job' of any job, anywhere in the world. These two sailors commanded the battalion for half of its twenty-one months in Spain. Their theoretical knowledge of war may have had some gaps, but their practical 'savvy' made them dangerous opponents even for the 'volunteer' regular officers from Italy opposed to them.

The battalion's first company was in action by the end of 1936. Ralph Fox, novelist and historian, and John Cornford, the young Cambridge poet, were among those killed while the other three companies were getting their one to six weeks' training. In mid-February, 1937, the full battalion, exactly 500 strong, butted into a Fascist offensive.

ON THE JARAMA

This was a full-scale drive to cut the last road into Madrid. At 'Suicide Hill', within distant rifle range of the Jarama River, the battalion found itself facing three times its numbers, with a gap of three miles in our line to the left of it, and a gap of 1,000 yards on its right. None of our machine-guns was less than twenty years old, and two of the three types jammed continually. The hill was held until near nightfall with rifles only; then we retreated – six hundred yards. This effort cost the battalion nearly half of its strength in casualties. But it was a necessary effort; for the timidly orthodox, clockwork strategist from the Reichswehr opposed to us did not think it right to move forces between our hill and the river until we were driven back, and therefore did not find the three-mile gap on our left until it was no longer a gap – Lister's division had filled it.

In subsequent days of bitter fighting the battalion gave ground only to regain all but 200 yards of it. Franco's offensive was stopped, and the Madrid–Valencia road remained open.

Followed ninety days in trenches without relief, and then the Brunete fighting, when the village of Villanueva de la Canada was carried. Copeman leading, by a night attack made in close formation as if an enemy ship was being boarded. Next month's attacks in Aragon cost the battalion two of its commanders.

RETREAT TO THE COAST

The capture of Teruel by the Government forces in December, 1937, was almost the only great action in which the 'English' could have taken part but were not called upon to do so. At the beginning of this year they were fighting in deep snow in the vain effort to hold Teruel. In the retreat of seventy miles that followed, from Alto Aragon to the coast, they were twice almost surrounded and got away by legs and luck. Twice they stood, at Caspe and Gandesa, to hold up for some days the drive to the sea; and near Gandesa they were ambushed by Italian tanks and Moorish cavalry. They lost a hundred captured, but fought so stiffly that the raiders withdrew.

In the recent Ebro battle they were among the first to cross the river and for sixty days resisted Franco's counter-attacks so successfully that he could not retake a sixth of the ground they had won.

Rather more than 2,000 men went out. The known dead are 432: with the missing the figure must be nearly a quarter of those who fought. Four-fifths of the remainder – over 1,200 – have been wounded, and of these nearly 500 have been invalided home. Care for the wounded and maintenance for the men now returning, until they can fit in to civilian life again, will need some thousands of pounds. But it will surely be difficult even for those taught to think of the brigades as 'international gunmen' (Dean Inge's kindly phrase) to resist the impulse to pay tribute to the courage and endurance of these men of our speech and our blood.

Tom Wintringham had commanded the British Battalion of the International Brigades during its first action at the Battle of Jarama in February 1937.

Monday October 17 1938   *p.12*

THE 10,000 SAIL
Italian Veterans Leave Spain

DE LLANO'S REGRET
Franco's Thanks for Their 'Collaboration'

Ten thousand Italians who have been fighting for General Franco in Spain for the past eighteen months left Cadiz on Saturday for home amid scenes of great enthusiasm. On Thursday they will arrive in Naples, will have flowers showered on them as they march from the port, and will be reviewed by the King of Italy and perhaps by Signor Mussolini as well.

The first ship sailed shortly after five o'clock in the afternoon and the others followed at half-hourly intervals. The troop-ships were escorted from the harbour by a number of Italian destroyers and one cruiser.

REGRETS AND THANKS

General Queipo de Llano, states Reuter from Cadiz, expressed regret at the departure of his 'comrades in arms', but said that international considerations made it necessary. He said that at the beginning of the civil war General Franco's war council refused the offer of Italian divisions and did not accept them until international brigades arrived in Madrid.

General Franco has sent a telegram to Signor Mussolini expressing gratitude for the collaboration of the 'volunteers' states Reuter from Burgos. The message wishes Italy greatness and voices faith in the solidarity of Italy with Spain in the future.

Mr. Francis Hemming, secretary of the Non-Intervention Committee, made a special journey to Cadiz to witness the departure of the Italian infantrymen at the invitation of General Franco. It is understood that he has drafted a long report for the authorities in London on what he saw.

Thursday October 20 1938 p.6

NO PARTITION IN SPAIN
Dr. Negrin's Speech

HOW PEACE COULD BE RESTORED

The following passages are taken from the official translation, now issued by the Spanish Press Agency, of the recent broadcast by the Spanish Prime Minister, Dr. Negrin:–

Faced by the failure of the plan of the London Committee for the withdrawal of volunteers, our Government announced in Geneva, the place where Spanish affairs with all other countries should have been dealt with, its decision to demobilise all the foreign volunteers – true volunteers these – who were fighting in our ranks.

In Geneva, in all places and at all times, our anxiety for peace is irrefutable. I know very well that there are those who attempt to compare our attitude with the offer of neutrality which may have been made by the insurgents to the official quarters of a certain Great Power through an aristocrat with many relations in England. But can a forced

265

and frightened declaration be confused with an effective gesture?

Is there anyone who will not understand that in the case of a European war the tactics of the rebels and their allies would lie in simulating a transitory neutrality in order to obtain our complete blockade and, with a supreme effort, succeed in ending our conflict and then place themselves with an army of two million men at the back of Franco and put chains across the Straits of Gibraltar?

MEDIATION

What we will not permit is another farce – that is to say, a simulation of evacuation by which will be embarked those who have been in our land for eighteen months, or the sick and wounded, or a limited number of Italians and Germans, which they are disposed to replace at the first opportunity.

This is not how peace will be attained. Neither will it be attained with attempts at mediation. Mediation between whom? Between us and the invaders? It is what we have been demanding in accordance with our rights for more than two years; and it is what those whose duty it was have not dared to do. Or is it mediation between the rebels and us which is to be attempted? That would be taking the control out of our hands, not mediation, and Spain is not a country of surrenderers.

The differences of Spaniards are settled between Spaniards. In no event will peace be attained by attempting to stabilise the fronts and weave artificial frontiers between the rebel and the loyal zones. This can never be. If any Spaniard permits it, even in hypothesis, he is guilty of the crime of high treason to his country and deprives himself of his nationality.

Listen well: we know that a Fascist triumph means our total extermination. Well, then our extermination rather than the division of Spain. If any apostle or envoy of peace knocks at our gate with proposals of mediation or partition our reply will be a courteous but dry and firm gesture of dismissal.

How then can peace be restored to us? By re-establishing violated international law. Force the withdrawal of the invaders. Restore to us our trampled rights as a legitimate Government. In a few months, perhaps in a few weeks, peace will arise spontaneously.

The peace policy of our adversaries is based on the annihilation of their opponents. Our peace policy is founded on a reconciliation with those who to-day are our enemies – a reconciliation which can only be carried out on the basis of collaboration in the future reconstruction and rebirth of Spain.

LETTERS TO THE EDITOR

RETURNING BRITISH VOLUNTEERS
Their Services to Spain

To the Editor of the Manchester Guardian

Sir,—Nearly a thousand survivors of the British battalion of the International Brigade will shortly be returning to this country in accordance with the decision of the Spanish Government to evacuate all foreign volunteers of whatever category serving in the Republican Army. The story of the International Column, as it was then called, dates back to November, 1936, when the arrival of the first contingent of volunteers from all parts of the globe coincided with a stiffening of the defence of Madrid and the halt of Fascism at the very gates of the city. The British battalion was founded as a separate unit in the following February and underwent its baptism of fire in the valley of Jarama, when it took a prominent part in repelling the Fascist onslaught on the Madrid–Valencia road, thus preserving essential communications between Madrid and the rest of Republican Spain. From that day, February 12, 1937, until the latest Ebro offensive the British battalion has blazed a path of glory. Many of this band of heroic Britons have fallen in the struggle for the freedom of Spain and for democracy the world over. They will never rise again, but the cause of liberty and justice which moved them to offer their services to the Spanish people will live for ever.

Those who have survived and who will be returning home shortly will come back with their heads held high. They have done something to redeem the honour of the British people, as a people that loves freedom and fair play. Many will be disabled, others wounded, and all will have a tale to tell of dangers braved and hardships undergone. Shell-fire and aerial bombardment were only a part of the tests which these men have faced. Beneath the burning Spanish sun, in the snow of Teruel, without food for days at a time in periods of heavy action, undergoing operations for the extraction of shrapnel often without anaesthetic, spending sleepless nights in digging trenches, dirty, lousy, weary, and hungry, these men have kept alive that fierce spirit of determination that democracy shall triumph over Fascism. They have known all the exigencies and perils of war plus extremes of privation and want, some of them due the policy of non-intervention which prevents the Spanish people from obtaining adequate food and medical supplies.

It is our duty to see that when they come home they shall have clothes, food, and other necessities to tide them over the period until they are able to obtain work. It is doubly our duty because these men, who have been steeled in the heat and fires of battle, have a leading role to play in the struggles that lie ahead of democracy in this country. We appeal, therefore, to your readers to help us immediately in collecting 3000 pairs of boots, overcoats, and suits. They can be sent direct to me, or if money is sent we can buy them at wholesale prices.– Yours, &c.,

FRED COPEMAN
(late Commander, 10th Battalion International Brigade),
National Memorial Fund, 1 Litchfield Street,
Charing Cross, W.C.2. October 25.

Saturday October 29 1938   *p.16*

INTERNATIONAL BRIGADES
Spain's Farewell

Bunting and flowers decorated Barcelona's streets when demobilised members of the International Brigades paraded yesterday for the last time in Spain, according to a Spanish Press Agency message from Barcelona. Pavements and balconies were packed by an enthusiastic crowd who welcomed the volunteers while Republican aeroplanes swooping low out of the clear sky scattered printed messages of 'Greetings to our International brothers'.

Dr. Negrin, the Spanish Premier, addressing members of the brigades, said that a special medal had been struck for those who had served in the brigades. 'It would be vain and petty of this Government to try to give adequate material proof of its gratitude,' Dr. Negrin told the men. 'But although this cannot signify anything approaching compensation for the great work done by the Internationals, the Government wants for them and for us a material and permanent remembrance. That is why a medal has been struck.

'The medal gives proof of your soldierhood and the right to ask for Spanish nationality on some future day.'

To the Italian Garibaldi Brigade he declared that they had 'demonstrated that the great Italian people is not a flock of sheep to obey the orders of a madman, and that that people will have a new renaissance.' Dr. Negrin said that the Spanish Government desired that an organisation should be formed to keep in touch with the volunteers and their families, and that a monument of the International Brigades should be erected.

THE NEW EBRO OFFENSIVE
Rebels in Strength

COUNTER-ATTACKS BY REPUBLICANS

Ebro Front, October 31.

Violent fighting started again at dawn to-day in the Sierra Pandols. It is apparent that the insurgents have concentrated an enormous strength of material and men in this sector, where they yesterday started their seventh counter-attack on the Republican line.

Concentrated artillery fire and bombing by successive masses of aircraft are preceding each infantry attack. The general direction of these attacks is towards the Sierra de los Caballos. Republican troops this morning twice dispersed the column thrown against their line. They have not, however, been content to resist, and they have several times counter-attacked during the day. In one counter-attack this afternoon a hill which was abandoned last night was reoccupied and is being held.– Spanish Press Agency.

FIERCE EBRO BATTLE
Franco's Gains

REBELS TALK OF 'FINAL STAGE'
British Ship Bombed

General Franco is throwing all his weight against the Republican forces in the curve of the Ebro to regain the ground lost in July. This is his seventh attempt, and it appears to be his greatest.

He has had some successes, the Republicans admitting that at the start of the offensive they lost three heights in the Sierra de los Caballos, the hills commanding the road from Gandesa across the Ebro. Last night they admitted the loss of another hill. The rebels are already talking of the 'final stage' of the Ebro battle.

REPUBLICANS CLAIM AIR VICTORY

The air communiqué issued in Barcelona last night claimed an outstanding victory in a fifty-minute air battle over the Ebro front. Seven squadrons of Republican 'planes engaged a large number of Italian machines and eleven Fiats were brought down for the loss of two Republican 'planes.

Meanwhile Franco's bombing in the Levant has reached a new intensity. In a raid on the waterfront at Barcelona yesterday by two squadrons the British ship Gothic, of Hull, and two Spanish vessels were seriously damaged. A single Government chaser, states Reuter, went up to tackle the two squadrons, which consisted of five 'planes each. It hit two of the bombers before crashing against a third and falling into the sea ten miles from the coast with its own wing ripped off. One person is reported to have been killed and two wounded.

The Gothic (2,546 tons) has been struck in air raids three times previously in the past month. Her master is Captain O'Neill, of Formby.

Last night the port zone of Valencia was heavily bombed three times. The casualties are not known, but the damage was great.

Friday November 4 1938 *p.11*

REPUBLICANS FALLING BACK TOWARDS THE EBRO
But No Slackening of Resistance

FRANCO'S RIGHT WING CLAIMS TO HAVE REACHED THE RIVER

Gradually, bitterly fighting all the way, the Spanish Republican forces are losing ground on the slopes that lead down to the Ebro.

Yesterday was the fifth day of Franco's seventh offensive, in which he has tried to win back the territory he lost in July. For three months he has failed to dislodge the Republicans, and as a result for three months his advance on Valencia has been held up.

The present offensive is bringing the rebels more success than most of the previous ones, and the position of the Republicans becomes more difficult as their foothold on the right bank of the Ebro lessens.

Last night it was reported from Saragossa that the right wing of Franco's army had reached the river in the region of Pinell.

There are two main attacks – one from the Sierra de Pandols, south of Gandesa, and the other along the road from Gandesa to Mora de Ebro and in the hills skirting the road.

Pinell was taken yesterday morning. The rebels swept down from the heights of the Pandols, and after a brief but bitter struggle the village was occupied. 'Mopping-up' operations went on in the hills themselves, where, reports Reuter from Saragossa, isolated Republican strongholds remain.

The insurgents claim that the road from Gandesa to Mora de Ebro has been cut by rifle fire at five or six points. The strategic cross-roads at Venta de Camposines, where two roads meet the main road, are now firmly in insurgent hands.

The manoeuvring, it is reported in Saragossa, seems to have dislocated the elaborate Republican defence system, and General Franco's commanders claim that the Republican troops are fleeing in considerable disorder pursued by aircraft. Batteries are keeping up a barrage against the bridges over the Ebro, the most important one of which is at Mora de Ebro.

MAINTAINING THE BRIDGES

One of the Republicans' main difficulties is to maintain communications with the forces on the right bank. The raft bridges are shelled and bombed throughout the day and have to be repaired by night, probably to be destroyed again the following day. At present the waters of the Ebro are rising after recent heavy rains, and it is becoming more and more difficult to maintain the bridges.

In spite of all, the Republicans are resisting strongly and only gradually are they giving ground.

Insurgent war 'planes were in action early yesterday. Four Republican 'planes, it is claimed, were brought down in the morning. General Franco's pilots state that never before this year has the Republican Air Force appeared in such strength. The claims of the number of 'planes brought down have proportionately increased.

Saturday November 5 1938   *p.16*

VICTORY FOR FRANCO
Italy's Determination

LORD HALIFAX'S STATEMENT

Following is the full text of an important passage in Lord Halifax's speech in the House of Lords on Thursday on the Anglo-Italian Agreement of which only a summary was given in yesterday's 'Manchester Guardian':–

I want to emphasise with all the force that I can summon

that it has never been true, and it is not true to-day, that the Anglo-Italian Agreement had the lever value that some think to make Italy desist from supporting General Franco and his fortunes.

Signor Mussolini has always made it plain from the time of the first conversations between his Majesty's Government and the Italian Government that, for reasons known to us all – whether we approve of them or not, – he was not prepared to see General Franco defeated. He has always made it plain, on the other hand, that he would assist, as he has been assisting, the work of the Non-Intervention Committee, and it is not his fault that greater progress has not been made by the committee in bringing its plans into operation.

The Anglo-Italian Agreement was signed on April 16 1938 and the declaration bringing it into force was signed in Rome on November 16 1938. The Agreement consisted of a protocol, eight annexes and exchanges of Notes. The protocol declared that Britain and Italy wished to place their relationship on a solid and lasting basis of friendship and to further the general cause of peace and security. The most important provision of the annexes was a reaffirmation of the status quo in the Mediterranean. In the exchanges of Notes, Italy pledged that she had no territorial or political aims in Spain.

Tuesday November 8 1938   *p.14*

REBELS TAKE KEY VILLAGE ON THE EBRO
Republicans Start Fresh Offensive

NEW ITALIAN DIVISION ALLEGED TO HAVE ARRIVED

Italian tanks in mass, Italian artillery, Italian 'planes in profusion, and, according to Senor del Vayo a new Italian division have not yet succeeded in completely pushing the Republicans back across the Ebro.

Yesterday, however, they had considerable success, taking Mora de Ebro, the most important village on the right bank that was held by the Republicans. But only after days of repeated attacks has the village been taken, and now most of the defenders have managed to escape across the Ebro. North of Mora de Ebro the Republicans still hold out.

The Republicans yesterday began a new offensive farther north, and succeeded in crossing the River Segre.

Early yesterday morning they crossed south from Lerida and captured Seros, Aytona, and Soses, east of Fraga, and cut the Fraga–Lerida road. They also claim to have cut the Balaguer bridge-head, north of Lerida, and have taken several hundred prisoners.

'NEW ITALIAN DIVISION'

Senor del Vayo, the Spanish Foreign Minister, yesterday declared, 'I have this morning received confirmation that fresh Italian units have arrived at the Ebro front since the last Note was sent by the Spanish Government to the British Government. It is estimated that an entirely new Italian division has appeared in the most recent fighting.

'Acts of piracy have been committed against two Spanish merchant ships by insurgent armed ships which have received assistance from German naval bases,' he stated. He appealed to all countries which had a wheat surplus, states the Spanish Press Agency, to put this at the disposal of Republican Spain for the relief of the civilian population.

AIR RAIDS

Eight people were killed and forty wounded in a Franco air raid on Upper and Lower Tarragona yesterday, reports Reuter from Tarragona.

'Dropping their bombs mostly on the village school', Republican war-planes are alleged to have caused '200 innocent victims' in the village of Cabra, in Cordova Province, at dawn yesterday, according to a Spanish Press Services dispatch received by Reuter. 'Cabra', adds the dispatch, 'has not a single military objective, not even barracks, and is situated nearly 45 miles behind the lines.'

Monday November 14 1938   *p.12*

EBRO STRUGGLE
Franco Throws In More Troops

'COMPLETE REPULSE'

Barcelona.

The reports of yesterday's fighting on the Ebro front in Spain are flatly contradictory.

The complete repulse of the rebel forces on the Ebro is

claimed in last night's Ministry of War communiqué issued in Barcelona.

A Reuter message from Saragossa, on the other hand, reports that General Franco threw another army corps into the Ebro battle yesterday, and that last night the Republican 'pocket' had been rolled up from the south-west for a distance in some places of four miles.

Earlier in the day 'very important results' were hinted at by the Nationalists following a vigorous spurt in their advance late on Saturday. Better weather helped the Franco troops. Brilliant sunshine again yesterday favoured the attackers, although morning mists and early twilight are now shortening each day's operations. The Nationalists, says Reuter's Saragossa correspondent, foresee a decisive victory in this sector as one way towards a speedy end to the war.

ITALIAN PRISONERS

A Spanish Press Agency telegram from Barcelona states that on the lower Segre east of Fraga the Republicans yesterday advanced 400 yards after a rebel counter-attack. The engagement opened with a three-hour bombardment of the Republican lines. Three battallions of rebel troops screened by ten tanks then advanced, but their attack was broken. In their advance during the counter-attack the Republicans are stated to have taken 36 prisoners, among them being two Italian non-commissioned officers who were members of the crew of one of three Italian tanks which were wrecked.

During the past week four Fiats, three Messerschmidts, two Heinkels, and a Savoia were shot down by Republican ground batteries, it is stated by the Spanish Press Agency. Ten German and Italian 'planes were also shot down by Government fighters in air battles on the various fronts.

The fighting on the Valencia front just south of Nules, where the Republicans have been attacking, appears to have come to a standstill.

Friday November 18 1938   *p.5*

ALL OVER ON THE EBRO
Whose Victory?

All rebel Spain was yesterday celebrating the end of the fighting on the Ebro. Franco's commentators are calling upon the Republic to surrender at once.

The Republicans, on the other hand, do not consider their withdrawal to the left bank as a great defeat, and in a long and detailed Note issued in Barcelona they give their reasons.

The Note points out that Government troops now occupy the positions they left when they went into the attack on the Ebro front on July 25. The advance across the Ebro nearly four months ago, the Note continues, stirred the imagination of the world; within 48 hours nearly 400 square miles of territory were occupied, and the insurgent armies threatening Sagunto were forced to abandon their offensive and turn to meet an attack which was approaching their own rear. The Note adds:

> The object of the offensive was to wreck the insurgent offensive against Valencia and to destroy international political plans which were based on an imminent insurgent success in the Levant. The Ebro army has proved its high morale and its technical qualities. To fight for four months with its back to a river such as the Ebro is not a feat possible to many armies, and it has been a struggle that would have been condemned from the first by orthodox military strategists.

'GREAT DEFEAT'

The Salamanca communiqué declares that the Ebro battle has been among the Republicans' heaviest defeats. It states:

> The operation which the Reds, through the medium of their propaganda, presented to the world as a great military success has constituted one of their greatest defeats. Our forces have taken 19,779 prisoners and given burial to 13,275 enemy dead. The enemy's total losses are estimated at over 75,000.

(The Republicans attacked along the river from the mouth to Mequinenza on the night of July 25. The crossing failed at Amposta and was most successful in the centre, Republican troops almost reaching Gandesa. They held out in this loop of the Ebro until the final offensive, begun a fortnight ago. Asco and Flix were the last villages to fall.)

REPUBLICAN SPAIN'S 13,000 VOLUNTEERS
Ready to Leave

Barcelona, November 20.

The total number of volunteers of the International Brigade to be withdrawn from Republican Spain under the League of Nations Volunteers Commission is 13,000, it was learned from a reliable source here to-day.

The volunteers represent 53 nations and are stated to include 800 British and 350 Canadians. Only 103 are Russians. Among the Canadians a large proportion are naturalised Europeans. The main body of the British and Canadian volunteers is now concentrated near the French frontier. It is understood that before allowing them to cross the frontier the French Government has asked for guarantees from the British Government that none will remain in France.–Reuter.

Catalonian campaign – December 1938–February 1939

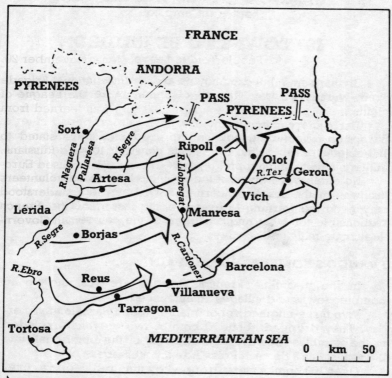

FRANCO GIVES WARNING
Bombing Campaign

100 TOWNS TO BE RAIDED
People Told to Leave

Civilians in a hundred towns and villages of Republican Spain were yesterday warned of imminent aerial bombardments.

The military announcements by wireless, reports Reuter's Burgos correspondent, took the unprecedented step of naming 100 objectives which the insurgents consider to be centres of military activity and supply depots.

No dates were given of the projected bombardments, but listeners in the zones concerned have been told that unless they heed the warning to evacuate, the insurgents cannot be responsible for what might happen in the course of raids on 'legitimate military objectives'.

FRANCO'S BOMBERS ROAM SPAIN

In the meantime Franco's 'planes are roaming Spain, bombing towns and villages unannounced.

Five three-engined rebel 'planes raided Barcelona yesterday. They dropped about 70 bombs, two of which exploded in the Ramblas (Boulevards). The rest of the bombs fell into the sea, states a Spanish Press Agency message.

Over 100 bombs were dropped by nine rebel 'planes over the region of Gerona, near El Pastoral. Three women were killed and a large number of people injured.

The Republican air communiqué yesterday reported a raid by a German 'plane, both bombing and machine-gunning, on the centre of Marmelejo (Cordova Province). Five women and two children were killed and twenty were wounded.

Ten Junker 'planes are also reported to have dropped 100 high-powered bombs on Tarrega (Lerida Province) on Wednesday, killing eight people and wounding 19 among the civilian population.

Four persons were killed and 18 others wounded when five foreign warplanes bombed the village of Torrejon, near Madrid on Wednesday.

WITHDRAWALS FROM LOYALIST
SPAIN VERIFIED
From our Correspondent

Geneva, December 4.

The international military commission that is verifying the withdrawal of foreign volunteers from Government Spain has almost finished its work in the Catalonia area and has announced that as far as that zone is concerned foreign volunteers have been effectively withdrawn from the front. More than five thousand foreign volunteers, including about two thousand French subjects, will have left Spain at the end of next week, it is estimated. The commission will then have to verify the departure from the Catalonian zone of a number of wounded and nationals of various countries.

The commission's report adds that foreign volunteers had, on orders of the Government, actually been leaving their units since the early days of October, and had been grouped according to nationality in concentration centres.

The report is based on investigations carried out by the commission in the different sections of the Catalonian front, in numerous districts behind the lines, in the military schools, general headquarters of inspectors general arms and services, aerial–defence units, organisations for passive defence, and aviation centres.

GENERAL FRANCO 46

Burgos, December 4.

General Franco to-day celebrated his forty-sixth birthday, and in conformity with the simplicity of his style of living spent the day quietly in his family circle at his modest villa home. The Nationalist press devotes its main pages to congratulations to the general and to assurance of loyalty and faith in his leadership.–Press Association Foreign Special.

BACK FROM THE SPANISH WAR
Welcome for the British Battalion

From our London Staff

Fleet Street, Wednesday.

The 300 and more British soldiers of the International Brigade who ended their journey from Spain at Victoria Station this evening had a tumultuous welcome from the thousands of people, many of them carrying banners, who crammed themselves into the space near the platform entrance, blocked up the station approach, or gathered in Buckingham Palace Road till the crowd there was so great that traffic had to be diverted.

Mr. Attlee had difficulty in reaching the platform, where the train had arrived twenty minutes before it was expected, and Miss Ellen Wilkinson, who tried to get through, gave up the attempt in despair. The crowds mainly unaware that the men had arrived, beguiled an hour of waiting by waving their banners, cheering and singing the 'Internationale', and the police did not seem to have much trouble in marshalling them.

The soldiers, some of them still suffering from wounds or sickness, had been travelling about France by such circuitous ways, they said, that the journey home took nearly two days. But before they could set off to enjoy a good meal at the Co-operative Wholesale Society's assembly rooms in Whitechapel, speeches were made at the station by some of the many well-known people there.

'We are proud of the great work you have done; you have worthily, on many a front, upheld the traditions of British democracy,' said Mr. Attlee.

'We unfortunately are ruled by a Government which desires not to help but to hinder the Spanish people and we ask you, now that you are back home, not to imagine that the struggle for democracy and freedom is finished but to realise that you may make a great contribution in the light of your vivid experience to help us to persuade the people of the country that, if Spanish liberty is to be maintained then the Chamberlain Government must go.'

Sir Stafford Cripps and Mr. Tom Mann also spoke, and two members of the battalion replied. The commander, Mr. Sam Wild, who was recently decorated with the Spanish Victoria Cross, declared: 'We intend to keep the promise we made to the Spanish people before we left – that we would change our front, but continue to fight in England for the assistance of Spain.'

Mr. Ben Cooney, the battalion's political commissar spoke of the five hundred men who had lost their lives. 'They need not have died,' he said. 'They have been killed by the policy of non-intervention.'

At last, after all the bustle of arrival and the poignant family greetings and the speeches, the men and wives and children trickled through a narrow lane in the wildly cheering crowd, and led by a bugle band, the battalion set off to march to Whitechapel. Long before they arrived many friends, including Mr. Wilfrid Roberts, Miss Ellen Wilkinson, and Professor Haldane, were waiting for them.

VIEWS ON THE FIGHTING

Impressions of the fighting in Spain were given to a 'Manchester Guardian' representative by two of the men. One Mr. Francis Webster, had spent fourteen months in Spain and the other, Mr. T. Bloomfield, eighteen months in two periods. They had been in the fighting on the Ebro.

They talked about Franco's great advantage in the air force and artillery. He made his advances always during the day, they said, when he could bombard the Government side heavily from land and air, but at night the Government troops were on level terms and could make their advance.

Both men spoke of the Spanish Government's weakness in anti-aircraft defence, except at the bridges. Mr. Webster said that Franco's men, when they saw one of their aviators coming down on the Government side, would shoot him in the parachute.

Speaking of the food shortage, they said the best food must go to the soldiers who needed it because they were badly clad. They had been distressed when in Barcelona for two days' leave to see food queues waiting for hours. 'But Franco', they added, 'will never win!'

The men of the battalion as a whole looked well, but as they said, they had had a long rest since leaving Spain.

Not all of the men of the British Battalion arrived home in this party. A further group of 67 men, many of whom had been taken prisoner on the Battalion's last day of action, were not released from Nationalist captivity until February 1939. (See report of Tuesday February 7 1939.)

THE LAST ROLL-CALL
Volunteers Return

BRITISH AND IRISH IN SPAIN
A Retrospect

(Three hundred British members of the International Brigade reached London from Spain on Wednesday. The writer of this article was formerly commandant of the British Battalion.)

By Tom Wintringham

The last of the British and Irish volunteers have left Spain. In this roll-call no attempt is made to give a picture of all the men who served, first in the Militia, then in little groups as part of the first battalions of the International Brigade, and finally with the British Battalion. It is a roll-call from one man's memory.

To give a complete picture of these men, all of them, would be as difficult as to picture the two thousand people who are packed in one stretch of sand on an English Bank Holiday or all the members of some widespreading organisation such as a co-operative society.

And my roll-call has a natural bias towards men who came my way or happened to have some characteristic or quality that made them different from the average. Yet it was the average volunteer who counted. It was Bert, who nearly dropped a handgrenade on me when we were practising, or Bill, who could produce 'stray' chickens from a dead-empty landscape, and many hundred other anonymous Berts and Bills who made up our companionship of fighting men. There was only one outstanding common characteristic, covering almost all of them: they hated war. They were trying to stamp out a spreading war as one fights a forest fire.

Most of them, though not all, were part of 'the Movement'. They had done the door-step work in uphill elections, gone on hunger-marches of the unemployed, worked to get new members for their trade unions in mills and factories, distributed leaflets, carried the trades council banner on May Day . . .

The exceptions, those who were not trade unionists or members of a working-class party, were not mainly moved by a desire for adventure. They had the ordinary man's feeling for fair play: they disliked Fascism as the man 'who can't be bothered with politics' does dislike it, everywhere.

EX-OFFICERS

Our best soldier was of that sort: George Montague Nathan.

His opinions were Liberal–Socialist. He had been an officer in the Great War; he was tall and thin and smoked a pipe and carried gloves and a stick. So he looked very like the typical English officer that foreign cartoonists put in their drawings. Anyone who saw him at once said: 'That's an Englishman.' Because of this and his extreme coolness in action, his way of looking after his men, and his marvellous eye for ground, he became a legend from the day he took into action the first British company, Christmas, 1936.

Just before he was killed at Brunete he was showing an American officer the lie of the land. An enemy machine-gun began dropping bullets on the road along which they were walking; these bullets first flicked the heel off the American's left shoe; then tore the sole off his right shoe. He started hopping a bit. Nathan watched him with surprise and, lighting his pipe, said 'When you've done, Bob, when you've quite done.'

Company commander in December, 1936, battalion commander in January, 1937, and Chief of Staff of our brigade next month, Nathan would doubtless have gone higher still if he had not been killed. Only one of our volunteers, I think, held a higher appointment than that Nathan reached: George Aitken, of the Amalgamated Engineering Union, who ranked as a lieutenant colonel.

Three others I remember who had been officers in the British army: Arthur Olerenshaw, the musician, who helped me run a training school for officers; young Cameron, who had fought on the North-west frontier, and Wilfred Macartney, author of 'Walls Have Mouths', the battalion's first commanding officer.

LABELS AND FACT

I have read with some surprise in a London paper that the International Brigades consisted of 'the lowest dregs of the unemployed' and of 'Marxist hordes that desecrated churches'. Desecrating churches has not been an English habit for 300 years. We had unemployed in our ranks whose courage and endurance proved what a waste it is to keep men of such quality eating their hearts out in idleness. But most of our volunteers gave up jobs to come to Spain.

Some of those who are buried in Spain would have enriched English literature if they had lived: Ralph Fox, as novelist: and four poets, John Cornford, Julian Bell, Christopher St. John Sprigg, and Charles Donnelly from Ireland.

Our brigades have been called 'international gunmen'. Let me run through names that seem strangely at variance with this and other labels stuck on us by those who choose to write without knowing the men they are writing about.

Traill, a journalist from Bloomsbury, Chief of Staff of the 86th Brigade; Bee, our map-maker, an architect; David McKenzie, son of an admiral; Giles and Esmond Romilly, relatives of Winston Churchill; Malcolm Dunbar, son of Lady Dunbar, our last Chief of Staff of the Brigade; Hugh Slater, journalist, and very neat with his anti-tank guns; Clive Branson; Peter Whittaker; Ralph Bates, the novelist.

Clem Beckett gave up the princely salary of a star dirt-track rider for a few pesetas and a grave on the Jarama; Noel Carritt and his brother came from the quiet of Boar's Hill, Oxford; Miles Tomalin became less interested in psycho-analysis than in the fireside sing-songs that he accompanied on a recorder; 'Maro', the cartoonist, drew his last sketch for us the night before he was killed.

Lorimer Birch was a scientist from Cambridge; R. M. Hilliard was known as the 'Boxing Parson of Killarney'. Lewis Clive, a descendant of Clive of India, was a Labour borough councillor and an active worker in the Fabian Research Bureau. Bill Alexander, who commanded the battalion at Teruel, was from the 'Fabian Nursery'. Chris Thornycroft, Richard Kisch, who fought in Majorca when the war was a month old, and all those others whom I have mentioned were neither 'gunmen' nor 'dregs of the unemployed'.

One boy brought me a letter of introduction from a Liberal M.P. – which might be thought a queer thing to bring to the adjutant if you are joining a 'Red' battalion. Another, from County Cork, wore a crucifix. Frank Ryan, who was in Franco's prisons for some months and is now 'missing', is a Catholic Irish Republican.

Last in the roll-call and, I think, representative of all those who fought in Spain, I remember Will Paynter, of the South Wales Miners' Executive, and three men whose graves are in Spain who were my company commanders in the Battle of the Jarama. In that battle our battalion helped to hold the last road into Madrid, a road open to-day. These three are William Briskey, a London busman, member of the Transport and General Workers' Union, a sergeant in the Great War; Harold Fry, from Edinburgh, at one time corporal in his Majesty's Brigade of Guards; and Kit Conway at one time of the Irish Republican Army.

They were known, by the man who commanded them and the men they commanded, to be the equals in courage and comradeship of those fighting men of the past whose names wake pride in the English, Scottish, and Irish peoples.

FRANCO'S 'INHUMAN BOMBINGS'
Spain's Bitterness at 'Cold Indifference of the Democracies'

ANOTHER APPEAL TO GREAT BRITAIN

A 'new appeal to the spirit of fair play and the traditional public uprightness of the British Government' was made by the Spanish Government yesterday in a Note handed to the Foreign Office by the Spanish Ambassador in London.

Britain is again asked to use its influence with Germany and Italy to put a stop to the continued bombing of the Spanish civil population by General Franco's Italo-German aviation.

LETTERS TO THE EDITOR

BRITISH BATTALION'S RETURN
A Double Appeal for Help

To the Editor of the 'Manchester Guardian'

Sir,–We desire to thank the press and the British public for the remarkable welcome accorded to us upon our return from Spain, and for the deep understanding displayed by all concerned. But the joy of our return is tempered by the sorrow of leaving for ever nearly five hundred of our comrades in Spain, and by the remembrance of the gaunt faces of Spanish women and children slowly starving to death. We will not rest until we are assured that the dependants of our fallen comrades are adequately provided for, and that the Spanish people receive the food they need.

So on behalf of the British Battalion we appeal to those who have displayed such great understanding to send food to Spain and give all the help they can to the Dependants' Aid Committee, a body which has done magnificent work in providing for our dependants while we have been in Spain, and which now has the task of providing for the widows and fatherless children of our fallen comrades. The secretary of this committee is Mrs. Charlotte Haldane, 1, Litchfield Street, London, W.C.2.–

Yours.&c.,

SAM WILD (Major) former Commander British Battalion,
MALCOLM DUNBAR (Major),   ROBERT WALKER (Captain),
JOHN POWER (Captain),   ROBERT COONEY (Commissar),
GEORGE FLETCHER   ALAN GILCHRIST (Commissar),
(Captain),   BEN RICHARDSON (Lieutenant).
(On behalf of the British Battalion.) London, December 12.

WHY FRANCO BOMBS
Says It Is a Short Cut to Peace

Burgos, December 22.

Replying to accusations that bombings from the air are inhuman, the insurgents declare that they are taking the shortest cut open to them to the obtaining of peace for the whole of the Spanish people, and that in bombing ports and towns which are stated here to be known sources of food and military supplies they are effecting this.

Insurgent authorities declare unequivocally that any attempts at mediation which do not have the effect of a 'complete moral and physical victory over the anarchist leadership of Republican Spain' will be rejected.–Press Association Foreign Special.

'IN BARCELONA BY EASTER'
Present Hopes of the Rebels

It was the fifth day of General Franco's new offensive in Catalonia, and on Franco's side already there is talk of the soldiers enjoying their abandoned Christmas hampers in Barcelona at Easter-time.

'The impetuous advance of the Spanish Nationalist forces has continued since dawn,' stated last night's report issued by the insurgent field headquarters. The advance has been carried forward an average of four miles, it is added. Fifteen hundred prisoners were said to have been taken yesterday, bringing the total since Friday to 7,000.

The immediate aim is still Borjas Blancas, 15 miles south-east of Lerida. The capture of this large village the Nationalists consider, would not only force a rapid retreat of the Republicans before Lerida, but would threaten to cut off the Ebro defenders by a quick drive down 40 miles of main road towards Tarragona.

At noon yesterday, states Reuter from Saragossa, the Nationalists had completely cleaned up the pocket at the junction of the Ebro and Segre, comprising an area of 280 square miles. This was accomplished when the Franco cavalry division, the Monasterios, forming the right wing, advanced from Almatret to the north bank of the Ebro. Several hundred prisoners were taken in the manoeuvre, it is claimed, and the right wing were brought in touch with the Moroccan Army Corps holding the south bank of the Ebro pocket.

The left flank, it is added, advanced in a general swing towards Borjas Blancas.

In the north near the Pyrenees the Franco troops captured the hydro-electric power plant at Mount Cabo (east of Sort). This gives them control of one of the few remaining sources of electric power for the textile towns west of Barcelona. The troops in this region are operating on the lower slopes of the Pyrenees with the temperatures six degrees below zero.

It is reported from Saragossa that a further 1,000 Republican prisoners have been drafted to the rear, bringing the total number taken since the advance began to over 5,000.

In answer to Republican allegations that Italian troops are forming the vanguard in this sector, the Nationalists state that the Catalonian Army Corps operating here consists of 80 per cent Spaniards and 20 per cent Italians.

A Ministry of Defence communiqué issued in Barcelona last night spoke of 'intense pressure' being continued by the insurgents in the Tremp sector. Italian troops 'to the known number of four divisions,' it is stated, obtained some advances, but were severely shaken by the fire and counter-attacks of the Government troops.

Tuesday January 3 1939   *p.15*

HARDEST BATTLE OF THE SPANISH WAR
Barcelona's account of Franco's Attack

ITALIAN DIVISION WITHDRAWN BECAUSE OF LOSSES

Barcelona, January 2.

The hardest battle of the war is how the fierce struggle that has been going on for the past eleven days is described in a communiqué issued to-day by the Minister of National Defence. After suggesting that the Nationalists were driven to launch the offensive by the refusal from abroad to accord belligerent rights and by the internal situation behind General Franco's lines, the communiqué proceeds:

Prisoners from each of the four Italian divisions have been captured in the last few days by Republican troops. Their statements make it clear that the offensive has been endowed with a wealth of assistance from Italy and Germany in the shape of

287

trained technicians and war material of every sort. Nevertheless, the invaders have only been able so far to advance behind a rain of shells in sectors of little military importance. They have only succeeded in engaging all their man-power in a strategic battle without being able to apply the principles of military science.

REPEATING EBRO OFFENSIVE

The Ebro fighting is being repeated in a much severer form. The Spanish infantry, armed with hand grenades, is attacking, holding and capturing the Italo-German tanks. They are withstanding attacks such as the invading forces have never before attempted. Following artillery barrages lasting up to five hours, in which tens of thousands of rounds are fired, the enemy is having to make four, five, or more attacks of this kind just to take a hill. Then the Republicans go singing into the counter-attack and, possessed by a burning patriotism, increase the cost to the invaders of every foot they hold.

The Spanish artillery, as the prisoners admit, spontaneously rakes with extraordinary precision the enemy concentrations and destroys the foreign tanks. The Republican air arm multiplies its efforts to compensate for its numerical inferiority, and while protecting the land army has brought down twenty Italo-German 'planes.

ITALIAN LOSSES

The insurgents have suffered extremely heavy losses. The first Navarran Division the best troops the insurgents have, has suffered, according to one prisoner, 30 to 40 per cent casualties. The Littorio Division, the best of the Italian divisions, was temporarily withdrawn when it was on the verge of complete annihilation. Every insurgent and Italian division has suffered very heavily, and the report in an Italian newspaper that Borjas Blancas had been taken is made ridiculous by the tenacity with which the Republicans have barred the invaders' progress.

Opposing an army which is in league with the enemies of Spain, whose soldiers are subject to a regime of terrorism and reprisals which they bitterly resent, and fighting a war for which they feel no enthusiasm, is the Republican Army. Its intention is to fight to the end, unshakably determined to bar the advance of the invaders and save the liberty of Catalonia and the independence of Spain.—Reuter.

EXPERIMENTING IN SPAIN
Germany Learns

From our Diplomatic Correspondent

London, Monday.

Germany's new Messerschmidt aeroplanes have been tested in the Spanish civil war.

The pilots are pledged before they leave Germany never to let their 'planes fall into the hands of the enemy. Each pilot has orders to set fire to his 'plane if it is brought down or has to make a forced landing on enemy soil. Each 'plane has a special tank of inflammable matter that can be ignited at once for this purpose.

The German pilots in Spain are used more in combined infantry and air attacks than in air raids, which are chiefly carried out by the Italians. The German military experts are particularly interested in developing the art of offensive operation by all arms combined, the air arm included, and Spain is proving to be a valuable experimental field. They are of opinion that the decisive blow in future wars will be delivered by combined operations of this kind.

Italian experts do not entirely share this view, but hold that the preponderance or superiority of one arm may be decisive.

ITALIANS DESTROYING ANOTHER SPANISH TOWN
Republicans Fight Against Great Odds

Barcelona, January 13.

It was admitted here to-night that General Franco's troops had captured Tortosa.

At the same time the Nationalists to-day exerted heavy pressure on the sector north-west of Tarragona, near the important road junction of Valls. This is about sixty miles from Tortosa in the direction of Barcelona.

I witnessed at close quarters the devastating barrage of shells and bombs with which the Nationalists were blasting the way for their offensive. The Nationalists were making a two-fold thrust towards Tortosa and towards Tarragona. It was evident that they hoped to cut off the Republican forces holding Tortosa and the line of the Lower Ebro. The Republicans, however, have eluded the trap by withdrawing their forces from Tortosa to a line reaching the sea at Hospitalet, 30 miles farther up the coast. Most of the civil population had already been evacuated from the enclosed coastal area, which is about 40 miles long and 12 broad.

From a hill close to the main road this afternoon I watched the battle north-west of Tarragona, where the Nationalists were pressing towards Valls. The ground trembled; it was as if a terrific thunderstorm were in progress. It seemed incredible that the Republicans should withstand the deluge of shells and bombs which the enemy were showering on them.

To-day the Italians were battering their way southward towards Valls from Montblanch, trying to force their way down the three roads which lead southward from Montblanch to the Mediterranean, and Valls must be added to the long list of pleasant little Spanish towns which have been wrecked by bombs and shells.

FOREIGN 'PLANES BUSY

Seeking the comparative safety of the olive trees on the hill, I heard the heavy drone of approaching bombers and saw nine Heinkels coming over in threes. They bombed and machine-gunned the congested highway, taking toll of refugee cars and telegraph wires, and raising immense clouds of smoke and dust. Then group after group of great bombers came over, raining bombs and bullets upon the roads beyond and raising fresh clouds of smoke from Valls.

During an hour and a half I counted more than 40 bombers, apart from the swarms of chasers, which kept diving and machine-gunning some target or other. Whereas the chasers dived at their targets, the bombers used the machine-guns without altering their courses.–Press Association Foreign Special.

Tuesday January 17 1939   *p.11*

ADVANCE ON BARCELONA
Franco's Progress

MACHINE-GUNNING REFUGEES
Italians Accused

Reports from Franco's Spain say that three insurgent armies are converging on Barcelona. They are, it is said, at an average of 42 miles from the city.

A message from General Franco urging the Catalans 'to lay down their arms in view of the inevitability of a Nationalist victory' was broadcast by insurgent wireless stations last night.

There has been much bombing round Barcelona, and yesterday five Italian 'planes bombed the fort and the poorer districts. According to the Spanish Government, the Italians bombed and machine-gunned refugees escaping from Tarragona. The Italians have done this in most of the big retreats in Spain.

At Geneva yesterday the League Council commented on the satisfactory progress made with the withdrawal of foreign volunteers from Government Spain. This has been verified by the Council's own commission which the Spanish Government invited to Spain. The importance of withdrawal from Franco's Spain was stressed.

Wednesday January 18 1939   *p.18*

LETTERS TO THE EDITOR

JUSTICE FOR SPAIN
The Republicans' Right to Buy Arms

To the Editor of the Manchester Guardian

Sir,–The Spanish struggle has entered a critical phase, the democratic Government of Spain has mobilised every man and woman to stem the last desperate offensive of the enemy against Catalonia. The determination of the Spanish people to resist is as great as ever, and its troops are successfully counter-attacking in the south.

It has now become clear that the Republicans are facing an overwhelming weight of arms, troops, and munitions accumulated by Italy and Germany in flagrant and open violation of their undertakings under the Non-Intervention Agreement. At least five Italian divisions with complete war material form the spearhead of the rebel advance in Catalonia. In Rome not only is this fact openly declared but the official 'Diplomatic Bulletin' announces that this aid will be increased as much as necessary.

The Prime Minister in Rome apparently accepted this position. The 'agreement to differ', according to the diplomatic correspondents, is that 'Britain will adhere to non-intervention while Italy adheres to intervention'. In other words, while the Republican Government is to continue to be deprived of its right to trade and purchase arms and has loyally fulfilled its

291

undertakings by withdrawing every one of its foreign volunteers, under supervision of the League of Nations Commission, the right has been recognised of the Italian Government to pursue military intervention in defiance of its repeated pledges.

British policy has been declared again and again to be 'to enable the Spanish people to settle their own affairs', yet now non-intervention has become a weapon by which Mussolini is to be allowed to impose his will on the Spanish people while Britain and France tie their hands.

Since, as seems implied by the results of the Rome visit, Mr. Chamberlain now admits that nothing further can be done to get the Italian divisions out of Spain or to prevent further Italian intervention in the degree Mussolini considers necessary, there is no possible basis in law or justice for preventing the restoration to the Republican Government of its right to purchase the means for its defence. The embargoes must be lifted and the frontiers opened by Britain and France forthwith.– Yours,&c.,

RICHARD ACLAND. ANTRIM.
KATHERINE ATHOLL, ALFRED BARNES, GERALD BARRY,
VERNON BARTLETT, GERALD BRENAN, VIOLET
BONHAM-CARTER, CECIL OF CHELWOOD,
PETER CHALMERS MITCHELL, MARGERY CORBETT ASHBY,
STAFFORD CRIPPS, MARGARET DEAS,
MARGUERITE NEVILLE DIXEY, E.K. DODDS,
A.S. DUNCAN-JONES, EBBY EDWARDS, R. FLETCHER,
MARGERY FRY, ALISON GARLAND, G.T. GARRATT,
DOROTHY GLADSTONE, VICTOR GOLLANCZ,
MILNER GRAY, J.B.S. HALDANE, PHILIP JORDAN,
KINGSLEY MARTIN, WALTER LAYTON, A.D. LINDSAY,
LISTOWELL, J.C. LITTLE, G. LE M. MANDER,
GILBERT MURRAY, LOGAN PEARSALL SMITH,
EILEEN POWER, D.N. PRITT,
MARGUERITE RATH-CREEDAN, RHONDDA,
WILFRED ROBERTS, W.J.R. SQUANCE, G.R. STRAUSS,
R.H. TAWNEY, J.B. TREND, ELLEN WILKINSON,
JOSIAH C. WEDGWOOD,
London, January 17.

BARCELONA SENDS GOLD TO FRANCE

Perpignan, January 20.

Seven lorries from Barcelona crossed the French frontier here this morning carrying 45 tons of gold and silver to Paris.– Reuter.

This brief report gives a telling impression of the gravity of the situation confronting the Republic.

REBELS REACH BARCELONA
Little Hope That the Catalans Can Save Their Capital

GOVERNMENT LEAVES THE CITY

General Franco has reached Barcelona. Last night he claimed that one column, advancing along the coast, was only a mile from the suburbs.

The Republican Government is reported to have left Barcelona, and may have gone to Gerona, sixty miles to the north-west. All the indications are that the war will be carried on from Gerona and other Catalan towns.

UNDER SHELL-FIRE

The Moors, advancing along the coast road, have won the race to Barcelona. (The Italians near Manresa are again lagging a little.) Yesterday afternoon General Yague's Moroccan Army Corps captured Gava, ten miles from Barcelona. They moved on without stopping and by evening Barcelona's aerodrome, lying to the south of the mouth of the River Llobregat, has fallen to them.

Last night Barcelona was under direct shell-fire; for hours rebel batteries were pounding the port. Again and again during the day the city was raided, but the anti-aircraft defences have been improved.

It is not certain whether the Catalans intend to fight in the streets to save their capital: the rebels believe they will not. Nor is it known whether Franco will try to enter the city as once or whether he will wait until the column from Manresa has surrounded Barcelona on the north-west and so cut off the Republican retreat.

THE GOVERNMENT LEAVES

Reuter reports that a very reliable American official who arrived in Perpignan last night from Barcelona declares that the Republican Government has now left Barcelona.

The diplomatists are withdrawing towards the frontier. The British Consul General for the present, however, will remain at Barcelona, as will also part of the French Embassy staff.

The British destroyer Greyhound, with a dozen women and children from the British Embassy in Barcelona on board, is on its way to Marseilles, but is being delayed by a fierce storm. The 40 Britons in Barcelona had been advised to leave the city aboard the Greyhound.

THE TRAPPED

But in the rapidly dwindling area of Republican territory in Catalonia there are millions of Spaniards who will not be able to escape. The sea is blocked to them by Franco's warships and the French frontier is closed.

It was learned in well-informed quarters in Paris late last night that the French Government, in reply to Barcelona's request, has stated that it cannot receive some 50,000 refugees from Republican Spain.

Saturday January 28 1939   *p.11*

FRANCO BOMBS REFUGEES
No Neutral Zone

FLIGHT TOWARDS FRANCE
Harried by 'Planes

General Franco yesterday declared himself opposed to the idea of setting up a neutral zone on Spanish territory for receiving refugees fleeing before Franco's advance, according to the Havas correspondent in Burgos.

Instead General Franco is bombing them; with the fear of his bombers hastening their steps, thousands of refugees were last night pouring into the towns and villages of Northern Catalonia. Franco's 'planes yesterday morning bombed the outskirts of Figueras, the new seat of the Republican Government. It normally is a town of 10,000 inhabitants, but now has a population of more than 40,000 – swollen by refugees from Barcelona.

The Republican authorities at Figueras, states Reuter's Perpignan correspondent, have sent an urgent request for medical supplies to the French authorities at Le Perthus. The road between Figueras and the French frontier, 15 miles away, is crammed with refugees. Some have already reached the frontier and have been allowed into France.

PITIABLE CONDITIONS

In Figueras there are scenes of indescribable confusion – Government officials trying to find their departments, Ministers hunting for their colleagues, crying mothers loking for lost children, small boys and girls begging piteously for bread. The refugees lack shelter from the bitter cold and fires to keep them warm.

Monday January 30 1939   p.12

15,000 REFUGEES CROSS THE FRENCH FRONTIER
46,000 More Expected Soon

Perpignan, January 29

Fifteen thousand refugees crossed the frontier from Spain into France yesterday, and to-day the flight from Franco continued. Forty-six thousand more are expected to reach the border shortly.

Among the thousands of refugees in the railway tunnel at Cerbère are about 100 former members of the International Brigade. They are waiting for the French authorities to allow them across the border.

One of the volunteers managed to work his way to the mouth of the tunnel at the Cerbère station this morning where he was able to speak with members of the International Evacuation Commission. They immediately sent him back to get a list of all the waiting internationals. The volunteer re-entered the 220-yard long tunnel and returned later with a list of over a hundred names, none British or American.

A great army of fugitives is still marching towards the frontier. Many, perhaps the majority of them, come from Barcelona, but some of them are fugitives from parts of Spain long ago in enemy hands. They have been driven from one place to another until at last they have been forced against the French frontier. Starting in groups from small towns, they have all converged upon the main highway, their numbers swelling until they have reached the frontier in a great flood.

Until late last night Reuter's correspondent watched the flood of exiles at the frontier village of Le Perthus. Once in that frightening jam of fugitives it was difficult to get out. In pouring rain refugees were streaming into Le Perthus in hundreds, homeless and starving and helpless, and terrified by false rumous that the enemy's mechanised troops were hot on their heels.

With great difficulty two cars carrying diplomatists tried to reach Figueras, but at Le Perthus they turned back when they heard that the roads on the Spanish side were completely choked with refugees coming up from the front and piling into one solid frightened mass. Along the roads are abandoned cars and mule-carts, but few abandoned mules, for the animals have been killed and eaten by starving people.

Wounded soldiers with their feet swathed in bandages and their arms in plaster casts and steel frames hobbled along; women reached safety carrying heavy suit-cases or bundles on their heads; old people and children huddled together in blankets on the station platform. Every particle of food offered to them was ravenously devoured by people who had not eaten for days.—Press Association Foreign Special.

p.12

'FINAL VICTORY' SOON
Duce to Franco

Rome, January 29.

In a telegram addressed to General Franco following the fall of Barcelona Signor Mussolini says:

The Italian people is enthusiastic at the news of your superb victory at Barcelona, which anticipates only by a short while the final victory destined to inaugurate in the world the era of the new Spain, united and strong.

At this moment in which the indestructible comradeship of blood has proved itself decisively once again, accept, with my greetings, my most fervent wishes for the future of your country. Arriba Espagna!
MUSSOLINI

To this General Franco replied:

The victory of Barcelona, crowning the brilliant operations in Catalonia, demonstrates the vitality of peoples when they are animated by a doctrine full of idealism.

As general and as a Spaniard, I am proud to number among my troops the magnificent Blackshirts which, at the side of their Spanish comrades, have written these pages of glory against international Communism.

With my best wishes for your Empire, kindly receive my most affectionate and cordial greetings!

GENERAL FRANCO

—Reuter.

MORE WOUNDED ITALIANS

Naples, January 28.

Some 600 soldiers of all ranks wounded in the recent fighting in Spain arrived here in the hospital ship Cradisca to-day. They were welcomed by the Prince of Piedmont and a crowd of onlookers who pressed cigars, cigarettes, and flowers on the men.—Reuter.

MORE ARMS FOR SPAIN
Dr. Negrin's Claim

'Although Spain is going through the most difficult phase of the war, the enemy's hopes that the republic would collapse with the fall of Barcelona are once more destined to be frustrated,' declared Dr. Negrin, the Spanish Prime Minister, in an address to the Spanish people, reports the Spanish Press Agency. He said:

Fresh reserves of troops and new material have now been put into operation. This war material arrived late, as it arrived late in Madrid, but it has now arrived in time, as it arrived in time in 1936. The Republic now has soldiers with ample war material and infinite courage.

When I could not give you hope I said nothing. To-day I can categorically assure you that we are safe. We have lived through disaster; we will survive this one also. Better times are coming, but everyone at the frontier and in the rear must take part.

CONTRASTS ON FRENCH FRONTIER
Clearing Up on the French Side: Misery Remains Over Border

From Nancy Cunard

Perpignan, January 31.

The taximan who drove me to Le Perthus to-day compared the exodus of refugees from Spain with the retreat of the Marne: 'The Marne was bad enough for us, but it was nothing at all comparable to this.' We stopped at the concentration camp at Le Boulou on the way. Here they said 18,000 refugees had been received and had been sent on between Saturday and Tuesday. Thousands more went direct to Perpignan.

Le Perthus has been thoroughly cleaned of the terrible mass of litter that such a tragic invasion as passed through these last three days must perforce leave. Chlorate of lime has been sprinkled along the street. The cafe, the only one, is less crowded. There are more French and Senegalese troops. In all, there is far more organisation. No longer does one see terrible masses of starved faces, cripples, and wounded soldiers waiting in the middle of the road.

RAGS

But immediately after the barrier into Spain the scene changes. Here is the region – it stretches for about a mile – that has been called 'Dantesque'. It rained for two days, and the litter of rags and filth lies sodden on the ground. Fresher rags drape the rocks along the road. A dead ass lies on one side. A van has fallen into the ravine and has caught against a tree.

A perspective of abandoned cars begins; there must be about twenty others that have fallen or been driven over the edge during those three days of the surge up the hill. To-day there are few people on foot. But a score of lorries passes during the hour or so it takes to walk down to La Junquera; all of them contain only women and children. The men, even many of the old ones, are sent back. People are camping out here too; as I return in the dark there are bright fires among the rocks.

I walk a little way with two old men. They are Asturian peasants. The one who does all the talking has a gesture of anger: 'I am 63, I was the mayor of my village. I am ready to fight on. Now they will neither let us into France now allow us to buy arms. What am I to do?' His companion says nothing but 'When we have the Spanish permits we shall be allowed in.' Meanwhile they trudge back to Spain, two ragged, weary, but proud old men. They have nothing to eat; they tell me they hope they may find 'something on the road someone might have thrown away'. But there is nothing.

I walk on. Mattresses and blankets that have been thrown away because they could be carried no farther are already beginning to rot. On a bridge is a typewriter. A Carabinero lolls in an armchair asleep in the sun of to-day. An officer controls my permit – already stamped. Another old man comes to tell me his indignation that 'some wounded were not let in at once; old people collapsed – why is all this?' They seem not to realise what a frontier means. There are laws and there are facts. And the facts are that thousands and thousands have got there before; the later thousands have to wait.

CAMPING IN THE OPEN

The rags begin again at the other end of La Junquera. People are camping out everywhere in the open fields. You cannot try even to assess their thousands. The winter sun of Spain shines on the fragment of mirror a man is shaving himself at, propped against a fallen lorry. Another man is cooking an omlette between some vines. The road, by comparison with three days ago, is just 'very full'. Cars can now pass on to Figueras. The whole migration is living here till it may come into France.

p.15

DR. NEGRIN'S PEACE TERMS
Disclosure that Arms Have Been Bought from Italy

Dr. Negrin, the Spanish Republican Prime Minister, in a speech in the Cortes, the Spanish Parliament, at Figueras yesterday, again laid down three conditions which he regarded as essential to the establishment of peace in Spain. These, which were among his 13 points laid down in May, were—

1. The independence of Spain should be guaranteed free of all foreign interference.
2. The Spanish people should be allowed to choose their own regime and destiny.
3. There should be no reprisals after the war.

'We shall fight to save Catalonia,' Dr. Negrin said, 'but if we cannot save it thousands of Spaniards are waiting for us in Central and Southern Spain by whose sides we will continue our struggle.'

'I know', Dr. Negrin continued, 'that soldiers and even officers have absented themselves from their posts, but we cannot for that call them traitors and cowards. They had for fifty days been fighting heroically with inadequate material. Many of those who fled knew what it was to wait in the trenches to seize the arms of a fallen comrade. The strongest men flinch in such circumstances.

'The lack of arms was always the most terrible problem they had to face, and in this they had to struggle not only against their enemies but against their friends who had turned themselves into 'policemen searching for contraband'.

'We have been forced', he continued, 'to deal in contra-band arms. We have even bought them – why not say so? – in Italy and Germany. Now we have received our contraband supplies while help has also come to us from the central and southern regions of Spain. This has reached us late, but not too late. Had we received help earlier Tarragona and Barcelona could have been saved. But we can still hold the enemy in Catalonia.

'This is not a war of ideologies: it is a fight for liberty and the future of all the democracies. We are defending not only our own interests against the totalitarian States but the interests of those who have made our struggle harder and who even in the present situation are pursuing a policy which they vainly think will save the peace of Europe. But how many days of peace will it bring? I say it is here in the crossfire on the Pyrenees that the world's future will be decided.'

Monday February 6 1939   *p.9*

FRANCE OPENS FRONTIER TO LOYALIST ARMY
End of Resistance in Catalonia

NEGRIN FLIES TO MADRID: OTHERS LEAVE THE COUNTRY

The Republican resistance in Catalonia has collapsed and there is now no organised force between Franco's armies and the Pyrenees frontier.

Franco last night told the French authorities on the frontier that he had withdrawn the Italians from the frontier to allay French anxiety.

It is stated that the Perpignan authorities yesterday asked

the rebel command to send its troops to the frontier immediately in view of the absence of any further Republican resistance in order to cope with the urgent refugee problem on the frontier. The Nationalists replied that they were advancing as quickly as possible, but they were hampered by the severance of road communications owing to the dynamiting of bridges by the retreating Republicans.

AZANA IN FRANCE

Last evening the frontier was opened to the retreating troops. Thousands are expected to cross. Five thousand volunteers were still on the Spanish side of the frontier last evening.

The Republican Prime Minister and the Foreign Minister have flown to Madrid, and Senor Azana (the President of the Republic) and the heads of the Catalan and Basque Governments have escaped into France. Yesterday 28 Republican aeroplanes were flown into France. The airmen will be interned.

The Italian general has telegraphed to Mussolini claiming that it was his division that captured Gerona. Spanish loyalist sources say that the occupying troops took savage reprisals on the civilian population, shooting many of them.

Figueras (where an attempt had been made to set up a Republican Government) is believed to have fallen also. The town was raided almost continuously, and many hundreds of refugees and other civilians have been killed. It is said to have been wrecked.

FASCIST GRAND COUNCIL

The Fascist Grand Council, meeting late on Saturday night, decided that Italian troops shall stay in Spain until Franco's victory is complete.

Dr. Gayda, who speaks for Mussolini, supplemented this in his paper yesterday. He made it clear that they are now to stay for political and diplomatic reasons. He says there must be a political victory and that the Italians will stop until there has been a 'final and thorough cleaning up of Red troops in Spain and in contiguous territory where they have been organised and until all improper political intervention has stopped.'

The Italian Supreme Commission of National Defence is meeting to-day to consider military problems arising out of the international situation.

REFUGEE SPANISH MINISTERS IN FRANCE

Not Entitled to Official Status – French Foreign Office view

REPORTS OF BRITISH EFFORTS FOR PEACE

Republican Rearguard Still Fighting

From our own Correspondent

Paris, February 6.

The defence of Catalonia is almost at an end. Unable to resist the immensely superior equipment of General Franco's forces, and perhaps also disheartened by the fall of Barcelona, a large part of the Republican Army has in the last weeks been rapidly retreating towards the north. Leading members of the Republican Government have also come into France. The rearguard of this Army is still fighting and holding back as far as possible Franco's advancing troops, but the bulk of the army has followed into exile the many thousand civilian refugees who crossed the French frontier last week.

The French Government, and M. Daladier in particular, has done the one thing that they could in all decency have been done in allowing the retreating Republicans to cross the frontier. The Spanish soldiers (all of whom are being disarmed at the frontier) and civilian refugees, who may together add up to something like 150,000 people, are going to be a great problem for France, and France is certainly entitled to the full co-operation of the other democratic countries, who, it is hoped, will share in the financial burden which the upkeep of these refugees will represent.

It is announced to-night that 40,000 refugees, soldiers and civilians, arrived in 24 hours.

CLAMOUR IGNORED

M. Daladier must be congratulated for having refused to yield to the indecent clamour of a large part of the press which, on the grounds that it was 'only' a civil war and that consequently belligerent rights and the right of internment did not apply to the Spanish Republicans, supported the monstrous proposals that no Spanish soldiers should be allowed into France, and should be driven back into Spain, where they could 'settle their differences' with General Franco as best they could.

Such a 'procedure' would in any case not have been

tolerated by French opinion. As it is, a large part of French opinion bitterly regrets the failure to stop the violation of non-intervention in Franco's favour without which the present tragic refugee problem might never have arisen.

Camps have been prepared for all the refugees, and the 'jam' at Le Perthus and Bourg-Madame is being cleared as rapidly as possible.

STATUS OF MINISTERS

President Azana has arrived on the Swiss frontier to stay with a relative whose home is there. Dr. Negrin, the Premier, and most of the other members of the Government have come to France. The newspapers to-day say that they must all consider themselves as refugees and must in no circumstances attempt to represent the Government of Spain while on French soil.

The French Foreign Office this evening declared that so long as the Spanish Government was on French soil and had not returned to what was left of Republican Spain France considered that 'there was no Spanish Government'. It is possible that Dr. Negrin and other Spanish Republican leaders will attempt to reach Madrid by air. Senor del Vayo, the Foreign Minister, is reported to have returned to Spain, after a talk on the frontier with the British Minister and the French Ambassador. It is not known exactly where Dr. Negrin is to-night.

The 'Temps' to-night asks Dr. Negrin to consider carefully whether the Spanish Republicans still wish to continue their desperate struggle in South-eastern and Central Spain or whether they had not better ask for an armistice, with the suggestion that the British (and possibly the French) Government would attempt to mediate such an armistice.

BRITISH VOLUNTEERS RELEASED FROM FRANCO'S PRISONS

Hendaye, February 6.

Dressed in a variety of coloured jerseys and trousers, but without shirts or socks, 67 British volunteers who a few hours before had been prisoners of General Franco left Hendaye to-night for home. They have been exchanged for Italians. To-day they had marched across the International bridge wearing Spanish Republican uniforms and singing 'It's a long way to Tipperary'.

Before leaving Hendaye the French medical authorities ordered them to be completely reclothed for sanitary reasons.

Later as each man climbed into his carriage at Hendaye railway station he received a parcel of food for the journey. They are due at Dieppe at noon to-morrow. Shaved and well fed the party were as happy as schoolboys breaking up for the holidays.

Thirty-one Canadians and eight English prisoners still remain in prison at San Sebastian and a further four Englishmen and three Canadians near Burgos.

The decision of the French that the men must be completely reclothed before leaving Hendaye was unexpected. The British consular authorities scoured the town for 67 shirts, underclothes, socks, and overalls, and 40 of the men who had already bathed for two hours sat naked waiting for the clothes. The 27 unbathed ex-prisoners sat in the sun in the station yard singing war songs and the Spanish melodies they had learned in prison.

The men were for the most part taken prisoners in April on the Ebro front. Since then they have been in prison at San Pedro. They relate how to pass the time they started a prison 'university'. Among their number they found sufficient 'professors' in the faculties of arts, philosophy, languages, physics, and electrical engineering. Though not allowed knives, they wrought for themselves twenty sets of chessmen. Out of cigarette cards they got together packs for bridge. Several men were wearing rings cleverly wrought and initialled and made out of toothbrushes.–Press Association Foreign Special.

Friday February 10 1939   *p.6*

REASONS FOR THE REPUBLICAN COLLAPSE IN CATALONIA
Great Rebel Superiority in Arms

SPIRIT OF BARCELONA BROKEN BY GERMAN AND ITALIAN 'PLANES

From our Diplomatic Correspondent

London, Thursday.

The Republican collapse on the Catalan front was, above all, the result of the immense superiority of the rebels in all the heavier armaments, a superiority that outweighed the marked inferiority of their infantry.

But there are subsidiary reasons as well. The rear positions of the Republicans were ill-prepared. The spirit of the civilian

304

population of Barcelona was depressed by air raids, by propaganda, by a well-developed system of hostile espionage, and by the shortage of food.

The Republican command made certain mistakes, as wisdom after the event reveals them to be. For example, well-fed but untrained Caribineros were detailed for the defence of key positions such as Montblanch. These Caribineros were fit in a physical but not in a military and political sense, and they retired without fighting before the Italian Littoria Division, whereas hungrier but more reliable Republican troops might have held that position successfully.

EXHAUSTED TROOPS

This retreat exposed the Tarragona road. It compelled the army of the Ebro to retire hurriedly. Indeed, the loss of the Montblanch position shook the whole Republican defensive system in Southern Catalonia. The army of the Ebro, however, retired in good order and without heavy losses. The command abandoned the town of Tarragona, hoping to make a stand along the line from Vendrell to Calaf, but the troops were completely exhausted, and the retreat through Manresa and Igualada could no longer be arrested.

The engagements in these sectors were dominated by the German and Italian aeroplanes. The rebels were able to send 350 aeroplanes with bombs and machine-guns into action on one vital point after another along this front. These air raids were followed by tank attacks and under cover of these the rebel infantry advanced along the valleys. In this way the rebels were able to outflank the heavily fortified mountain positions of the Republicans, who were again and again compelled to retire so as to avoid being encircled.

The staff work of the Republicans seems to have been poor: again and again units of their army lost all contact with the high command. Their defensive system was ill-conceived. Their high command believed that it was unnecessary to fortify the valleys on the assumption that they could be dominated from the heights, an assumption that was false.

TREACHERY

Treachery also seems to have operated on the Republican side, for a key position in front of Vendrell was suddenly abandoned for no apparent reason and without any orders from the high command.

Demoralisation grew in Barcelona with the approach of the rebel army. The effect of the aerial bombardments became devastating, in a psychological even more than a material sense. Although the general mobilisation in Barcelona was carried out efficiently, the Government was no longer sure of its troops. The antagonism between the Catalan Generalidad and the central authorities, dormant for so long, was reawakened by the imminence of disaster. The Generalidad opposed the proclamation of material law, and several military measures were made ineffective by this renewed conflict.

There was an immense overgrowth of bureaucracy that sometimes became stifling. There was widespread corruption that showed itself above all, in the unfair distribution of foodstuffs. The stubbornness of the Generalidad and of the Anarcho-Syndicalists prevented the removal of such evils.

A defensive position was hastily constructed on the River Llobregat, but it could not be completed in time. The concrete had not hardened when the first shells exploded. The trenches collapsed with every concussion. The Government meant to defend the city itself at first, but soon realised the situation was hopeless.

DEMORALISATION

Demoralisation spread rapidly. It was increased on January 25, when squadron after squadron of German and Italian bombing 'planes flew over Barcelona, though without dropping any bombs. This demonstration had an extraordinary psychological effect, for the inhabitants were helpless witnesses of the power of the enemy air force. They were made to realise the enemy's unchallengeable command of the air and to fear that bombing of unprecedented violence might begin at any moment. It was this aerial demonstration that finally broke the spirit of Barcelona. Republican aeroplanes did not dare to engage these forces. The anti-aircraft defences of the city had ceased to function the previous night.

There was little activity on the part of rebel supporters in Barcelona during the critical period. The Republican troops, marching through the streets on January 24 and 25, were fired on from the roofs. The Assault Guards cleared the Ramblas of these snipers on the afternoon of January 25.

The exodus from the city began on January 24. Tens of thousands trekked towards the French frontier. These dense, moving masses were machine-gunned by low-flying rebel aeroplanes. For many days afterwards the edges of the roads were lined with hundreds and hundreds of dead men, women and children. The fugitives were mostly of the working and lower middle classes. The greater part of the bureaucracy remained in Barcelona. Most of the officials of the Generalidad and of the Government departments remained with the intention of going over to General Franco. The fugitives who reached the French frontier are full of praise for the relief work done by the Quakers.

REPUBLICAN LACK OF ARMS

But the chief cause of the Republican defeat still remains the armed superiority of the rebels. Some Republican divisions of 8,000 to 10,000 men disposed of no more than a thousand rifles. Whole Republican units were without any ammunition for days. The rebels, on the other hand, had a superabundance of every kind of weapon. They outnumbered the Republican Air Force by about thirty to one.

International columns took part in the last battles. Several thousands of them were in camp and on the point of leaving Spain, most of them German, Yugo-Slav, Polish, and Italian. They were surprised by the rebel advance and volunteered to serve once more. Many were killed; the survivors are now on French soil.

Wednesday February 22 1939 p.6

FRANCO'S TRIUMPHAL ENTRY INTO BARCELONA
Italians Head the March Past

CRIES OF 'DUCE! DUCE!' GREET THE LEGIONARIES

Barcelona, February 21.

General Franco made his official entry into Barcelona in triumph to-day – twenty-five days after its capture. In brilliant sunshine he reviewed 50,000 troops, and this spectacular parade lasted three and a quarter hours. Barcelona had a public holiday for the occasion.

The march past General Franco in Barcelona's great boulevard the 'Diagonal' was headed by the entire Legionary Army Corps (Italians) with General Gambara in front. After them came Generals Moscardo, Yague, Solchaga, Unos, Grande, Valino, and Monasterio with their troops. Bombers and fighters were among the 250 'planes that roared overhead.

General Franco rode in an open car and was preceded by his picturesque Moorish bodyguard, their trappings jingling and glittering in the sun. He was greeted by shouts of "Viva Franco!' and thousands of hands were raised as the bands broke into the National Anthem 'Marcha Granaderos'.

To-day's display was in part a demonstration to Catalonia of the powerful military support which General Franco possesses for assuming rule over the whole of Spain. The entire

Nationalist Government visited Barcelona for the event, and the foreign Diplomatic Corps was well represented.

Until only a few hours beforehand great precautions were taken to keep completely secret the fact that the entry was about to take place. Thousands of troops of all categories lined the six-mile route through the streets of the city. They were assisted by the civil guard and public order officials. Sixty Moors in cloaks of scarlet and white – General Franco's personal footguards – were stationed on the terrace of a mansion decorated with exquisite tapestries. Their presence gave the first hint as to where the ceremony would centre. Sharpshooters from each of the regiments taking part were perched on top of every neighbouring building.

Standing in an open car General Franco arrived with General Davila, the commander of the Army of the North, and their appearance on a balcony was the signal for five minutes' ceaseless cheering and clapping. The first troops to arrive were those of the Littorio division (Italians), and their familiar green steel helmets were greeted with cries of 'Duce! Duce!'

Units of all types went by, including tanks and motorised light and heavy artillery.

The Green, Black, and Blue 'Arrow' divisions provided a striking microcosm of General Franco's army of 1,200,000 men. After the march past had ended – with the playing of the Italian, German, and Spanish national anthems – General Franco left for an unknown residence on the outskirts of the city.–Press Association Foreign Special.

Tuesday February 28 1939   *p.11*

GENERAL FRANCO RECOGNISED
UNCONDITIONALLY
Action by Britain and France

AMBASSADORS TO BE APPOINTED AT
ONCE
Commons Censure Debate To-day

Mr. Chamberlain announced in the House of Commons yesterday the British Government's decision to recognise unconditionally the Franco authorities as the legal Government in Spain. Last night Sir Robert Hodgson, the British Agent at Burgos, informed General Jordana, Franco's Foreign Minister, of this decision.

France's decision to recognise Franco was also finally taken yesterday and announced after a meeting of the Cabinet. Burgos will be informed as soon as possible.

The British and French Governments have not yet appointed their Ambassadors to Franco's Government, but there will be no delay in choosing them. Sir Robert Hodgson will act as Chargé d'Affaires in Burgos until the British appointment is made. It was suggested last night that Sir George Mounsey, an assistant Under Secretary of State, will be chosen.

Most countries in Europe have now recognised General Franco; the first among them were Germany and Italy, who sent Ambassadors to the rebels only a few months after the revolt began in 1936. The Soviet Union has not granted recognition, nor has the United States.

General Franco, speaking in Burgos last night, declared, 'The hour of truth has come. To-day England recognised us. To-morrow it will be the whole world.' He made no reference to France, but warmly praised Italy, Germany, Portugal, and Japan for their attitude towards the Spanish war.

It was announced in Madrid last night, reports Reuter, that Senor del Vayo, the Republican Foreign Minister, returned to Valencia from Paris yesterday and saw Dr. Negrin, the Premier. Both Dr. Negrin and Senor del Vayo are expected in Madrid shortly when an announcement of the Republican intentions will probably be made.

FRANCO'S ASSURANCES

The recognition of Franco by the British Government has been unconditional, but Mr. Chamberlain declared that the British Government

> have noted with satisfaction the public statements of General Franco concerning the determination of himself and his Government to secure the traditional independence of Spain and to take proceedings only in the case of those against whom criminal charges are laid.

The Opposition will to-day move a vote of censure on the Government during the debate on the recognition of Franco.

RESIGNATION OF AZANA
His Reasons

WORK IN PARIS FOR PEACE
'The War Lost'

From our own Correspondent

Paris, February 28.

The Spanish tragedy is moving rapidly to a conclusion. Senor Azana, the Republican President, to-day announced that he had handed his resignation to Senor Martinez Barrio, the President of the Cortes, who would normally become Acting President of the Republic for 61 days. But unless Senor Barrio returns to Madrid at once – and this was considered improbable to-night – the post of President of the Spanish Republic must to-day be considered vacant or rather non-existent.

It is probable that Senor Barrio agrees with President Azana's argument, which is in effect that the machinery of which the President of the Republic is part no longer exists. It is significant that President Azana's letter of resignation should be dated February 27, the day on which Britain and France recognised the Franco Government. He thus puts on them indirectly the responsibility for proclaiming the 'illegality of the Spanish Republic' – a melancholy conclusion to the whole policy of 'non-intervention'.

FRANCO ON HIS FRIENDS

Burgos, February 28.

'To-day Britain recognised us – to-morrow it will be the whole world,' declared General Franco in a speech in Burgos last night (briefly reported in our later editions yesterday). He declared:

When even those who fought against us now recognise us we should remember those who believed in us from the first. Let us pledge our friendship to those who gave their blood with ours, to those who set their honour at our side – to our sister nations, to Portugal, to our beloved Italy, to friendly Germany, and to those nations in America who also encouraged us.

Only the arms of Nationalist Spain had imposed the truth on an unwilling and hostile world, he went on. 'Our victory has not been over our own brothers, but over the world, over international forces, over Communism and Freemasonry.'– Reuter.

Saturday March 4 1939   *p.16*

SOVIET LEAVES COMMITTEE
Non-Intervention

From our Correspondent

Moscow, March 3.

A communiqué to-night announces the Government's decision, taken on Wednesday, to recall the Soviet representative from the London Non-Intervention Committee, which 'long ago ceased functioning' and is regarded here as meaningless.

By this act the Soviet Union is the only Power to take de jure cognisance of a situation which other Powers long ago accepted de facto. Other Powers have recognised Franco but neglected formal withdrawal from the Committee.

Their procedure is here described as the climax of the Western Governments' cynical attitude towards the whole non-intervention tragi-comedy. The Soviet representative was the only one who attempted to work honestly, it is claimed.

Tuesday March 7 1939   *p.6*

HOW THE NEGRIN GOVERNMENT WAS DISPLACED
Defence Council's Wish for Peace

BUT 'FIGHT TO THE DEATH' IF SPAIN'S INDEPENDENCE IS NOT ASSURED

Dr. Negrin's Government, it is now disclosed, resigned after a meeting in Alicante on Sunday night.

Differences of opinion have been evident among the Republican Ministers for some time. Reuter's Madrid correspond-

311

ent reports that three of the Ministers, Dr. Negrin, the Prime Minister; Senor del Vayo, the Foreign Minister; and Senor Vicente Uribe, Minister of Agriculture, supported by the Communists, were intent on following a policy of resistance.

The remaining members of the Cabinet favoured an armistice and peace on as honourable terms as possible without abandoning their anti-Fascist ideals.

Senor Barrio stated in Paris last night that the Permanent Committee of the Cortes had sent Dr. Negrin a note offering to collaborate with him on the condition that his efforts be directed exclusively towards ending the Spanish situation with the least possible damage and the fewest sacrifices possible.

'Our attitude was perfectly clear,' Senor Barrio declared. 'It may be that the knowledge of this note caused the coup at Madrid.'

DEFENCE COUNCIL SET UP

At any rate, by midnight on Sunday the politicians were no longer in control in Spain: the Army had taken the initiative, and the Council of National Defence, in which Army influence predominates, had been set up. It had at its head Colonel Casado.

The Socialists are represented in the Council by Senor Julian Besteiro and Senor Eduardo Valls, the Left-wing Republican by Senor Miguel San Andres, the Socialist General Union of Workers by Senor Wenceslao Carrillo, and the Anarcho-Syndicalist Workers' Confederation by Senor Gonzales Marin. Senor Besteiro is a moderate politician who was formerly Speaker of the Cortes.

Yesterday General Miaja joined the Council as president in reply to a broadcast appeal by Colonel Casado. The General returned to Madrid yesterday and conferred with members of the Council and the headquarters staff of the Army.

Colonel Casado is probably well disposed to negotiating a peace and thereby saving thousands of lives and avoiding useless destruction, but only if the national independence of Spain and freedom from reprisals are guaranteed.

COLONEL CASADO'S PEACE BROADCAST

Shortly after the Defence Council was set up he broadcast to Spaniards in the Franco Zone, declaring that their brothers in Republican territory sought a peace based on conciliation, independence, and liberty. He said:

You fight for nothing which we ourselves do not desire. We want a nation free from all foreign influence, unfettered by the imperialist ambitions of others.

312

In your hands lies peace, which Spain very badly needs, or war, which would enfeeble our country and thus place her at the service of invaders.

If you offer peace our hearts will generously respond, but if you continue waging war upon us we will fight to the death.

Colonel Casado, in a message to Spaniards in the trenches, says:

Our fate is decided. It depends only on us to get out of this impasse by our own will. Spaniards chose between fruitful liberty and lawless slavery, between peace for Spain's profit or war in the service of imperialist folly.

We have refused the intervention of any State. There are only Spaniards in our Army. Seek only the interests of our fatherland Spain. It is the only thing which matters. It is the only aspiration which we can legally have. Our struggle will not end as long as the independence of Spain is not assured.

The Spanish people will not put down their arms until they have the guarantee that a peace without reprisals will be established.

A manifesto issued by the Council strongly attacked, 'the lack of foresight shown by Dr. Negrin', and declared, 'To prevent preparation from being made for a comfortable and lucrative flight abroad while the people fight the new Defence Council has been formed.' Members of the Council, it added, 'promise they will not shirk their sacred duties, will not desert, and will not tolerate desertion.'

SENOR BARRIO ON PEACE

The Defence Council's determination to try to obtain peace was emphasised by Senor Barrio in Paris last night. He said that leaders throughout Republican territory were in full agreement with him and the Defence Council in seeking peace. 'General Miaja', he said, 'is the only man who can come to an understanding with General Franco and bring peace back to Spain. Our agreement with the Madrid Council is absolute. From this movement we expect peace for all Spaniards.'

It was reported in Paris yesterday that Colonel Casado had offered surrender provided Republican leaders were guaranteed safe conduct and no Italian troops entered Madrid. This report said that 500 Republicans who fear reprisals have already fled from the Central Spanish zone by sea and air.

REPUBLICANS ESCAPE

Dr. Negrin and Senor del Vayo arrived at Toulouse yesterday evening, having travelled from Central Spain in a Spanish civilian aeroplane.

Later six other members of the Cabinet arrived in two aeroplanes. All said that they were going to Paris on the night train.

Senor Alberti, the Under Secretary for Air in Republican Spain, arrived at Oran with Air Force officers and civilians in two 'planes from Albacete. A third 'plane with eight passengers, mostly Russians, also arrived with a woman on board who is believed to be the famous woman Communist deputy to the Cortes, Senora Dolores Ibarruri, 'La Pasionaria'.

The change from the Negrin Government to the Defence Council has been accomplished peaceably. Madrid was quiet last night. Although as a precaution 6in. guns and machine-guns had been mounted at strategic positions on street corners and troops were being held in readiness at their barracks, there were no signs of revolt, disorder, or popular disapproval of any kind.

Troops were guarding Communist centres, which no unauthorised person was allowed to approach or to enter.– Reuter and Associated Press messages.

Wednesday March 8 1939 p.6

THE COMMUNIST RISING IN MADRID FAILS
Appeals by Army Leaders

REPUBLICAN 'PLANES HELP TO PUT DOWN THE NEW REVOLT

Madrid, March 7 (Midnight).

Republican 'planes bombed a group of soldiers who, headed by Communists, attempted to revolt to-day, declares a broadcast statement, which adds that the Communists were deceived into believing that the Air Force was under their control. It said that this was entirely false, as all but four 'planes which helped La Pasionaria and others (including Colonel Lister) to escape abroad remained loyal to the Defence Council.–Exchange Telegram.

314

OTHER NEWS ABOUT THE REVOLT

Madrid, March 7.

The Communist rising broke out in Madrid at dawn to-day. Communist forces had gathered in the old Hippodrome building and in the working-class quarter of Cuatro Caminos. A certain amount of gunfire and rifle-shots were heard during the morning, but by this afternoon the calm that prevailed all last night had been restored.

It was not until half-way through the morning that the people of Madrid generally learned that anything was wrong. The Madrid wireless station then announced that Communists in Madrid were making a desperate attempt at a coup, but it was declared that elsewhere in Republican Spain all was quiet.

Colonel Casado, Defence Minister in the Council, broadcast an appeal to soldiers who had been 'tricked by Communist leaders into holding out against the National Defence Council' to change sides. Wireless appeals to the Communists who are alone in opposing the military Junta, were also made by General Miaja, by Senor Besteiro, Socialist Minister of Foreign Affairs and by the Anarchist leader Lieutenant Colonel Mera.

To-night the rising had been crushed in the capital itself, but at one or two isolated points on the outskirts the Communists were still holding out. 'Republicans are steadily dominating the position and the movement will soon be crushed,' Major Epeardo Medrano chief of the Press Propaganda Department said.

The Madrid radio announced that Republican bombing planes under the order of General Miaja were bombing the remaining centre of Communist resistance. The broadcaster announced that 'planes which fly over the city are in the service of the National Defence Council. The population is not alarmed.' After the 'planes began bombing the noise of firing stopped.– Reuter and Associated Press.

CASADO, THE MAN BEHIND THE EVENTS IN MADRID
His Former Work With Communists

FUTURE OF THE 'CONTRADICTORY ALLIANCE' HE LEADS

From a Correspondent recently in Spain

Paris, March 8.

Thirty-two and a half months after the 105th pronunciamiento in Spain's history – better known under the name of Franco's civil war – another young Army chief, Segismundo Casado, has overthrown his legal Government, thus raising the number of rebellions of his country to 106. The Spanish Army is incorrigible.

Even if people abroad have seldom heard of Casado, his name is not unknown to close observers of recent events in Spain. He is hardly forty-five years of age. His career includes, however, more than one rebellion against the established Government.

A brilliant student of Spain's Sandhurst, the Alcazar Military Academy of Toledo, Casado distinguished himself both by his outstanding gifts for modern tactics and for his revolutionary – that is, democratic – spirit. As a captain scarcely 30 years old he led in the garrison of Ciudad Real during the summer of 1926 one of the first Republican insurrections which were eventually to break General Primo de Rivera's military dictatorship. He had to pay for his coup by several years' solitary confinement in one of Primo de Rivera's much-dreaded fortresses.

CASADO'S MOTIVES

What exactly is then behind Casado's coup? His formula of 'Peace with honour, or resistance, to the last', is, after all, no different, on the face of it, from what Negrin said. As for Casado's anti-Communism, it seems to be quite a sudden discovery for a man whose entire military career was linked during the war, and mostly in the defence of Madrid, with the names of Modesto, Lister, Galan, and the International Brigades. His close co-operation with the F.A.I. (the Anarchists) and Anarcho-Syndicalists does not point to a precisely moderate tendency.

The chief reason for his present anti-Communist attitude

316

may be that yesterday's Defence Council and to-day's Miaja Government – the outcome of Casado's rebellion – represents all the forces who in Republican Spain wish resistance to come to an early end. Julian Basteiro has been a champion of 'mediation' ever since the war began, and the young Republican leader San Andres represents the Azana school of thought. The Miaja Government is further supported by representatives of the opposition Socialist of the Largo Caballero group, who are among Negrin's chief enemies. Finally it is supported by the Anarchists, who since 1936 had a marked tendency to consider Socialism and Communism as worse enemies than a Franco dictatorship under which they could still keep their principle of individualist and terrorist action.

It is more than likely that this new alliance, contradictory in itself though it is, will carry out a 'purge' in order to open the doors wide to 'conciliation'. These people believe that conciliation will be prepared once the diehard supporters of unconditional resistance such as Negrin and 'La Pasionaria', have been eliminated.

THE FUTURE

Will 'peace with honour' really come out of Casado's bold move, which represents, among other things, a rebellion of the professional principle of war army officers against the new militia chiefs, and perhaps also a revolt of Madrid 'regionalism' against the military and political authorities who came back to Central Spain after the collapse of Catalonia? Will Casado's move mean more bloodshed or will this shy and smiling colonel prove the mystery man of mediation – assuming that General Franco is willing to deal with him at all?

Saturday March 11 1939 *p.17*

MADRID BATTLE GOES ON
Stubborn Communists

REINFORCEMENTS FOR MIAJA

Madrid, March 10.

Sections of General Miaja's mobile army which arrived in Madrid this morning are pushing groups of armed Communists into the open country outside the city. After the entry of the column into Madrid there was stiff fighting with the Communists, who had taken up strong positions. The fighting developed into a battle, in which the Communists relied chiefly on hand grenades. The Republicans replied with tanks, mortars, and field artillery, and their onslaught drove the Communists back. However, they went on putting up a stiff resistance, but heavy mortar fire tore big gaps in their ranks.

During this mortar bombardment the mobile army threw out sections of machine-gunners on both flanks, keeping the Communists under a continuous stream of fire from three sides. After twenty minutes' fighting the Communists showed signs of weakening. In another five minutes the rest threw down their arms, shouting 'Long live the Republic!'

FRESH FIGHTING

Madrid, March 10.

Special squads of men with motor-lorries to-night carted from Madrid's streets the bodies of men which had lain where they fell for the past two days. New Communist disturbances broke out even as they worked, but they were reported quickly quelled by detachments of tanks and machine-gunners from mobile troops who fought their way into the city to Miaja's aid to-day.

The Government announced that 14,000 Communists had surrendered in the last 24 hours, that many Communist strongholds had been captured, and that a number of prisoners taken by the rebels had been released.–Associated Press.

Monday March 13 1939   *p.9*

MADRID REVOLT OVER?
Rebels Surrender

DEFENCE COUNCIL'S CLAIMS
Peace Plan Now

The Defence Council in Madrid claimed late last night that the Communist rising, which broke out on Tuesday had been totally crushed and that all 'rebel' strongholds had surrendered without conditions.

After the surrender of the Communists the Council under General Miaja held a five-hour meeting at the end of which it was announced that 'the plan drawn up before the rebellion' was now to be carried out. The plan was simply peace, it was stated.

The statement issued by the Defence Council announcing the surrender had declared that 'now that the events which paralysed its political life are finished the council will be free to devote itself without loss of time to the accomplishment of its patriotic aims'.

General Miaja on Saturday night made thorough preparations for an attack on the Communists. A sharp battle early yesterday morning was followed by the surrender of their main stronghold in buildings on the site of the old racecourse. The 'rebels' in Chamartin village, another stronghold on the northern edge of Madrid, also gave themselves up during the morning. The General Staff 2nd Army Corps, which revolted under its commander Lieutenant Colonel Buenos, surrendered on Saturday.

MADRID ALMOST NORMAL

The streets of Madrid were almost normal yesterday, reports Reuter, but were crowded with people visiting the scenes of the fighting. No bread rations were issued yesterday, but they are promised for Tuesday.

Communist 'rebels' in armoured cars attempted to drive through Valencia on Saturday, but were prevented by forces of carabiniers, who captured two tanks and forced the rest to retreat. The Communist groups are reported to have been marauding previously in villages round Valencia.

Communists are being ejected from all public institutions throughout the whole of Spanish Republican territory. The United Socialist Youth Organisation, which was formerly under Communist influence, has been taken over by the purely Socialist leaders, states Reuter.

The Burgos Government officially denied yesterday that attacks have been made on Madrid, but it is believed that General Franco will soon launch an offensive.

Wednesday March 15 1939   *p.6*

MADRID'S HOPE OF PEACE
No Response Yet

The National Defence Council in Madrid prepared for peace, while Franco carries on his preparations to attack Madrid.

Colonel Casado, the Defence Minister in the Council states:–

The National Defence Council is busy planning a liquidation of the war. We do not yet know what General Franco's attitude is. We are trying to negotiate an honourable peace, if possible on the basis of the independence of Spain and no reprisals.

But in a broadcast from the radio station in Burgos, states Reuter, the Nationalist spokesman declared that there could be no differentiation between the Communists and adherents of the National Defence Council in Madrid. Both factions, the spokesman added, were 'part of the Red horde' responsible for the assassination of thousands of their fellow-countrymen.

Saturday March 18 1939   *p.17*

MADRID TO FIGHT
Peace Talks Fail

St. Jean De Luz, March 17.

Madrid intends to fight on, according to information received by the Press Association special correspondent to-night from the capital. The National Defence Council, it is stated, desired the evacuation of General Franco's chief political enemies as a condition of surrender. Britain was prepared to carry out the evacuation if General Franco agreed.

As, however, General Franco remains adamant in demanding unconditional surrender this proposal has fallen to the ground. General Miaja and Colonel Casado will therefore defend Madrid to the last.–Press Association Foreign Special.

Madrid, March 17.

Lieutenant Colonels Luis Barcelo and Emilio Bueno, the principal leaders of the recent Communist revolt in Madrid, were sentenced to death to-day.–Reuter.

Friday March 24 1939   *p.11*

PEACE TALKS IN BURGOS?
Italian Reports

Rome, March 24.

Reports received early this morning by Italian newspapers from their correspondents in Burgos state that an aeroplane landed at Burgos yesterday evening carrying envoys from the Madrid Government. The envoys are stated to be entrusted with the task of negotiating a conditional surrender of Madrid and Valencia.

The reports add that negotiations were going on late last

night between the Madrid envoys and representatives of General Franco's Government.–Exchange.

Monday March 27 1939   *p.11*

MADRID NOT TO SURRENDER
Burgos Breaks off Talks

OFFENSIVE BEGUN

The Madrid wireless announced last night that General Franco had broken negotiations for the surrender of Madrid.

Senor Jose del Rio, secretary to the Republican Defence Council, told listeners of the course of negotiations with General Franco. He stated that yesterday when terms were being agreed upon General Franco had suddenly and inexplicably insisted, in view of an alleged Republican delay, on an immediate unconditional surrender of a symbolical portion of territory on all fronts to his advancing troops.

General Franco declared that it was no longer possible to hold back that offensive: on the Cordova front, in the South of Spain it was begun yesterday morning.

SURRENDER TERMS

Senor del Rio began by explaining the terms on which the Republicans had offered surrender. He said:

The Council for National Defence, following its plan, entered into negotiations with the Burgos Government, to which it submitted conditions for the surrender of Republican Spain. The principal points in these conditions were:

1. The Nationalist Government shall respect the integrity of Spanish territory.

2. Military and civilians who took part in the struggle shall be treated with consideration.

3. A guarantee shall be given that no reprisals shall be taken against anyone, and that only regular courts shall try delinquents.

4. Respect for the life, liberty, and interests of military and public servants and militia.

5. A minimum delay of 25 days to allow the departure abroad of those who wish to leave.

6. Italian and Moroccan troops to be withdrawn from Spain.

The Burgos Government, which had in its turn put up conditions, agreed that Spaniards who wish to do so should be enabled to leave the country and agreed to guarantees demanded by the Council for National Defence, but suddenly negotiations were broken off.

The alleged delay referred to in the broadcast may refer to the question of surrendering the Republican air force, for Senor del Rio read telegrams exchanged between Franco and the Republicans. The first, to General Franco, ran:

To-morrow (Monday) we are sending our air force as a symbolic surrender. Please arrange time.

The second was:

From the Council of National Defence to the Nationalist Government: It is perhaps possible for us to effect the surrender this very afternoon (Sunday).

To this General Franco replied:

It is most urgent you give up your arms in view of the imminence of our offensive, which has already begun on certain fronts. Order your troops to hoist the white flag.

Announcing the breakdown of negotiations, Senor del Rio said:

At six o'clock this evening representatives of the Burgos Government received orders to break off negotiations, and the two officers representing us were told to regain the Republican lines. We emphasise before the world and before all Spaniards that the entire responsibility rests with the Nationalist Government, which in this way is prolonging the carnage which has ravaged Spain in the last two years.

FRANCO'S PROMISE

Before these announcements in Madrid General Franco had broadcast to Spaniards in the Republican zone appealing for them to surrender before the 'final great offensive'. He pointed out that after the Catalonian victories the whole world, even the Republican chiefs, recognised that a final victory by the Nationalists and the surrender of the Republicans were inevitable. He declared:–

The Nationalist Government repeats all its previous offers of a generous pardon for all who have not committed crimes. Neither military service with the Republicans nor the fact of belonging to anti-Nationalist political parties will be regarded as reasons for criminal proceedings. Legal tribunes alone will deal with crimes committed during the Republican occupation. Surrender to the Fatherland is honourable, but it would be criminal lunacy to shed further blood for a lost cause and for a few interested individuals.

The appeal said that with the Republican Navy lost and the coasts blockaded a sterile resistance and delayed surrender with the waste of the lives of innocent soldiers would be folly. If the Republicans are 'wishful to avoid greater ills they should raise the white flag and surrender in order that they may have in the future a Spain great and free and just for all Spaniards'.

CORDOVA OFFENSIVE

General Franco began an offensive early yesterday morning on the Cordova front, Southern Spain, according to an official communiqué issued in Burgos.

The Nationalists last night claimed to have advanced over an average depth of 25 miles. Prisoners and deserters taken in the operations were said to number 10,000.–Reuter messages from Madrid, Paris, Burgos, and Salamanca.

Tuesday March 28 1939   *p.11*

EVACUATION OF MADRID
Franco Begins His Attack

NO RESISTANCE?

General Franco yesterday began his 'final great offensive' after the failure of the negotiations for the surrender of Madrid. He is attacking on several fronts, and has made considerable advances.

In face of this threat the National Defence Council decided to evacuate thousands of families from Madrid, and the work of evacuation began yesterday afternoon. Broadcasting last night Senor del Rio, a member of the Council, said that the evacuation would have to be based on 'absolute obedience.' 'Madrid must show', he said, 'that she knows how to lose.'

Reuter reported from Madrid early this morning that the demobilisation had been ordered of all Republican recruits awaiting instructions to join up. This move was regarded as confirming that the Republicans do not intend to offer any resistance.

General Miaja, Commander-in-Chief of the Spanish Republican Army, arrived in Valencia last night with two other Republican generals.

FRANCO'S GAINS

On Sunday Franco had opened the fighting on the Cordova front, in the south of Spain; yesterday he struck again near Toledo, south-west of Madrid, and a Burgos message received by way of Paris last night declared that Franco's troops were entering the suburbs of Madrid proper.

On the Cordova front Moors and the Andalusian Army Corps have already penetrated the Republican lines to a depth of 25 miles, it is claimed. The Nationalist troops, it was announced last night, have captured the Almaden mercury mines, the richest in the world, which have been held by the Republicans since the outbreak of the civil war.

A Burgos dispatch states that the Republicans are offering only feeble resistance. More than ten thousand prisoners are claimed to have been captured.

Franco's troops are said in Burgos to have crossed the Tagus in the region of Toledo without meeting with resistance, and the Republicans are said to be in disorderly flight near the bridgehead of Toledo. The communiqué from G.H.Q. talks of the 'irresistible advance' of the Nationalists.–Reuter.

Wednesday March 29 1939 p.11

MADRID GIVES ITSELF UP TO FRANCO
Mussolini and Hitler Rejoice

DUCE DECLARES: 'SO WILL ALL ENEMIES OF FASCISM END'

Madrid has surrendered. The rebels who in November, 1936, had fought to enter and failed walked in yesterday as troops of the generally recognised Spanish Government and not a shot was fired at them.

The supporters of Franco in the city, the 'fifth column' he once spoke of, had been waiting for this moment for more than two years. They came out in the streets wild with excitement to welcome the troops marching in. General Franco is expected to enter in triumph on Saturday.

Valencia may follow Madrid in surrendering. The National Defence Council is already there discussing the question of handing over the city.

Italy and Germany, as they did prematurely in November, 1936, are celebrating the fall of Madrid. In Rome last night Signor Mussolini appeared on his balcony and told ten thousand cheering people:

Franco's infantry and the Italian legionaries have entered Madrid, and the Spanish war can thus be considered finished. It finished with the collapse of Bolshevism. So will end all enemies of Italy and of Fascism.

Signor Mussolini's appearance on the balcony was greated with shouts of 'Tunis, Tunis', and the Duce smiled.

Herr Hitler has also welcomed the news. His telegram to General Franco conveys his heartiest congratulations on 'the final defeat of nation-destroying Bolshevism'.

Thursday March 30 1939   *p.11*

THE END IN SPAIN
All Is Franco's

32 MONTHS AFTER REVOLT BEGAN
Hurry to Surrender

The civil war in Spain is over – 32 months after it began. Last night Franco announced that he was in control of all the 52 provinces. All that remains is for him to wipe out isolated centres of resistance.

Cities, towns, and villages throughout Spain hurried to follow the example of Madrid. Ciudad Real and Cuenca were the first to announce their surrender – at one o'clock in the morning. The 'fifth column' of Franco sympathisers in the towns had risen and taken control.

Shortly after dawn Falangists (Spanish Fascists) and Civil Guards in Murcia captured the town hall and the public buildings and all the barracks. The garrisons agreed to join them. Most of the Republican authorities had already fled.

GUADALAJARA

Then Guadalajara, north-east of Madrid, went over, where two years ago this month the Republicans had inflicted a great defeat on the Italians. Jaen followed in the south, awaiting the arrival of General Queipo de Llano's troops, which were only a few miles away.

Berlin was the first to report the surrender of Almeria, the port that German warships shelled two years ago, killing and wounding 74 people, as a reprisal for the bombing of the Deutschland. A German News Agency report says that the rising of the Nationalists began in the harbour district, where several ships hoisted the Nationalists' flag. The rising quickly spread to the rest of the town. Hundreds of Nationalists were released from prison: Republicans who had failed to escape were arrested.

VALENCIA

At noon Valencia surrendered; five hours later General Franco's troops entered.

Valencia was twice in the civil war the capital of Spain. As one of the chief ports through which arms and supplies reached the Republic, it has suffered since January, 1937, numberless shellings from the sea and bombings from the air. In the harbour lie many ships, among them British ships, either sunk or disabled.

All through the night, reports the Havas correspondent in Valencia, members of Republican organisations and political parties as well as military chiefs were leaving the city. Lorries rumbled through the streets continuously, but the greatest order prevailed. Trade union and political organisations issued appeals to all their supporters who wanted to leave Spain to present themselves at the evacuation offices. Soldiers could be seen awaiting evacuation, but there was no sign of panic.

Yesterday a British ship, the Atlantic Guide, reports Reuter from Valencia, was approaching the port and negotiating to take on board refugees. A Franco aeroplane machine-gunned the crew.

Just before the city surrendered General Miaja, commander of the Republican forces, and other Republican leaders fled in 23 'planes to Oran, the French port in North Africa. In Burgos, states Reuter, it is declared that all the members of the National Defence Council except General Miaja and Colonel Casado have been detained in Valencia.

Falangists came out of their hiding, rose against the Republicans, and forced the surrender of Alicante. A wireless broadcast announced that the city was ready to receive the conquerors.

In the evening Cartagena submitted. Until the flight of most of the Republican fleet it had been the Government's main naval base.

Albacete was the last important town to go over. The civil population rose against the Republican garrison and forced their surrender. Then they told Burgos by wireless that they would receive Franco's troops.

So without bloodshed roughly a third of the country went over to Franco yesterday, and last night in nearly all the cities, towns, and villages the red and gold flag of Nationalist Spain was flying. The revolt that Franco began in July, 1936, was over.

Appendix 1: Spanish political parties

A list of all of the political parties active in Spain immediately prior to the outbreak of the civil war is provided below, together with information on their leadership and political persuasion. Not all of these parties are mentioned in the 'Manchester Guardian' reports but the reader might find it helpful to have some indication of their character as their presence contributed to the problems confronting the Republic.

Parties of the political Left

Republican Left: Led by Manuel Azaña. A strongly democratic, anti-fascist and anti-clerical party arguing for progressive social reform.

Republican Union: Led by Diego Martinez Barrios. Adopted a position marginally to the right of the Republican Left.

Catalan Left (Esquerra): Led by Luis Companys. Virtually identical in character to the Republican Left but emphasising the autonomy of Catalonia as an independent Republic.

Galician Federation: Led by Santiago Casares Quiroga. Social policies akin to those of the Republican Left it merged with that party despite placing emphasis on the autonomy of Galicia as an independent Republic.

Socialist Party: Led by a triumvirate, Francisco Largo Caballero (Left), Indalecio Prieto (Centre), Julian Besteiro (Right). Seeking a collective form of government with the socialisation of production.

Communist Party: Led by José Diaz. Seeking a democratic republic with the ultimate goal being a workers' and peasants' state built on Soviet lines.

Unified Socialist Party of Catalonia (Partit Socialista Unificat de Catalunya – PSUC): Led by Joan Comorera and M. Valdes. A merger of Catalan Socialists and Communists.

Iberian Anarchist Federation: Led by Buenaventura Durruti, Juan Garcia Oliver and Angel Pestaña. Advocating 'libertarian communism' and opposing all forms of state control.

Workers' Party of Marxist Unification (Partido Obrero de Unificacion Marxista – POUM): Led by expelled Communists Andrés Nin and Joaquim Maurin. Vehemently anti-Communist with a strong Trotskyist influence.

Parties of the political Centre

Radical Party: Led by Alejandro Lerroux. Strongly anti-Socialist and an ally of the Fascist parties.

Conservative Party: Led by Miguel Maura. Some way to the right of the Radical Party.

Liberal Democratic Party: Led by Melquiades Alvarez. More a group than a party and of an avidly reactionary character.

Parties of the political Right

Spanish Confederation of Autonomous Right Parties (Confederación Española de Derechas Autónomas – CEDA): Led by José Maria Gil Robles and José Calvo Sotelo. A right-wing coalition of reactionary Republicans and Monarchists under pro-fascist leadership.

Popular Action (Acción Popular): Led by José Maria Gil Robles. Strongly pro-clerical and pro-fascist.

Agrarian Party: Led by José Martinez de Velasco. Strongly pro-clerical and a defender of the interests of the larger landowners.

Spanish Regeneration (Renovación Española): Led by Antonio Goicoechea and José Calvo Sotelo. Seeking the restoration of Alfonso XIII and pro-fascist.

Spanish Phalanx (Falange Española): Led by José Antonio Primo de Rivera. An overtly fascist party based on Italian and German lines.

Carlists (Traditionalists): Strongly clerical and reactionary. Since 1833 had been followers of the line of Don Carlos, the brother of Fernando VII, who pretended to the throne against Isabel II. Opposed to Alfonso XIII.

Basque Nationalist Party: Led by José Horn. Pro-clerical and reactionary with Carlist sympathies and seeking limited autonomy for the Basque Provinces.

Catalan Regionalist League (Liga Regionalista Catala): Led by Francisco Cambó and Juan Ventosa. A regional party of a strong conservative persuasion and standing in marked opposition to the Catalan Left.

Two trade unions were also of unquestionable political significance.

General Workers' Union (Unión General de Trabajadores – UGT): Led by Left Socialists and Communists.

National Confederation of Labour (Confederación National de Trabajo): Led by anarcho-syndicalists.

Appendix 2: Major political figures in the Spanish Civil War

A list of the major political personages referred to in the 'Manchester Guardian' reports, together with other actors not mentioned, is given below.

Alcalá-Zamora, Niceto: President of Provisional Government (which held office April 14–June 29 1931); elected first President of Second Spanish Republic, December 19 1931; impeached, April 7 1936.

Alfonso XIII: King of Spain May 17 1888–April 14 1931.

Alvarez del Vayo, Julio: Socialist, former minister to Mexico; Foreign Minister and Minister to League of Nations.

Azana, Manuel: leader of Republican Left; Minister of War in Provisional Government; Premier October 1931–September 1933 and February 19–May 10 1936; elected Second President of Republic May 10 1936.

Batet, Domingo: Nationalist general, one of the leaders of the 1936 insurrection.

Besteiro, Julian: leader of the right-wing of the Socialist Party and former Speaker of the Cortes.

Cabanellas, Miguel: Nationalist general, one of the leaders of the 1936 revolt.

Calvo Sotelo, José: extreme right-wing monarchist; Minister of Finance under Primo de Rivera; assassinated July 13 1936.

Cambo, Francisco: leader of Catalan Regionalist League.

Casares Quiroga, Santiago: leader of Galician Federation (defunct by July 1936), Minister of Marine in Provisional Government; former Minister of Interior and Public Works; member of Republican Left; Premier May 13–July 18 1936.

Chapaprieta, Joaquin: conservative; Premier, September 25–December 9 1936.

Companys, Luis: leader of Catalan Left; President of the Catalan Generalidad.

Diaz, José: general secretary of The Spanish Communist Party.

Durruti, Buenaventura: anarchist leader.

Fanjul, Joaquin: Nationalist general, one of the leaders of the 1936 revolt; executed August 17 1936.

Franco, Francisco: Nationalist general, one of the leaders of the 1936 revolt, eventual supremo of Nationalist cause; former Chief of Staff during Gil Robles War Ministry.

Gil Robles, José Maria: fascist; leader of Popular Action Party and CEDA; Minister of War May 6–December 9 1935.

Giral Pereira, José: Republican Left; former Minister of Marine; Premier July 18–September 4 1936.

Goded, Manuel: Nationalist general; leader of 1936 revolt in Balearic Islands; executed, August 12 1936.

Goicoechea, Antonio: fascist, formerly a monarchist, and leader of Renovación, Espanola.

Gonzalez Peña, Ramon: Socialist; one of the leaders of the October 1934 Astunian revolt.

Herrara Orio, Angel: pro-clerical fascist; baker of Gil Robles and organiser of Acción Nacional in 1932.

Iglésias, Pablo: founder of Spanish Socialist Pary and UGT.

Largo Caballero, Francisco: leader of Socialist Left Wing; Secretary of UGT; former Minister of Labour; Premier September 4, 1936 to May 16, 1937.

Lerroux, Alejanaro: reactionary, leader of Radical Party; Minister of Foreign Affairs in Provisional Government; four times Premier between October 1933 and September 1936; in alliance with Gil Rbles 1934–36.

Miaja, José: most famous of the Republical generals.

Martinez Barrios, Diego: leader of The Republican Union after severing his links with The Radical Party; Minister of Economy in the Provisional Government; Speaker of The Cortes from March 16, 1936; Premier for eight hours approximately on July 18, 1936.

Maura, Miguel; leader of Conservative Party; Minister of Interior in Provisional Government.

Maurin, Joaquin: co-founder of POUM.

Mola, Emilio: most renowned of Nationalist generals; leader of 1936 revolt in Old Castile.

Negrin, Juan: socialist; former Minister of Finance; Premier after resignation of Largo Caballero.

Nin, Andrés: co-founder of POUM.

Pestaña, Angel: anarchist leader.

Portela Valladares, Manuel: independent Right; Premier from December 30 1935–February 19 1936.

Prieto, Indalecio: leader of centralist faction of Socialist Party; Minister of Finance in Provisional Government; former Minister of Public Works; become Minister of Air and Marine on September 4 1936.

Primo de Rivera, Miguel: right-wing military dictator of Spain from September 13 1923–January 28 1930.

Primo de Rivera, José Antonio: fascist, leader of Falange Española and son of Miguel.

Queipo de Llano, Gonzalo: Nationalist general; one of the leaders of the 1936 revolt and famous as the 'Radio General' for his broadcasts from Seville.

Samper, Ricardo: Basque Nationalist Party leader and Premier from May 2 1934–October 1 1934.

Sanjurjo, José: Nationalist general; leader of the 1932 right-wing revolt and killed in a 'plane crash on his way to join the 1936 revolt.

Uribe, Vicente: secretary of the Communist faction in the Cortes and appointed as Minister of Agriculture on September 4 1936.